The World Cup
as World History

William D. Bowman
Gettysburg College

ROWMAN & LITTLEFIELD
Lanham • Boulder • New York • London

Executive Editor: Susan McEachern
Assistant Editor: Katelyn Turner
Higher Education Channel Manager: Jonathan Raeder

Credits and acknowledgments for material borrowed from other sources, and reproduced with permission, appear on the appropriate pages within the text.

Published by Rowman & Littlefield
An imprint of The Rowman & Littlefield Publishing Group, Inc.
4501 Forbes Boulevard, Suite 200, Lanham, Maryland 20706
www.rowman.com

6 Tinworth Street, London SE11 5AL, United Kingdom

Copyright © 2020 by The Rowman & Littlefield Publishing Group, Inc.

British Library Cataloguing in Publication Information Available

Library of Congress Control Number: 2019949884

ISBN 978-1-4422-6718-3 (cloth : alk. paper) | ISBN 978-1-4422-6719-0 (pbk. : alk. paper) | ISBN 978-1-4422-6720-6 (ebook)

♾™ The paper used in this publication meets the minimum requirements of American National Standard for Information Sciences—Permanence of Paper for Printed Library Materials, ANSI/NISO Z39.48-1992.

Contents

Acknowledgments

Over the course of several years of thinking about the content of this book and writing it, I have acquired many intellectual debts. First and foremost, I would like to thank my students at Gettysburg College, who for a generation now have sharpened the way I look at both world and sports history. Many of them have discussed formally and informally the ideas contained in this text, which is intended for classroom use and is therefore dedicated to them. Ryan Bilger, a recent graduate of the college, deserves particular thanks as he helped with the selection of many of the photos in the book. His encyclopedic knowledge of football made him the perfect sounding board in the late stages of editing the book.

My colleagues in the History Department at Gettysburg College, Abou Bamba, Michael Birkner, Peter Carmichael, Scott Hancock, Dina Lowy, Karim Samji, Magdalena Sánchez, and Tim Shannon have been a source of inspiration over the course of a long academic career and have listened patiently to my ideas about world and sports history. Some of them even share my passion for football. To all of them, I express my gratitude. The library staff at Gettysburg College, especially Clint Baugess, has supported my work at every stage by finding texts, sources, and online resources. Elizabeth Carmichael did an expert job of providing an index for the book.

I have also learned much from a whole generation of world and sports historians, too numerous to mention in an acknowledgments section. I would, however, like to thank several scholars—Michael Adas, Pamela Crossley, Xinru Liu, Patrick Manning, Howard Spodek, and Peter Stearns, among others—who came over the course of several summers to institutes in Gettysburg to discuss world history concepts and content. Ane Lintvedt, a longtime advocate of world history, also participated in those institutes and has discussed ideas with me on numerous occasions, including in the final stages of finishing this book.

I have also benefited greatly from my long association with J. Megan Greene of the University of Kansas. Megan worked with me on an earlier world history textbook and has offered her guidance and encouragement on this book through weekly conversations over the past year.

Finally, I want to thank the publishing staff at Rowman & Littlefield. Susan McEachern has been the ideal editor. She has shepherded this project for the past several years, shown great patience, and improved the book in numerous ways. Katelyn Turner was extremely helpful in the editing process and especially with securing permission for the photographs in the book. Janice Braunstein expertly guided the manuscript through the last steps in its production. Amanda Jackson did heroic work copyediting the text and preparing it for publication. The book has also benefited from the comments and critiques of anonymous readers engaged by Rowman & Littlefield.

As with all academic publications, I am solely responsible for the content of this book.

Introduction

Football is the world's most popular sport. It has more leagues, players, and fans than any other athletic activity. The World Cup is football's preeminent international tournament. It is held every four years in locations around the globe. Billions of viewers watch it on television or on their electronic devices. Millions of dollars in advertising are spent sponsoring the competition. Players and teams become famous or fall from grace because of their performances in it. The World Cup of football is truly a world-historical event. Nevertheless, scholars and academics, including world historians, have not always fully recognized the global significance of the competition or analyzed it in terms accessible to students.

Over the course of the last several decades, world history courses have gradually become the introductory classes in many universities, colleges, and high schools in North America. Administrators, teachers, and the wider public have realized that the increasingly interdependent world in which we live demands our reorientation in studying the past. Classes and discussions that focused too narrowly on historical developments or eras in one part of the world, be it Asia, Europe, Africa, or North or South America, could not adequately capture the complex political, economic, cultural, social, and environmental interactions and encounters of the past or the present. Scholars have developed a world-historical perspective to analyze consequential and contested issues such as trade, the exchange of diseases, global labor movements, technological innovations and their applications, and the spread of religions, philosophies, and ideologies. World historians have been hard at work creating new analytical frameworks to capture the diversity of human experience and study the global past.[1] In the process, academics have engaged in much healthy debate about appropriate chronology, approaches, themes, and focus for world history courses and texts.

The development of world history and the intense debates among its practitioners have opened up whole new areas of inquiry and refocused older ways of looking at the past. For example, geographical regions that are not limited to one continent—such as the Atlantic World, the Indian Ocean, or the Pacific Rim—have been used to look at trade networks, the movement of peoples, or the spread of disease. World historians have used commodities such as tea, coffee, or silver to show how connected and interdependent important regions of the globe were in certain eras. Environmental approaches that focus on climate, agriculture patterns, industrialization, nitrogen cycles, and land use have also become common. Through their research and writing, world historians have deepened and transformed ideas about empires, imperialism, colonialism, and decolonization. Scholars have used patterns of exchange and diffusion to understand the impact of the spread of ideas, language, medical knowledge, and legal codes. From the lens of world history, diplomatic and military encounters often take on richer contours than if they are viewed exclusively through the vantage point of a single nation-state or region. Race, gender, economic exchange, political interactions, and the spread of cultural developments have proven to be among the more useful categories for world history analysis. In short, world history has revolutionized the way we look at the past.[2]

One area of global significance that world historians have not yet fully incorporated into their approaches is sports. To be sure, world historians have conducted some good studies of individual sporting activities and there is a growing awareness of them as important cultural practices.[3] On the whole, however, world historians have not yet fully acknowledged how sports work in many different global settings.[4] This is somewhat surprising because the field of sports history has made significant strides over the course of the last several decades, especially from the 1970s to the present. World and sports history as academic pursuits have largely come of age at the same time. Scholars have created social, political, cultural, and economic models to look at the overall development of sports and leisure activities and the particular evolution of specific sporting practices. Sports historians have been especially active in their work on the nineteenth, twentieth, and twenty-first centuries. They have, for example, researched and written about the history of football, basketball, baseball, the modern Olympic movement, cricket, bicycling, swimming, track and field, and many other sports in the modern era. Some of the best work done in sports history takes a global or international approach and employs categories such as race, gender, economic exchange, political organizations, and cultural diffusion in its analysis.[5] Much sports history, however, remains focused narrowly on the development of an individual athletic activity and its importance to a locality, community, region, or nation and does not especially use world historical contexts.[6] The two fields, world and sports history, have not fully discovered each other. This is especially true in the case of world history, which often attempts to cover so many chronological periods, themes, and contexts that it can overlook a fruitful analytical discussion of sports that would reveal important contours about global developments.

The World Cup as World History brings together the two rapidly developing fields of world and sports history. It does so, however, by using a tightly focused approach on one sport, football, and in one setting, the World Cup. The book uses the foremost footballing event in the modern era to analyze not only how a sport has grown and evolved to become a global game, but also to understand how football as a cultural practice, a contested political arena, an economic commodity, and a cultural spectacle can serve as a vehicle to achieve new insights about world history. Some of the most important themes of world historians working on the modern era, especially globalization, race, ethnicity, gender identity, and the rise of a consumer and leisure-time culture, are also the analytical categories that have driven sports historians, including those who work on football in the modern era. A history of football and the World Cup can show the deep connections between two fields, world and sports history, that have developed over the course of the past several decades but that have not fully discovered and embraced one another.

Thus, by bringing together the intellectual and topical concerns of world and sports historians, *The World Cup as World History* aims to become an accessible and important supplement to standard world history textbooks. The book is therefore relatively short and thematic. It covers five significant developments in the history of the World Cup: the origins and evolution of the game prior to the first World Cup in 1930; the politics of World Cup competitions, including discussions of how sites are selected and charges of corruption at the very heart of the process; the economics of the World Cup; race, ethnicity, and gender and the World Cup competition; and the World Cup as a sporting spectacle, with an emphasis on the cult of star athletes in the modern era. Each of these chapters contains tables and photographs that are intended to provide additional context and material about the topics that can be used for further discussion of football as world history. Finally, each chapter ends with a short list of documents and a guide to further reading that will allow students and teachers to pursue the topics in greater depth should they choose to do so.

The first chapter of *The World Cup as World History* focuses on the evolution of kicking and ball games in many different global settings—China, Japan, and Mesoamerica, for example—until the creation of the modern game of football in the nineteenth century. Rules and codes for playing football were established first in the United Kingdom and then spread rapidly to other parts of Europe and South America. The game quickly reached many other parts of the world and became one of the most popular sporting practices of the modern era. Chapter 1 concludes with a discussion of the introduction of the first World Cup in Uruguay in 1930.

Chapter 2 details the growth of the World Cup from relatively humble origins in the pre–Second World War era to a truly global sporting event after 1945. The chapter focuses primarily on the political dimensions of the game's foremost tournament. As a sport, football became so important that virtually every aspect of the World Cup—the selection of sites, the playing of games, and the outcome of the matches—was of political significance. Politicians from Benito Mussolini in the 1930s to Vladimir Putin in 2018 hoped to use football's immense global popularity for their own political purposes. In addition, chapter 2 highlights the creation and role of the Fédération Internationale de Football Association (FIFA), world football's international governing body, in the management of the World Cup. FIFA has become one of the most powerful and controversial sporting organizations in the history of the modern era.

Chapter 3 looks at the economics of the modern World Cup. From a relatively small beginning in 1930, the competition has grown into a huge financial undertaking. The tournament has several different ways in which it generates money, including ticket sales, television rights, advertising arrangements, and the sale of merchandise. Each of these sectors has grown to make the World Cup a major economic juggernaut. In addition, the bidding process to host the tournament and the broadcasting of the draw of teams into playing groups for the final round of matches have become sources of World Cup revenue. These activities, too, have grown in size and significance in recent decades. Finally, the World Cup benefits financially from the long qualifying tournaments that countries now have to navigate to reach the final round of play. The World Cup of football is truly a massive global business undertaking.

Gender, race, and ethnicity are the themes in chapter 4 of *The World Cup as World History*. In countries around the world, the ethnic and racial composition of national teams for the World Cup has often been a topic of intense scrutiny. In some cases, World Cup competitions have shown clearly that racial bias, discrimination, and animosity went hand-in-hand with football in the modern era. At other times, football's foremost global tournament has been a sporting arena to showcase progress in diversifying the ethnic and racial dimensions of national sides. The World Cup of football showcases the sharply contested debates over race and ethnic identity in the modern era.

The progress of women in world football has been slow and uneven since the sport's inception. At the time the game of football was codified and put on a modern footing in the 1860s and '70s, prevailing attitudes about the supposed physical weakness and limited social and cultural spheres of activity for women made it difficult for them to play the game on the same basis as men. Although there were women football enthusiasts from the inception of the modern era, they did not always find help from national sporting organizations or clubs to promote them athletically. Gradually, some of the institutional and social barriers to women playing sports weakened over the course of the twentieth century. In addition to many other physical activities, women played football in increasing numbers in the 1970s, '80s, and beyond. The introduction of a FIFA World Cup competition for women in 1991 was an important breakthrough and has solidified and expanded their role in global football in recent decades. As a consequence of this competition, some women football players, such as Marta of Brazil or Abby Wambach of the United States, have become international stars. Women's experience and gender roles and identity help one to understand much about the history of football in the modern era.

Finally, chapter 5 discusses the cultural significance of both the men's and women's World Cup. As a sport, football brings together large crowds that experience the game through its sights and sounds. To witness a football match in person is to be part of a crowd whose emotions and reactions affect the way we perceive the athletic event. Football has the ability to impact us on an emotional level. The drama of World Cup matches has been played out in stadia that have become famous in their own right as cultural cathedrals of the game. Moreover, a number of players have through their World Cup performances become icons of the game. They have become well known to fans, commentators, and scholars alike. Through their performances, players such as Pelé, Diego Maradona, Bobby Moore, or Lev Yashin have created a shared memory of the game, its evolution, and its importance as a cultural undertaking. Football's World Cup and its famous players have become part of global culture and history in the modern era. Chapter 5 analyzes the impact and performances of several famous football players during the World Cup to get at the spectacle of the game and its cultural significance.

In five thematic chapters, therefore, *The World Cup as World History* traces the history of modern football in the nineteenth, twentieth, and twenty-first centuries. It uses many important contemporary analytical categories, such as globalization, gender analysis, international economics, modern political developments, and sport as a cultural spectacle as they relate to the world's game, football. By focusing on the World Cup and not the entire history of football, the text keeps a tight focus and allows for an integrated discussion of its core issues and themes. This focus allows the text to remain relatively short and accessible to students of world history or sports history.

NOTES

1. Students and teachers of world history could start their exploration of the field with the *Journal of World History*. Jerry H. Bentley was the founding editor of the journal, which contains a rich variety of articles, reviews, and other materials relevant to the study of world history. Bentley, who passed away in 2012, is the coauthor (along with Herbert F. Ziegler and Heather Streets-Salter) of the highly respected *Traditions and Encounters: A Global Perspective on the Past*. Other world history texts often used in North American classrooms are: Richard W. Bulliet et al., *The Earth and Its Peoples: A Global History*; Valerie Hansen and Kenneth R. Curtis, *Voyages in World History*; Robert B. Marks, *The Origins of the Modern World: A Global and Environmental Narrative from the Fifteenth to the Twenty-First Century*; Howard Spodek, *The World's History*; Robert W. Strayer and Eric W. Nelson, *Ways of the World*; Peter Stearns et al., *World Civilizations*; and Robert Tignor et al., *Worlds Together, Worlds Apart: A History of the World from the Beginnings of Humankind to the Present*. All these books have been published in multiple editions and, generally speaking, are reissued in regular cycles. Of course, the list of world history titles grows continually, and newer texts, such as Ross Dunn and Laura Jane Mitchell, *Panorama: A World History*, which was first published in 2015, may become widely used over time.

2. Some scholars, foremost among them David Christian, have even gone so far as to suggest that one should employ a "Big History" approach to the past and see human activities against the background of eons. Such an approach is a further invitation to transform the way we look at the past. See, for example, David Christian, *Maps of Time: An Introduction to Big History* (Berkeley: University of California Press, 2004); David Christian, *Big History: Examines Our Past, Explains Our Present, Imagines Our Future* (New York: DK Publishing, 2016); and David Christian, Cynthia Stokes Brown, and Craig Benjamin, *Big History: Between Nothing and Everything* (New York: McGraw-Hill, 2014).

3. The Advanced Placement exam on world history for 2008, for example, included a document-based-question (DBQ) on the modern Olympic movement from 1892 to 2002. The 2012 DBQ was on the history of cricket and politics in South Asia from 1880 to 2005. The Bridging World History online series has a very good section on modern football as part of its treatment of global popular culture.

4. A survey of recent editions of the texts cited in note 1 reveals that they contain little or no treatment of sports topics. The 2017 edition of Bentley, Ziegler, and Streets-Salter, for example, has references to games—Mayan ball games, Panhellenic festivals, and the ancient Olympic Games—but nothing on the history of football per se. Bulliet et al. (2019) has no sections or references to sports, football, or games.

Strayer and Nelson (2016) has no sections on games, sports, or football, although it does have one reference to the use of rubber balls. Hansen and Curtis (2017), on the other hand, does have some treatment of Amerindian ball games, the ancient Olympics, and one reference to the history of football. Overall, however, most of the world history texts in wide circulation have not recognized sports as a major topic for analysis or discussion. Of course, these books are trying to cover an immense number of concepts and eras and do a tremendous amount of good work in numerous world historical contexts. Nevertheless, sports should be added more regularly and systematically to the list of topics included in world historical texts.

5. See David Goldblatt, *The Ball Is Round: A Global History of Soccer* (New York: Riverhead, 2006); Laurent Dubois, *Soccer Empire: The World Cup and the Future of France* (Berkeley: University of California Press, 2010); and Tamir Bar-On, *Beyond Soccer: International Relations and Politics as Seen through the Beautiful Game* (Lanham, MD: Rowman & Littlefield, 2017) for examples of analyses of the global dimensions of football. Most of the panels at a very important conference on football, "Soccer as the Beautiful Game: Football's Artistry, Identity, and Politics," held at Hofstra University in April 2014, took global or international perspectives on their topics. Several important essays from this conference were later published—see Brenda Elsey and Stanislao Pugliese, eds., *Football and the Boundaries of History: Critical Studies in Soccer* (New York: Palgrave Macmillan, 2017).

6. See the *Journal of Sport History*, for example, which contains many articles and reviews focused on the career or development of an individual athlete, town or city, or national setting. The *Journal of Sport History* does, however, also show the evolution and diversity in the field as it regularly has articles and reviews featuring global and international perspectives.

Chapter 1

The Origins of Modern Football and the First World Cup

Football is without a doubt the most popular game in the world and has been for most of the twentieth and twenty-first centuries. In the second half of the nineteenth century, when the modern rules of football were first codified in England, there were many contenders for the title of the world's most popular sport. Horse racing, hunting, fighting games—including boxing—and many other popular leisure-time activities could be found around the globe. Moreover, any number of new or newly reorganized games and pastimes, such as golf, cricket, and cycling, competed or would compete for the attention of participants and spectators alike. The playing field in the modern era, from the late eighteenth century onward, was really quite crowded. This was especially true beginning in the second half of the nineteenth century. At that time, industrialization, urbanization, overseas trade, cultural diffusion, and the growth in leisure time began to transform many global relationships. These developments, in turn, provided space and opportunity for sports to modernize and establish themselves and grow within a large number of countries around the world.

Yet it would be football that would gradually and definitively become the world's game. Regardless of how one measures the impact of a sport and its influence, football became the dominant game in the twentieth century. Currently, it boasts more players, leagues, sponsors, spectators, viewers, gamblers, and global impact than any other sport in the world. The creation of the World Cup of football, first played in Uruguay in 1930, helped expand the reach of the sport. The tournament was itself the result of a long historical process that confirmed the growing influence of the game in athletic competitions. The World Cup, especially after the Second World War, would in turn expand the popularity of football and make it a truly global sporting phenomenon.

Of the many reasons one might cite for football's popularity, perhaps two stand out. First, around the globe many different cultures and nations can and have laid claim to a "footballing" legacy or even see themselves as the originators of the game. That is, the prevalence of kicking and ball games throughout the world and in many different epochs has allowed different societies to create a "history" or sometimes a mythology that links them to the origins of the world's game, football. Even though these many ball games differed greatly in style and meaning from one another and from the modern game of football, a growth industry has popped up to link ancient cultures to contemporary football.[1] Second, and more directly linked to the rise of the World Cup, is football's simplicity. Once its contemporary rules were codified in the nineteenth century, football could spread globally because it was an easy-to-understand game that demanded little in the way of equipment and could be played anywhere time and space allowed. This introductory chapter explores briefly some of the earliest history and cultural background of football and then analyzes in greater detail the origins of the modern game around the world, culminating in the creation and spread of the World Cup itself as a primary vehicle for the popularity of football in the contemporary sporting landscape.

KICKING GAMES AROUND THE WORLD

Over the last several decades, world historians have become used to turning to the expertise of a wide range of scholars in order to understand the past better. Certain eras and developments can sometimes be better researched with the tools of geology, anthropology, or archaeology, to name but a few fields, than with the traditional text-driven sources of classical historical inquiry. Although the present study does not hearken back to the dawn of human time, it is helpful, even for the student of history looking primarily at a modern development such as the World Cup, to survey briefly some of the earliest cultural and sporting forerunners of football. To do so, this overview of footballing traditions does not attempt to sort myth from history or to seek a definitive answer to the question of who were the world's first football players. As noted above, a wide variety of ball games played for a diversity of reasons created the deep cultural background and sometimes collective memory and identity against which modern football has established itself. Nevertheless, there are few, if any, direct historical connections between these early games and pastimes and the contemporary sport of football. That is, ancient Chinese or Mesoamerican ball games are not the immediate forerunners of modern football, but they indicate that for centuries people have played a wide variety of kicking games.

This suggests that ball and kicking games are deeply rooted in the human experience. Even if one cannot draw direct historical links between these early sporting practices and modern football, there is something culturally significant about these games, which ties them to our contemporary sporting culture. They also helped to create historical narratives for nations and people to refer to when they did adopt football as a national sport in the nineteenth or twentieth centuries. Central and Latin Americans, for example, could hearken back to Mesoamerican cultures to find a "history" of football, if they were so inclined, even if the games the Olmecs, Mayans, and Aztecs played were quite different from the modern game. Thus, it is important to explore briefly the historical background against which modern football has developed.

Sports historians who have looked at the early history of kicking and ball games have highlighted the role they played in many ancient cultures. Using evidence drawn from archaeology, anthropology, and art history, in addition to printed sources, they have reconstructed many aspects of the games played in China, Japan, Australia, North America, and Mesoamerica, to name but a few places where sporting activities and leisure pursuits were a critical part of social, cultural, or religious practices. In China, for example, a game called *cuju* was played, beginning with the Han dynasty (206 BCE–221 CE), for many centuries.

The game was probably of even earlier origins, but it was seemingly only organized formally under the Han. The contests involved two teams, a marked field with goals, and a leather ball. One could apparently advance the ball in many ways, including using one's hands, but kicking the ball was the primary way of moving it forward. The game had a long history in China as cuju was known during the Tang (618–907 CE) and Song (960–1279 CE) dynasties. It does not, however, appear to have thrived or even survived the rule of the Ming (1368–1644 CE). In the centuries when the game was still popular in China, it was exported and spread along trade routes and lines of imperial expansion. Variations of cuju, played with different rules and meanings, reached such places as the Malay peninsula. Cuju was almost certainly also the forerunner of the Japanese medieval ball game known as *kemari*.

Japanese scholars may claim ancient indigenous roots for this game, but the island empire probably adopted and adapted it from the Chinese. Kemari became especially important among the Japanese elite, who played the game enthusiastically. For this reason, the game became associated most firmly with Japan's medieval past and became marginalized when the country began to modernize and industrialize under the Meiji Restoration that began in 1868.[2]

Independently, the ancient cultures of Mesoamerica also developed kicking games that were central to their societies. The Olmecs, Mayans, and Aztecs all knew and sponsored kicking and ball games in their empires. Indeed,

Cuju Illustration

Kemari, Tokugawa Japan

through their influence such games were spread far north into what would be modern-day Arizona and as far south as Central America to the edges of contemporary Colombia. The various games played by these Mesoamerican cultures have been well documented, as archaeologists have recovered or reconstructed many of the courts on which they were played.

Artwork and many physical objects also attest to the importance of the game in Mesoamerican religion and mythology. Finally, when Europeans, primarily Spaniards, came to the Aztec empire in the sixteenth century, they were interested in the games the locals played, which were infused with cultural meanings. Several of the Europeans, including Catholic religious figures, recorded what they saw and interpreted the games for European audiences. What impressed many of the outside observers was that the game was played with balls made of rubber, which was indigenous to the region. The balls made the Mesoamerican versions of games fast and demanded high levels of skill.

Archaeological evidence indicates that kicking games in Mesoamerica began at least as early as 1500 BCE and were played throughout modern-day Central America more or less continuously until the collapse of the Aztec empire in the early sixteenth century. This is indeed a very long legacy. The use of rubber balls was almost as old as the games themselves, which had religious as well as secular meanings. So central were games to Mesoamerican cultures that they feature in some of the defining myths of the people in that

Mesoamerican Playing Grounds (*Wikimedia Commons, tato grasso*)

region of the world. The *Popol Vuh*, which is a classic of Mayan and world literature, has at its heart the story of two hero twins, Hun Hunahpu and Vucub Hunahpu, who must play ball games against the gods of the underworld. By outplaying the gods, the twins became foundational figures in Mayan mythology and cosmology.[3]

By the time of the Aztecs, ball and kicking games were more ritualistic and secular in nature and often played for sporting and gambling purposes. The games could also be quite rough and even violent, with players occasionally losing their lives. Despite the Spaniards' early fascination with Aztec ball games, they did not fare well during the encounter with the Europeans. On the one hand, the ritualistic nature of the games made them suspicious to the Spaniards, who did not understand Mesoamerican culture well. On the other hand, European conquistadores and Catholic clergymen worried about the rowdy and rambunctious style of the games. In the long run, however, it would be disease that did the most to disrupt the ball games of Mesoamerica and the culture that was associated with them. Much of the indigenous population was wiped out as it was exposed to European epidemic illnesses. Thereafter, it was impossible to sustain the indigenous culture, including its athletic practices, in the same manner as before the Europeans' arrival. A few places in the region, however, maintain the historical connections to the ancient ball games of the Mesoamericans, but these are not the roots of the modern sport of football in the area. The main football stadium in Mexico City is called the Azteca, which has been the site of many important football matches, including two World Cup finals (1970 and 1986). It is only a few miles away from Tenochtitlan, the old capital of the Aztec empire. The stadium is, however, a cultural reference to a past society; it is not a direct historical link from that society to the present-day Mexican obsession with football. Nevertheless, even indirect cultural reference points form part of the deep background for understanding football as the world's game. History and myth can flow together and reinforce each other in historical interpretations.[4]

Many other global societies can lay claim to a sporting legacy that includes kicking and ball competitions. In Latin America, further south than the reach of Mesoamerican cultures' influence, there are records of ball games among various peoples as far as Patagonia on the southern tip of the continent. Native Americans in what would be the contemporary United States also had their versions of kicking games, as did the indigenous people of Australia. Certainly, world historians working with evidence drawn from archaeology, anthropology, and art history will over time learn even more about these cultural practices and how they fit into global patterns and developments. But these games, all of which are evidence of a strong cultural attachment to kicking and playing with a ball, will almost certainly remain only indirectly connected to the background of modern football.

THE CREATION OF MODERN FOOTBALL

Modern football originated in England in the mid-nineteenth century. Kicking and ball games had been known in Great Britain for centuries, too, but these were popular pastimes with a wide variety of rules, traditions, and customs. In the public schools of England, which were the reserve of the social and economic elite, students played several varieties of "football" in the first decades of the nineteenth century. The desire to standardize the game and make it more rational and modern led gradually to the codification of rules for football. This development, in turn, would allow first for competitions between schools and then later between clubs. Recent scholarship on the origins of football in England has tended to complicate or even downplay the role of public schools in its creation. Some scholars have argued that it was the sporting culture beyond their walls, in places such as Sheffield and Lancashire, that did the most to spread the popularity of the new nineteenth-century rules of football and to commercialize it for a wider public by using professional players.[5] Paid players certainly did not fit with the sporting ethos, with its emphasis on amateurism, of the public schools. One can see, however, these developments as being part of an unfolding historical process and working together. English public schools helped to codify the rules of modern football, which could, in turn, be taken to sporting contexts in middle- and working-class settings far beyond elite academic institutions. Thus, these developments reinforced one another and helped to spread the popularity of the game quickly through English society. By the end of the nineteenth century, the game had grown very rapidly indeed and had become popular with wide social strata. As administrators, soldiers, teachers, and businessmen exported the game, football was changing the sporting landscape in Great Britain, on the continent of Europe, and in places around the world.

An important step in making football into a modern sport that could be exported to different places came in 1848 with the establishment of the so-called "Cambridge Rules." At Cambridge University to the north of London, representatives from many of England's most powerful public schools—Eton, Harrow, Rugby, Winchester, and Shrewsbury—met to draw up a set of common rules to play football. This influential step was not met with universal acceptance, and various versions of football still existed throughout England in the 1850s and into the 1860s. At the same time, many new clubs, playing by different rules and customs, were founded outside of the framework of England's public schools. As the popularity of the sport spread, so too did the desire to create even more unified systems of play. This was in keeping with the nineteenth century's increasing reliance upon modern, rational mechanisms for conducting everyday life, including people's work and leisure schedules. This desire to codify and regulate the game also clearly grew out of a hope to standardize the game so that matches between a wider circle of schools or clubs could be held. These same forces of modernization and rationalization of a sport would not only create football as we know the game today; they would also help to spread it to far-flung parts of the world.[6]

A further decisive step in the history of football came in 1863, when, after a series of meetings in London, the Football Association was formed. These meetings produced a relatively comprehensive set of rules that gave more shape to the game.

The association also began sponsoring a cup competition in 1872, the oldest continuous footballing event of its kind in the world. The name "soccer," in fact, is a derivation from the word association and dates its history to the meetings, rules, and competitions set up beginning in 1863 by the Football Association. Of course, outside of North America and Australia, the game is known as football, a name that reflects that gradually all forms of "handling" of the ball—advancing it with one's hands—were outlawed from the game. As the rules were codified, football could now be distinguished from other emerging games, such as rugby, which was also being rationalized and standardized in the second half of the nineteenth century and which, of course, allows the use of one's hands to advance the ball. Tackling and other means of obstruction also became the reserve of rugby as they were outlawed in the game of football.

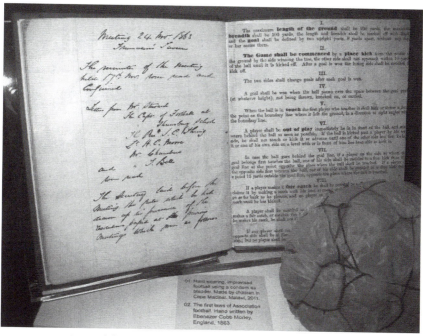

Laws of the Game (*Wikimedia Commons, Adrian Roebuck*)

The newly codified version of the sport would spread very quickly in the British Isles. The first international match, played between England and Scotland, was in 1872, only nine years after the formation of the Football Association. A league to organize teams and regulate play was founded formally in 1888 in Birmingham, one of England's fastest-growing cities. The original league featured primarily teams from the north and England's midlands.[7] Its first champion was the team Preston North End, which now plays its football in the lower tiers of English football. The league was the forerunner of all the organizational efforts that have followed and in some ways served as a model for the international development of the game as it made its way rapidly across the channel and on to the continent of Europe in the last decades of the nineteenth century. The game's popularity spread such that by 1900, football became the sport of urban businessmen, tradesmen, and the working class. As the game continued to grow, new clubs were founded, early forms of professionalism (paying players) emerged, and larger and more elaborate grounds and stadia were built to accommodate the expanding fan base. The game quickly became further commercialized, too, as advertisements sprung up around or outside of football grounds. The business side of football, however, was still in its infancy, and only later would the sport generate vast amounts of money and revenue.

FOOTBALL'S EXPANSION IN EUROPE

Britain's economic, political, and cultural connections to the European continent became the conduits through which football as a game was introduced to countries such as France, the Netherlands, Belgium, Germany, Switzerland, and Austria. British practitioners of the sport or newfound enthusiasts on the European continent then exported the game to yet other countries. For example, in Vienna, the capital of the Habsburg Monarchy until the end of the First World War, English gardeners working for the Rothschild family introduced football. From Vienna, the game spread quickly to other parts of the old empire—modern-day Hungary, Czechia, Slovakia, and Croatia, for example—or people in these regions became familiar with the sport through their own business or cultural connections within the Austrian Empire.[8]

France's fascination with football was part of a sporting boom in the modern era. Of course, the French have participated in and supported many sports in the nineteenth and twentieth centuries. One can hardly forget, for example, the importance of cycling in French culture.[9] Football would also firmly establish itself in France and in the Francophone world—those areas that fell under French colonial or cultural influence. In fact, a Frenchman, Jules Rimet, would be at the heart of the creation of the original World Cup, and the trophy or cup awarded at the end of the competition would eventually be named after him.

Football had been exported to France from England in the late nineteenth century and was being played at the club level as early as the 1870s. The game would quickly become popular, although mostly in the northeastern and southeastern regions of the country. In the decades before the First World War, many new football clubs would emerge in these parts of France, and leagues and competitions would begin to be organized. Nevertheless, a truly national French footballing culture that involved all regions of the country did not develop until after 1918.[10] As in Britain, the game could be played anywhere a ball, or a facsimile thereof, and an open space could be found. There were reports in the nineteenth century of spontaneous games being played in public spaces in Paris. The spread of football in urban areas would be one hallmark of the sport's growth throughout Europe and the world. As cities expanded and as urban dwellers carved out some leisure time, the desire to play grew, and football provided one possible outlet for this pent-up energy.

In France, as in Britain and throughout much of the modernizing, industrializing world, the growth of football was fueled by two immensely important social and cultural developments. Although the game was seen as a rough sport, many educators, businessmen, churchmen, and social elites thought it could be used as a vehicle of social control to tame and direct the energies of not only the sons of the elites in schools but also of the emerging working and middle classes of the late nineteenth century. In other words, football, with its rules, codes, and emerging traditions, could be used to discipline and direct the sporting culture of those who played it. In practice, this meant a type of balancing act developed in footballing circles. The frequently rough and spontaneous nature of the game was to be checked and guided by firm discipline. The goal was to produce a greater number of useful citizens and disciplined workers for the state and society. To be sure, the balance between rough play and sporting discipline was not always maintained, and rowdiness sometimes won out everywhere the game was played. Police reports in Europe, for example, show that the authorities were not always in control of a game that was spreading like wildfire throughout the continent. Incidents of violence and unruly behavior, charges of professionalism, and reports of gambling were part of this early footballing culture. Moreover, football throughout the continent was and could be played well beyond the reach of leagues, schools, and similar organizations. Exactly who, if anyone, was in control of this new and expanding sport, its energy, and its social and cultural meanings was not always clear. Football was not then or now simply a vehicle for social control and discipline.

Another major and global phenomenon driving the expansion of football in the nineteenth century was imperialism. As European countries, such as France and the United Kingdom, sought to extend their political, economic, and cultural influence globally, they also took their games with them. Thus, the French introduced football to parts of the Caribbean and west Africa in the era before the First World War. Wherever British or French settlers, soldiers, or businessmen established themselves, they brought the new sport to the colonial populations and to regions and people coming into contact with their spreading imperial influence. This development would be immensely important to the global growth of the game. After the Second World War and the era of decolonization, however, the former citizens of the empire would also strike back. Several former French and British colonies would establish footballing traditions and teams strong enough to contend with or defeat their one-time colonizing metropolitan states. For example, Senegal would famously win its match against France at the 2002 World Cup. Equally significant would be the migration of players from throughout the colonial and post-colonial world, especially after 1945, to Europe to play football at the club and national levels. This profound movement of players has been an important global phenomenon within footballing culture for the past several decades.[11]

In the late nineteenth and early twentieth centuries, however, football in the colonial world carried with it the idea of the "civilizing mission." Just as the sport was supposed to help direct, guide, and control the energies of the

European urban youth in the continent's cities and towns, it supposedly would also bring colonials closer culturally to the colonizers. Football could be seen as a vehicle for spreading European values and customs to places like the Caribbean or Africa. Of course, Europeans ran the risk of the sport spreading so widely and becoming so popular that the colonials could literally beat them at their own game. This was a worry even in the decades before the First World War and showed clear assumptions about supposed racial and social hierarchies in global encounters. As Pierre de Coubertin, one of the founders of the modern Olympic movement, said, victories by the "dominated race over the dominant race . . . could have dangerous implications."[12] The spread of football globally, therefore, demonstrated a two-edged quality. As a codified game with a set of rules and a supposed discipline, football could be used as a mechanism of social and racial control. As a sporting contest whose style of play and outcome could never fully be predicted or directed, football could also represent a danger to the very social and racial hierarchies it supposedly reinforced.[13]

The First World War (1914–1918) greatly influenced the history of modern football. Massing million-man armies to fight on several fronts brought together large numbers of men who were exposed to the game for the first time. Soldiers who were already football enthusiasts before the war successfully popularized the sport among the uninitiated. Again, the simplicity of the game helped. It could be played anywhere a ball and some open ground away from enemy lines could be found. There are ample reports during the First World War of balls being sent to the front and of officers sometimes kicking a ball out in front of the lines into "no man's land" in order to encourage their troops to move forward. There is also the famous "Christmas match," during which hostilities were temporarily suspended so that German and Allied soldiers could play a game.[14] Although one should be careful not to romanticize such developments or to overstate the political influence of football during the First World War, the sport was clearly establishing itself in ever-wider social and national circles. Moreover, it was taken to new peoples. Colonial subjects who had not been exposed to the sport before the First World War and who were caught up in the global conflict as soldiers, sailors, and workers learned about football for the first time and took the game back to their home territories, provinces, and countries.

As the sport spread globally—be it to France, Austria, Italy, Brazil, Argentina, or Africa—it followed the example set in England: association rules were adopted, clubs were founded, leagues were set up, and competitions were regularized. Soon, in much of Europe, including the southern-tier countries of Portugal, Spain, and Greece, domestic league and cup competitions were established. Many of Europe's and South America's most famous clubs were established in the years right around the turn of the twentieth century or before and after the First World War, as is evident in table 1.1.

Table 1.1. Sampling of Foundation Dates of Major European and South American Club Teams

Club	Country	Year
Bayern Munich	Germany	1900
Borussia Dortmund	Germany	1909
Borussia Mönchengladbach	Germany	1900
Schalke	Germany	1904
Admira	Austria	1905
Austria	Austria	1911
Rapid	Austria	1899
Grasshoppers	Switzerland	1886
Zürich	Switzerland	1896
Lyon	France	1899
Marseille	France	1899
Saint Étienne	France	1919
Monaco	Monaco	1890
Ferencváros	Hungary	1899
Honvéd	Hungary	1909
MTK	Hungary	1901
Újpest	Hungary	1885
Atlético Madrid	Spain	1903
Barcelona	Spain	1899
Real Madrid	Spain	1902
Sevilla	Spain	1890
Benfica	Portugal	1904
Porto	Portugal	1893
Sporting Lisbon	Portugal	1906
Inter Milan	Italy	1908
Juventus Turin	Italy	1897
Lazio	Italy	1900
Milan	Italy	1899
Panathinaikos	Greece	1908
Olympiacos	Greece	1925
PAOK	Greece	1926
Boca Juniors	Argentina	1905
Newell's Old Boys	Argentina	1903
River Plate	Argentina	1901
Botafogo	Brazil	1904
Flamengo	Brazil	1895
Fluminense	Brazil	1902
Santos	Brazil	1912
Nacional	Uruguay	1899
Peñarol	Uruguay	1891

Note: Foundation dates may not always correspond to the date on which a club played its first official match.

Sources: Tom Dunmore, *Historical Dictionary of Soccer* (Lanham, MD: Rowman & Littlefield, 2015), 27–28, 35, 36–37, 41, 43, 44, 128, 152, 156, 183, 199, 208–9, 220, 221; footballhistory.org; Worldfootball.net.

So explosive was the growth of football in Europe and South America that an international organization to govern its rules and competitions was formed in Paris in 1904. This was FIFA, the Fédération International de Football Association. The creation of FIFA was a key moment in the history of modern football. On the one hand, the organization adopted association football's

Table 1.2. Foundation Dates of National Football Associations, Dates of Joining FIFA

Country	Founded	FIFA
Argentina	1893	1912
Australia	1911 (1961)*	1954 (1963)*
Austria	1904	1905
Brazil	1914	1923
Cameroon	1959	1962
Canada	1912	1913
Chile	1895	1913
China	1924 (1949)*	1931
England	1863	1905–20, 1924–28, 1946*
France	1919	1904
Germany	1900	1904
Ghana	1957	1958
Greece	1926	1927
Ivory Coast	1960	1964
Japan	1921	1921
Korea, Republic	1933	1948
Mexico	1927	1929
Nigeria	1945	1960
Russia	1912 (1992)*	1912–17 (1992)*
South Africa	1892 (1992)*	1910 (1992)*
Spain	1913	1904
Sweden	1904	1904
Turkey	1923	1923
United States	1913	1914
Uruguay	1900	1923

Note: Political developments have affected the standing of national football associations and their affiliation to FIFA in the modern era. For example, Russia and China both experienced communist revolutions that changed the countries' relationship with FIFA for long periods of time. South Africa's history of racial oppression (apartheid) greatly complicated its relationship to FIFA in the twentieth century. England and Australia have had on-and-off-again relationships with FIFA as well. Dates with an asterisk (*) in the table indicate that in some instances national football associations were founded and refounded or that they changed their affiliation dates with FIFA. On the other hand, FIFA usually considers France and Spain to be founding members of the organization, even though their official national football associations were founded after 1904.

Sources: FIFA.com; fff.fr (France); rfef.es (Spain); www.thefa.com (England); safa.net (South Africa); www.rfs.ru (Russia); FootballAustralia.com.au (Australia); Tom Dunmore, *Historical Dictionary of Soccer* (Lanham, MD: Rowman & Littlefield, 2015), 53.

rules and was helpful in sponsoring and organizing international competitions, such as the World Cup. Over time and partially because of FIFA's influence, football would clearly become the world's game, with more players, fans, sponsors, and media outlets than any other global sport. A FIFA study from 2001 claimed that at least 240 million people around the world played football regularly.[15] On the other hand, FIFA has left a huge trail of controversial political and economic decisions, especially in the last forty years or so, that have come to a head in recent years. Today, the future of the organization and its leadership are under careful scrutiny and great international pressure. The politics of the world game, including recent FIFA controversies, are discussed in greater detail in chapter 2.

FOOTBALL'S SPREAD TO SOUTH AMERICA

An important part of the expansion of football came when the sport spread from Europe to South America. This expansion was a complex story, but it followed certain recognizable global patterns. The game was primarily a British export that came to the port cities of the River Plate region as early as the 1860s and 1870s and then spread rapidly in northern Argentina, southern Brazil, especially in the Rio de Janeiro and São Paulo urban areas, and in Uruguay. British expatriate businessmen and their employees, who came to places like Buenos Aires, Montevideo, and the Brazilian cities as part of the expansion of European economic and cultural influence in South America, played football. The British had no need to put governmental officials or military personnel into independent South American nations because the former's financial and trade influence was so strong in the latter. The British controlled, for example, most of the developing railways in Argentina and had many other business interests and investments throughout the continent.[16]

Football in the River Plate area—the delta that includes Uruguay, northern Argentina, and southern Brazil—underwent a number of important evolutions in a rapidly changing society in the decades before the First World War. Clubs, competitions, and eventually cups were set up in its major urban areas. By the turn of the century, international competitions between Argentina, Uruguay, and Brazil were established. At first, the game was played primarily by the British abroad and the elites who sought to imitate them and to attach themselves socially to the economically powerful Europeans in their midst. Some combination of British and South American elites established most of the earliest South American clubs. The English-language schools in the area also cultivated and spread the game among the high-ranking sons of the region. Quickly, however, the popularity of the game spread to artisans, workers, dockhands, and even the urban poor. Before the First World War, factory clubs were founded in Brazil, for example, and the social basis and support for football expanded greatly. Although the social elites of Latin America remained largely in control of the club infrastructure, new football teams, players, and spectators began to open up and spread the game to wide social and racial sections of Brazilian, Uruguayan, and Argentinian society. With these developments, questions of race, class, and status became quite important in the sport and were points of contention throughout most of the modern era.[17]

Football came somewhat later to the countries of Chile, Bolivia, and Paraguay than it did to the River Plate region. The pattern of its spread was similar, however, as it was waves of European, especially British, businessmen, financiers, and their sons that brought the game into these countries as well. By the earliest decades of the twentieth century, they had all developed strong footballing traditions. Further north, the sport established itself in Ecuador more firmly than in Venezuela, where baseball would become the emerging sport of choice. In Colombia, the history of football was initially somewhat mixed as it caught on in the coastal cities but not in the interior municipalities of Bogotá, Medellín, and Cali. In addition, the geography of the area, mostly rough mountainous and jungle terrain, made it difficult for competitions between urban areas to develop. The distances from Colombia, Peru, and Ecuador to the heartland of South American football in the River Plate region also meant, in the early decades of twentieth century, that there would not be much initial exchange in footballing culture.[18]

Because South America did not participate in the First World War, football in the region would go through several important transformations. First, the power of British money was greatly weakened after 1918 because of the monetary losses the United Kingdom experienced during the Great War. This meant that football clubs' reliance upon local elites and groups for financial support increased. It also increased the nationalistic sentiment and fervor within many South American clubs and associations. Staying out of the war meant, too, that the organizational efforts of South American clubs to stage international events could go on without interruption. For example, the first continental football association in the world, CONMEBOL (Confederación Sudamericana de Fútbol), was formed for South America in 1916.

Football was developing rapidly in South America and becoming embedded deeply in the organizational life and daily culture of several of its nations. Two huge and important global developments, immigration and urbanization, strengthened the dramatic boom in the sport in late nineteenth- and early twentieth-century South America. Immigrants from Europe and Asia arrived in South America in large numbers during this period. They came as members of the economic elite, middle-class entrepreneurs, lower-class artisans, the working class, the rural poor, and the economically marginalized. They came not only from Britain but from many other European nations, such as Italy. They also came from Japan and China and, taken as whole, dramatically transformed South American societies. At the same time, this influx of immigrants combined with the movement of people from the countryside, what historians call "internal migration," and caused explosive growth in many of South America's cities. In these booming urban areas with their increasingly complex racial and ethnic mixtures, football established itself as the game of the elite and the commoner alike and became wildly popular. Football's simplicity, the visual attractiveness of the sport, and international competitions all helped to grow a strong fan base for it in South America. Although it was somewhat surprising when the first World Cup was played in Uruguay in 1930—a development examined in detail below—no one could doubt the public's passion for football in the River Plate region.[19]

FOOTBALL'S SPREAD TO AFRICA AND ASIA

Although it has become the sport of much of Africa in the twentieth century, football does not seem to have quite the same deep cultural roots to kicking games there as was the case in China and Mesoamerica, for example. To be sure, Africa had a rich sporting culture in pre-modern times. From Egypt in the north to the tip of modern-day South Africa, many physical activities and leisure-type pursuits were known. However, most of these games did not involve balls and even fewer involved kicking. Of course, this is a huge generalization about an immensely large geographic area, and one could find exceptions to it, but it does seem to hold for most of the continent. On the other hand, once modern-day football reached Africa through the difficult and complex colonial encounter with European nations in the nineteenth century, it took on deep roots, first among white-settler and African elites, but quickly also among working-class white and black Africans in regions like southern Africa and the west and north African coastal regions. It would take until the interwar period, the 1920s and '30s, for the game to spread further inland to territories where European culture was less pervasive or had been nonexistent until the late nineteenth and early twentieth centuries.

Football would soon provide playing and political opportunities for many African peoples and, after decolonization, nations. Clubs formed early in British-controlled areas of the African continent, for example. These organizations were not the preserve of white elites, as football culture made its way deeper and deeper into the sporting ethos of Africans both in the north in places like Egypt, which had a flourishing football scene, and in modern-day South Africa. Organized football spread more slowly into French-controlled regions of Africa, which was perhaps a reflection of French culture not adopting as early or forcibly games and competitions as part of its educational system as in Great Britain. Nevertheless, significant clubs and important competitions would develop in places like Algeria, Tunisia, and Morocco, all under French influence. Indeed, international matches in this region of North Africa could rival the density and frequency of those taking place in South America and Europe by the 1930s. Against this background, it is not surprising to learn that French club and national teams in the interwar years recruited players such as Raoul Diagne of Senegalese descent but born in French Guiana and Larbi Ben Barek (Larbi Ben Mbarek) from Morocco. The movement of players from Africa to Europe began quite early in the history of world football.

The importance of the development of football in Africa can hardly be underestimated. The elaboration of the game, its spread into urban and rural areas, the establishment of clubs, leagues, and domestic and international competitions would give Africans of many different racial, ethnic, or social backgrounds a realistic playing field, upon which they could measure themselves against their European colonizers and each other. In the process, football became a possible venue for the assertion of African self-confidence, status, and even regional and national identity. This was especially true in the 1950s and '60s, when much of the continent began the formal, painful, and often violent process of decolonization, which would go on for several decades. Newly emerging African nations were anxious to join FIFA, football's world governing body, and to compete internationally, even if political difficulties still blocked their path to a competition such as the World Cup. Through football, African peoples and nations had the opportunity to engage heavily in organizational activity, to establish a base of support for their political and national movements, and to nurture and expand feelings of independence from their colonial overlords. For example, in South Africa football clubs eventually became associated with the anti-apartheid movement. Newly independent African nations would use their national football associations to pressure FIFA to ban white-controlled South African teams from international competitions in the early 1960s. The Confederation of African Football (CAF), which had formed in 1957 and had already begun to sponsor continental competitions among African nations, expelled South Africa, because of its apartheid system, from its ranks in 1961. The ban would stay in place until the early 1990s, when the political tide turned in South Africa, a black majority government was installed, and apartheid officially came to an end. Less than two decades later, FIFA, which by now included a large number of member organizations from Africa, would award the 2010 World Cup to South Africa. Politics and the game of football were in this case deeply intertwined.[20]

The pattern of development of football in Asia differed quite markedly from that of Africa in the modern era. Although there were obvious sites of European colonialism in Asia through which the sport could be introduced and spread (Vietnam, India, and Indonesia, for example), football's initial steps in making cultural inroads into Asia were slow. Moreover, the game was slower to grow in much of Asia than it did in Africa in the twentieth century. Finally, in large parts of Asia today, football either competes with other sports for national status (China, for example, where numerous other sports, including basketball, are played popularly and at high levels) or has not become part of the national sporting scene. India, for example, adopted cricket and not football from the British as the dominant sport. Nevertheless, today the culture of football is very important in many parts of Asia, especially when one measures its economic impact through viewership and merchandising deals. Thus, it was a logical move on the part of FIFA to stage a World Cup, the 2002 competition, in Japan and South Korea, the only time up to that point that it had been co-hosted. (Canada, Mexico, and the United States will jointly host the 2026 cup.) The first FIFA Women's World Cup of football was played in China in 1991. China, Japan, and South Korea have established themselves as football nations in women's football in recent decades. Japan won the Women's World Cup of 2011 and finished second in the 2015 competition in Canada. Overall, the impact of football in Asia has been more diffuse than in Africa or South America, but its influence, which continues to grow, is clearly part of the global history of the world's game in the modern era.

The history of football in Asia has also been affected by a number of world historical events. The experience of imperialism, for example, was quite varied in places such as India, China, and Japan. In Japan, for example, western colonialists did not establish direct political power until the short-lived American occupation following the Second World War. To be sure, Japan followed western patterns of economic modernization and industrialization beginning with the Meiji restoration in 1868, but it remained fundamentally in control of its cultural life and developments. When western sports did make their impact in Japan, it was mostly through the spread of an American sport, baseball, in the interwar years. Football did not become well established in Japan until well after the Second World War, but the recent success of its women's national team, the establishment of professional leagues for both men and women, and its co-hosting, along with South Korea, of the World Cup in 2002 significantly raised the sporting profile of football in Japan.[21]

India, of course, had a long and complex history of colonial interaction with the British. The British East India Company was heavily involved in the Indian subcontinent long before British political administrators and formal representatives of the crown took over direct control of governing India in the wake of the Sepoy Rebellion of 1857. India under the Raj, the British name for the governmental system that was introduced after 1857, was indeed the "jewel in the crown" of the empire. It must be remembered, however, that Indian influence upon British ways and customs was at least as profound as vice versa. Britain brought Christianity and its educational systems to the region, but these did not convert the majority of peoples to western ways and manners. As world historians have been pointing out for the last several decades, India's influence upon the British diet, language, literature, and culture was quite profound, and this was long before significant numbers of people from the region began migrating to Britain after the Second World War. To this day, football, which made its way to so many other parts of the British Empire, has not fully established itself in India, Pakistan, or Bangladesh as the national sport, although there are signs of its growing popularity in these countries, too. Cricket, on the other hand, has become wildly popular in these countries, so much so that they have often come to dominate the English at their own game.[22]

China's history with football presents yet another case of interaction with colonialism and western culture. World historians are well acquainted with the standard narrative of opium wars, treaty ports, spheres of influence, and the "opening up" of China in the nineteenth century. To be sure, China's turmoil and even chaos in this period could be quite severe—witness the destruction caused by the Taiping Rebellion in the 1850s—but China never fully lost political control of much of its empire for long periods of time, nor did European cultural practices, including sports, make widespread inroads into Chinese society in the nineteenth century. China's problems were real enough, but they were often perceived by the various regimes as internal problems of control and stability. Contact with European militaries, missionaries, merchants, and cultural messengers was just one of the challenges facing China in the late nineteenth and early twentieth centuries. It also had to deal with internal competing political interests, ethnic minorities, economic instability, and famine. In this environment, football and other western sports did not make many advances beyond the port and coastal cities well into the early twentieth century.

The next few decades, the interwar period, were also a time of intense political and economic instability in China. Warlordism, communism, and encounters with Japan's imperial ambitions all challenged China's fundamental ability to function. In the wake of the tremendous suffering of the Second World War, a civil war broke out between nationalists and communist forces in 1949. None of these developments provided a firm ground upon which a new sport might be played and grow in popularity. When football clubs and competitions did finally establish themselves in China after the civil war, they did not have to wait long for further upheaval. Mao Zedong's dual internal revolutions, the Great Leap Forward from 1958 to 1961 and the Cultural Revolution from 1966 to 1976, did much to disrupt the organizational life of the country and daily culture that might have fostered football's growth. For many Chinese, especially those with some notion of western orientation, the Cultural Revolution was a period in which one had to worry about physical survival, not sporting practices. Thus, it is not surprising that football has only established itself slowly in China in the decades since Mao's death, along with the gradual liberalization of society and the growth in wealth and leisure-time pursuits. In recent decades, football in China has grown in stature and popularity, but it competes against any number of other sports—table tennis, gymnastics, basketball, etc.—for influence and audience. China has become a footballing nation, but its involvement and obsession with the global game is not on par with much of the rest of the world. Certainly, it is not the dominant sport in China that it is in most of Europe, South and Central America, and large parts of Africa.

FOOTBALL IN CANADA, AUSTRALIA, AND SOUTH AFRICA

The spread of football to Great Britain's so-called white dominions—British-controlled Canada, Australia, and South Africa—presents a number of vexing questions for sport and world historians. On the one hand, nowhere was the initial and sustained cultural connection between Britain and its dominions greater than in these globally far-flung and diverse lands. In an uneven and never complete global process, the English language, religion, literature, laws, and much more were brought to these places, which over time set up political and economic systems that favored white settlers. These settlers, in turn, saw themselves over generations as the "native" and natural leaders and authorities in these lands. In order to make it so, the white settler communities often displaced or decimated the original aboriginal or native populations. This displacement process was never complete. In Australia, for example, the influx of white settlers largely destroyed the native population. Aboriginal people struggled to maintain their lives and culture under challenging circumstances. In these white dominion societies, one might therefore suspect that football, a British leisure-time activity with codified rules, would come to dominate the sporting culture of these lands. However, the competition for national sport standing in all of these countries has been quite contested, and nowhere in these former British dominions does football reign supreme as the number one popular and professional sport.

The reasons for the contested place of football in the white dominion states have much to do with historical and cultural context. Global patterns are always complicated by local, regional, and national differences and by historical contingency. For example, timing was a crucial factor in the way football was either received or rejected in many of these countries. By the time the modern, codified version of the game reached Australia in the 1870s, there was already a thriving culture of Australian Rules football, which had established itself first in the city of Melbourne and then spread to most of the rest of the southeastern part of the country. Moreover, rugby would become wildly popular in Australia and serve as another important sporting alternative in the late nineteenth century and throughout the twentieth century. Cricket was also played widely in Australia and used there as a marker of elite status in society, especially in the late nineteenth century. By the time the provinces formed themselves into a federal union in 1901 and created the modern state of Australia we know today, the sporting scene in the newly established country was quite crowded. In many places, football would struggle to gain and maintain a foothold or was seen as the sport of the working class or of recently arrived immigrants. Thus, it was not surprising that Australia remained on the margins of global football and the World Cup competitions throughout the first half of the twentieth century.

Football's popularity increased in Australia in the 1950s and '60s, when new waves of immigrants, coming primarily from southern and southeastern Europe, came to the country. They were needed for the continued stability and growth of the economy. Their enthusiasm for football caused a boom in the number of recreational and professional clubs that were formed in the 1950s and '60s, and they helped develop the sport such that Australia qualified for the World Cup in 1974. The new immigrants, however, were not always easily accepted or assimilated into society and maintained much of their old-world identity, be it Croatian, Serbian, or Jewish. Despite more international success in recent decades, football in Australia remains very much one sporting option among many, and there have been several fallow periods in its contemporary cultural and historical significance.[23]

Canada experienced its own idiosyncratic encounter with football. First, its relatively early date of independence—in 1867, Canada achieved control over most of its internal or domestic political and economic affairs—meant that it could develop its own independent sporting traditions. Second, ice hockey, as any casual sporting fan will certainly know, became quite popular in Canada and in many places enjoys national sport status. Quebec, with its attachments to French culture, was not initially enthusiastic for what was then seen as a British game. Finally, Canada was and is influenced by the spread and adoption of sports, such as American football, coming from the United

States. Thus, Canadian sporting culture, much like Australian, is quite varied, and football has to assert itself within a broad mix of athletic pursuits and competitions; it often takes a backseat in terms of popularity and standing to a sport such as ice hockey.[24] Nevertheless, there have been a number of football highlights for Canada in recent years, especially the hosting of the Women's World Cup in 2015. Canada will also co-host, along with Mexico and the United States, the men's World Cup in 2026.

In South Africa, the mix of historical context, political developments, and sporting practices has also been quite profound. Football came to the southern tip of the continent in the last decades of the nineteenth century, but so did rugby and cricket, which became the sports of the white elite. Football was associated with lower-class workers and the employees of European businesses. Quickly, football also became quite popular among the majority population of indigenous black Africans, who would form themselves into teams, clubs, and leagues. Race considerations, which permeated all aspects of South African society, would also be a defining factor in the evolution of sports in that country. Some of the economic and racial barriers have been broken down in recent decades with the formal abandonment of apartheid in the early 1990s, the election of Nelson Mandela—former opposition leader— as president of South Africa, and the coming of the World Cup in 2010. The country remains today, however, a divided society, and social and economic conditions weigh heavily upon sporting practices.[25]

FOOTBALL IN THE UNITED STATES

The history of football (soccer, as opposed to American or "gridiron" football) in the United States can be likened to a roller-coaster ride over the course of the nineteenth and twentieth centuries. By the 1870s, '80s, and '90s, when football was being exported to the European continent and to South America and parts of Africa, the United States had been free of direct British political influence for a century. There was, of course, much economic and cultural exchange across the Atlantic between Great Britain and the United States. Many forms of American sports, including boxing, horseracing, and cockfighting, could trace their origins or parts of their roots back to English practices. By the time football in its modern form made its way across the Atlantic in the second half of the nineteenth century, it encountered a dense sporting scene. Baseball had already established itself as a popular and professional sport. American football, a rugged game sometimes played to fatal conclusions, was making its way into collegiate athletics. In addition, the older sports mentioned above, especially boxing and horse racing, were still popular in many circles. Football, therefore, was a relatively minor sport in the United States in the last decades of the nineteenth century.

Football received a fresh jolt of enthusiasm and participants with the influx of migrants to port cities throughout the United States in the last years before the First World War and into the interwar period. This was when the first World Cup would be played in Uruguay in 1930. The United States was among the teams that participated in that inaugural event. Indeed, the United States enjoyed a certain place in world football based on its showings in the 1930 and 1950 World Cups. The United States beat England 1–0 in the latter competition and finished third in the former, which was only played by thirteen nations.[26]

After the Second World War, however, football in the United States took a nosedive in terms of international standing as other sports, such as baseball, American football, and basketball, grew in stature. The country did not qualify for the World Cup from 1954 until the 1990 competition. Moreover, the game itself had a hard time competing financially for broadcasting and advertising dollars at a time—the 1960s—when television was beginning to dominate the cultural landscape. Baseball, and later football and basketball, came to be the prized commodities of commercial and, eventually, cable television and the Internet. With the introduction of many star players from the 1970 and 1974 World Cups, there was, however, a new football boom in the United States that manifested itself in the craze for the North American Soccer League (NASL). The NASL came to prominence rapidly in the mid-1970s, then seemed to die out just as quickly in the early 1980s. Poor financial planning hit the league, and money was no longer available to attract aging global football superstars to the United States.[27]

A new base of popular and professional commitment to football in the United States was established in the 1990s. Four major developments have made it relevant again in the United States in the last twenty years. First, there was the successful staging of the World Cup in the United States in 1994. Second, along with that competition, a new and vigorous professional men's league (Major League Soccer, MLS) was founded officially in 1993, began playing games in 1996, and has begun to flourish in recent years. Once again, aging European and South American superstars, along with a younger cohort of American and foreign-born players, have competed for the attention of the US sporting public. Third, the success of the US women's national team, which has now won four World Cup competitions (1991, 1999, 2015, and 2019), has grown the game among young women and men alike and led to the creation of several women's professional leagues, the most recent of which is the National Women's Soccer League (NWSL). Fourth, there has been a dramatic surge in young people, both boys and girls, playing football in recent decades. It has become a suburban phenomenon in the United States. Some parents seem to prefer its team-oriented nature over the individualistic aspects of sports such as baseball. The fear of serious injury in football is also less than in a sport such as American football. As a consequence of these four factors and more, football's popularity as a sport that is played at the youth, high school, and college level in the United States has grown significantly since the 1970s and '80s. Perhaps a residual boom from the glory days of the NASL and its original football superstars has also played a role in this development. Certainly, the introduction of Title IX in 1972, which bans discrimination against women's sports at the collegiate level, has helped women's football to grow in the United States. Since the early 1970s, many young women have joined intercollegiate football, and some have gone on to play professionally—a select few for the US national team.[28]

THE FIRST WORLD CUP: URUGUAY 1930

After surveying the spread of football from Britain to Europe and to much of the world and discussing in brief its influence and position in many different countries, let us focus more systematically on the run-up to the first World Cup of 1930 and on some of the political, economic, and cultural reasons for the further popularity of football in the early twentieth century. By the end of the First World War, in 1918, it was truly a global phenomenon. Although it was not yet played throughout the world, its popularity in Europe, the Americas, and in large parts of Africa could not be denied. It had also gained a foothold in Canada, Australia, and the United States. Teams, leagues, and competitions had been established that gave the game a strong organizational base. As we have seen, FIFA was founded in 1904. Many countries around the world already had a national football association or federation by the early twentieth century, and they attached themselves to FIFA (see table 1.2). In addition, football had established itself as a spectator sport capable of drawing large crowds to matches in many different countries. That tendency would only grow as the 1920s and '30s experienced a further football boom globally. Leisure-time pursuits, games, and sports were exploding in popularity in the interwar period. Newspapers had been reporting regularly on sporting results since the late nineteenth century. Now, photographs and extensive commentaries and editorials often accompanied their stories. Teams traveled further to play each other and sometimes went on tours to distant continents, all of which helped promote the spread of the game. Sports were growing exponentially and becoming an increasingly large and important part of global culture in the interwar period.[29]

Against this background, football would stage some of its earliest international competitions, which would culminate in the first World Cup being played in 1930. Of the many reasons for the creation of the first tournament, four stand out. First, there was, as we have already seen, the dramatic global growth in popularity of the sport between the 1860s and the 1920s. Second, the game had proven its ability to draw large audiences and be a revenue-generating sport. The game was already becoming big business at the club and international level by the 1920s and '30s. For example, football drew some of the largest audiences at the Olympic Games in 1928, in Amsterdam, for its matches.[30] Third, an important change in footballing culture made it difficult if not impossible for the Olympics to be the primary international arena for the game. Some countries had already introduced professionalism into domestic football leagues.[31] In many others, paid service for players was conducted off the books but was still a part of the game. Thus, professionalism, open or concealed, was becoming part of world football early in the twentieth century. The aristocrats and European elites who had reintroduced the Olympic Games to their late nineteenth- and early twentieth-century societies wanted, however, to stick to their "amateur" ideal of the athlete. According to this ideal, athletes should compete only for the love of the game and not for money or payment of any kind.[32] One can, of course, question to what extent the Olympic Games themselves were living up to this amateur standing even in their early history, but the ethos of those games was coming increasingly into conflict with football's culture as it was developing in the early decades of the twentieth century. Professionalism in the sport would remain a thorny issue—some national associations and clubs would reject it until well into the twentieth century—but its presence in the game was also a hallmark of the modernizing world. Players were becoming specialized workers who more and more dedicated their time and energy to the discipline of the sport. To be sure, most players still held jobs or practiced occupations beyond the pitch, but a trend toward professionalization and specialization was evident in world football. To include players both professional and amateur, a new type of competition—the World Cup—would have to be invented.

Fourth, high-ranking officials of FIFA and various national associations were ready and even anxious to create a global competition separate from the Olympics. This book includes much about the politics and economics of the World Cup, but obviously they were important considerations from the outset of the competition that have to be discussed briefly here in the story of the run-up to the first tournament in 1930. Jules Rimet of France, who is always cited as one of the driving forces behind the creation of the World Cup, worked hard to form a new global competition for football. He became a legendary figure on the international scene.

Jules Rimet, 1930 (*History and Art Collection/Alamy Stock Photo*)

Rimet and the circle of officials around him were in uncharted waters in the late 1920s when they had to persuade the athletic world to go along with the World Cup.[33] They also realized that a new global football tournament, separate from the Olympic competition, would strengthen the organizational hand of FIFA as the controlling body of football. Further, they hoped that the new international competition would not only become a sporting centerpiece but also eventually be of economic benefit to FIFA, its member associations, and hosting countries. These political and economic issues have woven themselves into the very fabric of the World Cup ever since and have remained highly contentious, especially in the last several decades.

The first World Cup in 1930 also highlighted a number of other modern developments in the history of sport. For example, one of the hallmarks of any modern sport is an obsession with statistics. It is not surprising, therefore, that one of the most covered aspects of all World Cup competitions is the reporting of results. Virtually every action of every match—goals, fouls, penalties, corner kicks, offside violations, etc.—would come to be analyzed in painstaking detail. This is especially true today when modern technology—slow-motion cameras, digital recordings, computers, and the like—makes it possible to examine games and competitions over and over again. Even the earliest World Cup competitions, in 1930, 1934, and 1938, generated a wealth of good and reliable statistics. In 1930, reports of the cup competition came from fans inside the stadia; fans gathered outside to hear the reaction of the crowd, the radio, or newspapers, whose editorial offices were sometimes besieged by fans eager to learn the results. Despite the reluctance of European nations to show up and compete, the 1930 competition was a sporting success—if one measures the amount of interest it created. Fans crowded into the Centenario, the stadium built especially for the World Cup, and waited anxiously to learn the outcome of the final match. Numerous reports confirm that Buenos Aires, the capital of Argentina, was nearly shut down so that its fans could follow the team in the final. Many of them traveled by boat or barge to Montevideo to try and attend the match live.[34] The spectacle of sport and the drama the world's game could create were much on display in the first tournament in 1930. In many ways, the first World Cup would establish a political, economic, and cultural blueprint for the competitions that would follow, but the tournament would also evolve greatly over the course of the next several decades.

At the first World Cup, which was an abbreviated version of what the competition would later become, certain clear global patterns were established. A model for bringing teams from the Americas and Europe to a sporting competition had been created. It would take several decades, but eventually this model would be opened up to include teams from Africa, Asia, and Oceania. Formal mechanisms for qualifications would be introduced and revised in the future, but they would have been pointless without a first World Cup to use as a basis for the growth and development of the fast-growing game. Mass media in the 1930s meant primarily radio and newspapers, but a connection between the competition and reporting and digesting its results had already been established. In the future, this connection would become much more complex and involve substantially more money as the game reached ever larger audiences. The 1930 cup was an early marker in the history of football and its reporting by the mass media, which would evolve and develop greatly over the course of the twentieth and early twenty-first centuries. A game that had only taken on its modern form in the mid-nineteenth century had in less than a century developed domestic and international competitions, culminating in the World Cup of 1930. It had moved quickly from being an elite sport to a popular sport, which in some places was being played by professionals. Finally, it was becoming a sporting spectacle that could capture the imagination of thousands of players and fans alike. Behind this dramatic process in the expansion and growth of football in the modern period were key globalizing developments, such as the migration of people, cultural diffusion, and economic changes that created leisure-time activities and the wherewithal to sponsor and attend sporting events. Further, political shifts meant that governments hoped that staging global sporting competitions might bring prestige and recognition to their various countries. These globalizing trends, among many others, would remain very much a part of the history of the World Cup for the rest of the twentieth and into the twenty-first century.

From the first men's tournament in 1930 until its most recently played version in 2018, the competition would continue to grow and evolve in many respects. In the early 1990s, a FIFA-sponsored Women's World Cup would be introduced. From relatively humble beginnings, the World Cup has grown into a truly global competition with huge economic, political, social, and cultural consequences. At present, there are more countries and territories represented in FIFA than in the United Nations, which is, at some level, a startling commentary on the modern world. It is also, however, clear evidence of the global spread of football. The World Cup, a centerpiece of the game now for several decades, offers a good window onto many recent world historical trends, including shifts in politics, economics, and gender and racial identity, all of which form the basis for analysis in the rest of *The World Cup as World History*. In the last chapter of the book, football as sporting spectacle is analyzed to see how it has embodied different cultural ideas and ideals over the past near century.

DOCUMENTS AND ARTIFACTS RELATED TO THE ORIGINS AND DEVELOPMENT OF FOOTBALL

A. Football Association Tribute to the Cambridge Rules, University of Cambridge. https://www.cam.ac.uk/news/football-association-tribute-to-the-cambridge-rules

   1. From these rules, how was football to be played in mid-nineteenth-century England?
   2. How did these rules help to distinguish football from other sports (rugby, for example) that were also developing in the mid-nineteenth century?

B. David K. Brown, *Association Football: The Game, and How to Play It, Rules and Constitution of the Dominion Football Association*. Toronto: J. R. Robertson, 1879. HathiTrust Digital Library. https://hdl.handle.net/2027/aeu.ark:/13960/t1sf36r24

   1. For whom was this book intended? What was a "dominion" and what was its relationship to Great Britain in 1879?
   2. According to David K. Brown, how was the game of football to be played? What descriptions of players and formations does he provide?

C. C. W. Alcock, *Football: The Association Game*. London: George Bell & Sons, 1906. HathiTrust Digital Library. https://hdl.handle.net/2027/nyp.33433066624655

  1. What insights about the growth of the association game (soccer, football) to 1906 can you gain from Alcock's book?
  2. According to Alcock, how should one play "modern football"? To what extent had the game evolved from the 1870s (Brown's treatment) to 1906 (Alcock's description)?

D. The Greater Game, Football and the First World War, National Football Museum, Manchester, UK. https://www.nationalfootballmuseum.com/exhibitions/the-greater-game-2

  1. How did organized football try to cope with the serious challenges created by the First World War?
  2. What was the "Christmas Truce" of 1914? What does it tell us about the state of football at the time of the Great War?

E. Rimet Cup, 1930, FIFA. https://www.fifa.com/worldcup/history/jules-rimet-cup.html

  1. How does an artifact such as the Rimet Cup help us understand the history and evolution of the World Cup?
  2. What was the history of the cup after it was created for the 1930 tournament?

SUGGESTIONS FOR FURTHER READING AND RESEARCH

Archer, Michael. *History of the World Cup*. London: Hamlyn, 1978.

Bondy, Filip. *The World Cup: The Players, Coaches, History, and Excitement*. New York: Mallard Press, 1991.

Campomar, Andreas. *Golazo! The Beautiful Game from the Aztecs to the World Cup: The Complete History of How Soccer Shaped Latin America*. New York: Riverhead Books, 2014.

Cantor, Andrés, and Daniel Arcucci. *Goooal! A Celebration of Soccer*. New York: Simon and Schuster, 1997.

Chyzowych, Walter. *The World Cup*. South Bend, IN: Icarus Press, 1982.

Dauncey, Hugh, and Geoff Hare. *France and the 1998 World Cup: The National Impact of a World Sporting Event*. London: Frank Cass, 1999.

Duarte, Orlando. *The Encyclopedia of World Cup Soccer*. New York: McGraw-Hill, 1994.

Finn, Gerry P. T., and Richard Giulianotti, eds. *Football Culture: Local Contests, Global Visions*. London: Frank Cass, 2000.

Foer, Franklin. *How Soccer Explains the World: An Unlikely Theory of Globalization.* New York: Harper Perennial, 2010.

Glanville, Brian. *The Story of the World Cup.* London: Faber and Faber, 2014.

Goldblatt, David. *The Ball Is Round: A Global History of Soccer.* New York: Riverhead Books, 2008.

Goodman, Michael E. *The World Cup.* Mankato, MN: Creative Education, 1990.

Holt, Richard, J. A. Mangan, and Pierre Lanfranchi. *European Heroes: Myth, Identity, Sport.* London: Frank Cass, 1996.

Horne, John, and Wolfram Manzenreiter. *Japan, Korea, and the 2002 World Cup.* London: Routledge, 2002.

Jackson, Robert B. *Soccer: The International Sport.* New York: H. Z. Walck, 1978.

Lewis, Michael. *World Cup Soccer.* Wakefield, RI: Moyer Bell, 1994.

Los Mundiales de Fútbol: Desde Uruguay 1930 a Francia 1998. Barcelona: Océano, 1997.

Mangan, J. A. *Europe, Sport, World: Shaping Global Societies.* London: Frank Cass, 2001.

Merrill, Christopher. *The Grass of Another Country: A Journey through the World of Soccer.* New York: H. Holt, 1993.

Morrison, Ian. *The World Cup: A Complete Record, 1930–1990.* Derby, UK: Breedon Books, 1990.

Murray, Bill. *The World's Game: A History of Soccer.* Urbana: University of Illinois Press, 1998.

Robinson, John. *Soccer: The World Cup, 1930–1998.* Cleethorpes, UK: Soccer Book Publishing, 1998.

Rollin, Jack. *The World Cup, 1930–1990: Sixty Glorious Years of Soccer's Premier Event.* New York: Facts on File, 1990.

Snyder, John. *Goal! Great Moments in World Cup History.* San Francisco: Chronicle Books, 1994.

Trecker, Jim, and Charles Miers. *Soccer! The Game and the World Cup.* New York: Universe Publishing, 1998.

NOTES

1. This book will use the term "football" for the game that is called "soccer" in the United States, for the former term is how most of the world knows the sport.

2. On cuju and kemari in China and Japan, respectively, see David Goldblatt, *The Ball Is Round: A Global History of Soccer* (New York: Riverhead Books, 2008), 5–8.

3. Andreas Campomar, *Golazo! The Beautiful Game from the Aztecs to the World Cup: The Complete History of How Soccer Shaped Latin America* (New York: Riverhead Books, 2014), 9–18.

4. Campomar, *Golazo!*, 9–18.

5. Adrian Harvey, "The Myth of the Public Schools as the Inventors of Modern Soccer: The Ultimate Revisionism," *Soccer and Society* 19, no. 1 (2018): 50–58.

6. A written version of the Cambridge Rules from 1856 can be found in the document section of this chapter. On the foundations of football in nineteenth-century England, see Paul Gardner, *The Simplest Game: The Intelligent Fan's Guide to the World of Soccer* (New York: Collier Books, 1994), 7–8.

7. Gardner, *The Simplest Game*, 8–14.

8. Tom Dunmore, *Historical Dictionary of Soccer* (Lanham, MD: Rowman & Littlefield, 2015), 30.

9. Christopher S. Thompson, *The Tour de France: A Cultural History* (Berkeley: University of California Press, 2008).

10. Goldblatt, *The Ball Is Round*, 158–59.

11. Matthew Taylor, "Global Players? Football, Migration, and Globalization, c. 1930–2000," *Historical Social Research* 31, no. 1 (2006): 7–30.

12. As quoted in Laurent Dubois, *Soccer Empire: The World Cup and the Future of France* (Berkeley: University of California Press, 2010), 26.

13. Many global cultural phenomena, when examined historically and analytically, reveal a dual function. Education, for example, can be used in a colonial setting to create allegiance to the culture of the colonizing forces. Colonials can also use education to throw off the influence of the colonizers.

14. Goldblatt, *The Ball Is Round*, 173–76.

15. FIFA.com.

16. Bernard Porter, *The Lion's Share: A Short History of British Imperialism, 1850–2004* (Harlow, UK: Pearson Longman, 2004), 19–20.

17. Campomar, *Golazo!*, 21–126.

18. Joshua H. Nadel, *Fútbol: Why Soccer Matters in Latin America* (Gainesville: University of Florida Press, 2014), passim.

19. For more on the development and expansion of football in South America, see Goldblatt, *The Ball Is Round*, 125–37.

20. Paul Darby, *Africa, Football, and FIFA: Politics, Colonialism, and Resistance* (Portland, OR: Frank Cass, 2002).

21. On the history and economics of football in East Asia, see John Horne and Wolfram Manzenreiter, eds., *Football Goes East: Business, Culture, and the People's Game in China, Japan, and South Korea* (London: Routledge, 2004).

22. An account of the spread and popularity of cricket in the region is beyond the scope of this book. On cricket in India, see Ramachandra Guha, *A Corner of a Foreign Field: The Indian History of a British Sport* (London: Picador, 2002), passim. Television audiences for cricket matches between India and Pakistan may soon top the one billion mark.

23. Chris Hallinan and John Hughson, *The Containment of Soccer in Australia: Fencing Off the World Game* (London: Routledge, 2010).

24. Colin Jose and William F. Rannie, *The Story of Soccer in Canada* (Lincoln, ON: W. F. Rannie, 1982).

25. Darby, *Africa, Football, and FIFA*, 136–91.

26. FIFA, "1950 FIFA World Cup Brazil," FIFA.com, https://www.fifa.com /worldcup/archive/brazil1950/index.html.

27. The NASL was officially in operation from 1967 to 1985, but its heyday was clearly the period from 1975 to 1980.

28. The growth of women's football globally and in the United States is discussed in chapter 4.

29. William Bowman, "Hakoah Vienna and the International Nature of Interwar Austrian Sports," *Central European History* 44 (December 2011): 642–68.

30. Joel Rookwood and Charles Buckley, "The Significance of the Olympic Soccer Tournament from 1908–1928," *Journal of Olympic History* 15, no. 3 (November 2007): 6–15.

31. For example, Austria introduced a fully professional league in 1924.

32. David Young, "How the Amateurs Won the Olympics," in *The Archaeology of the Olympics: The Olympics and Other Festivals in Antiquity*, ed. Wendy J. Raschke (Madison: University of Wisconsin Press, 1988), 55–73.

33. Bill Murray, *The World's Game: A History of Soccer* (Urbana: University of Illinois Press, 1998), 61–62.

34. Campomar, *Golazo!*, 134–40.

Chapter 2

The Politics of the World Cup

In the previous chapter the discussion focused on ball and kicking games in the pre-modern era, the evolution of the modern game of football in nineteenth-century Britain, the spread of that game globally, and the growth in the game in the early decades of the twentieth century. That story culminated in the high-level international competitions held as part of the Olympic Games and finally the first World Cup in 1930. As part of that discussion, global political and economic aspects of the history of football in the late nineteenth and early twentieth century were brought in to help understand the world historical importance of football in the modern era. This chapter will focus on the political contexts surrounding the World Cup matches after Uruguay in 1930 to Russia in 2018. The object of this close political reading of a sport in its foremost international competition will be to connect the history of the game to world historical questions and issues. Such an examination allows the reader to see the ways in which sports and world history, through the lens of political developments, intertwined in the modern era.[1]

Each World Cup competition brought with it a host of fascinating political developments and knotty problems. Individual rivalries were often played out during the matches, staged every four years. Much about the particular political objectives, perspectives, and disappointments of numerous countries worldwide could be worked out through looking at individual World Cup games. There are thousands of good political stories from football's foremost tournament. And, when appropriate, these stories, and smaller developments, will be included in *The World Cup as World History*. For the most part, however, the narrative in this chapter will focus on the major political dimensions of the World Cup. Moreover, the most important political developments and lines of continuity will be those that link the game and its evolution in the World Cup to global patterns and world historical contexts.

Finally, no discussion of politics in football would be complete without some treatment of FIFA, football's global governing body, which has evolved remarkably from its early days before the First World War to its current configuration in the early twenty-first century. Thus, FIFA's history, and especially the role of some of its major presidents, will be discussed in brief in this chapter as well. As it is currently reorganizing itself and trying to clean up its inner workings after years of corruption, it will be impossible to finish the story of FIFA and politics in this book, but the political and economic underside of world football cannot be overlooked.

JULES RIMET, STANLEY ROUS, AND THE FIRST SEVERAL DECADES OF FIFA

The early history of FIFA and the World Cup cannot be understood without the near legendary Jules Rimet, longtime president of the former and key sponsor of the latter. Rimet's career shows the political promise and limitation of football as it evolved over the course of the first half of the twentieth century. He was born in 1873 in Theuley, France, in territory close to the border with Germany. He served in the French military in the First World War. This was a formative experience for him in a number of different ways. On the one hand, he seems to have been exposed to soldiers coming from a large number of places in the old nineteenth-century French empire and to African American soldiers from the United States. These encounters gave him a certain cosmopolitan perspective on global affairs. His perspective, while progressive for its day, was still very much Eurocentric in nature. On the other hand, his exposure to the trenches and the fearsome fighting that marked the Great War caused him to long to create a forum in which national conflicts could be worked out without resorting to death and destruction. After the conflict was over, he would find such a vehicle in FIFA and the World Cup.[2]

FIFA was created in 1904 primarily as a continental European organization. British nations opted out of it at its inception and would have an off-and-on relationship with it throughout most of the pre–Second World War era. Other nations, however, including ones from South America, quickly joined the organization, although much about the practical relationships between individual national associations, continental bodies, and FIFA needed to be worked out in the first decades after its founding. Much of the early work of FIFA was dedicated therefore to coordinating organizations and procedures; it did not sponsor international competitions per se, as that was left up to individual national and regional associations such as CONMEBOL, the organization of South American football-playing nations, which had already begun to sponsor cup competitions as early as 1916.

This situation would change when the men's World Cup competition was introduced in 1930. FIFA would be its primary sponsoring body. Jules Rimet was at ground zero for this development, which was, as we saw in the introduction, spurred on by many factors, including the international growth of the game, the success of the Olympic competition, nascent underground or aboveboard professionalism in several national leagues, and the desire to stage a world championship of football open to all countries. It would be several decades before the World Cup could grow and expand to meet, for the most part, some of these grandiose objectives.

Rimet and his allies, including Henri Delauney, had to convince European teams, for example, to attend the inaugural competition in Uruguay in 1930. He watched as the cup, while adding many important European teams to the tournaments of 1934 and 1938, was also appropriated for political purposes, especially the fascist aims of Benito Mussolini in Italy. The scheduled competition for 1942 obviously could not take place as the continent erupted into another global conflict that gave the lie to Rimet's optimism about sports providing an arena for political conflicts to be worked out peacefully. His vision would take a back seat as his home country was occupied and divided in two: a directly controlled and German-occupied half, centered on Paris, and a collaborationist French-administered section, run by Philippe Marshal Pétain from Vichy. Rimet, who also headed the French football association for decades (1919–1942), found himself for the time being literally sidelined politically as the game in which he had invested so much was either suspended during the time of conflict or used for political propaganda reasons, as when the Nazis staged football games within their concentration camps. The Second World War era was a low point in the history of international football, especially in Europe.

Rimet would work hard to promote his global vision of the world's game and its foremost international event, the World Cup, at the conclusion of the Second World War. And he and his allies in FIFA, working with various national associations, were quite successful in reestablishing the tournament, first in Brazil in 1950 and then in Switzerland in 1954. When Rimet retired as head of FIFA in 1954, he handed the reins of power to Rodolphe Seeldrayers, who died after only a few years in office. Seeldrayers was succeeded by Arthur Drewry (1955–1961) from England. Thereafter, Stanley Rous, another Englishman with long-standing connections to his native Football Association, became FIFA's president. Rous had already been an important functionary within FIFA as he had worked for many years in the organization's refereeing division. He was a steady hand who believed that his primary role

Table 2.1. FIFA Presidents (excluding acting presidents)

Robert Guérin	1904–1906
D. B. Woolfall	1906–1918
Jules Rimet	1921–1954
Rodolphe Seeldrayers	1954–1955
Arthur Drewry	1955–1961
Stanley Rous	1961–1974
João Havelange	1974–1998
Josef (Sepp) Blatter	1998–2015
Gianni Infantino	2016–

Source: FIFA.com.

was to make world football better regulated by training coaches and referees, which he himself had been for several decades in England.

Unfortunately, neither Rimet nor Rous had the type of flexible global vision that would have allowed FIFA to embrace the political changes going on in the world after the Second World War. Rimet may have been relatively open and progressive in his political vision, but it was still a Eurocentric vision that had a difficult time adjusting to the changing political landscape of decolonization in the post-1945 era. Rous was none the better at adjusting his worldview to allow for or accommodate emerging Asian and African nations into FIFA's structures, and to give them more opportunities to play in the World Cup. In fact, he would lose a power struggle in the 1960s and '70s to João Havelange of Brazil over the political representation of former colonies in football's governing body. The political imagination of Rimet and Rous was not subtle or quick enough to adjust to changing global political realities. They had both done good service for FIFA and the World Cup. Without Rimet's political support and involvement, it is doubtful that the competition would have ever been launched. For his work, the cup given at the end of the tournament would come to bear his name. Nevertheless, he and his immediate successors would give way to far more aggressive political actors, such as Havelange and his protégé, Josef (Sepp) Blatter, who would take the world's game to another level of political and economic expansion.

THE HAVELANGE AND BLATTER REVOLUTIONS AND THE FURTHER HISTORY OF FIFA

In the last several decades, certain key individuals have stood out as the driving forces of FIFA's political culture. Two such figures are João Havelange and Sepp Blatter.

João Havelange, 1982 (*Nationaal Archief Fotocollectie Anefo*)

Sepp Blatter, 2012 (*International Students' Committee*)

Together, they helped create a sporting organization that is unrivaled for its global reach and its corruption. Investigations into FIFA's internal workings and finances are ongoing. What has thus far been discovered is stunning in its dimensions, but it is too soon to say for certain what will be the outcome and legacy of these investigations. After initially agreeing to exit the world stage, Blatter, the Swiss businessman and executive, tried to maintain his power and influence behind the scenes. Eventually, however, international pressure forced FIFA, in February 2016, to ban Blatter from any executive role in football for six years. He gave way to Gianni Infantino, an Italian Swiss, who has struggled to move FIFA and his own reputation beyond the recent scandals. In January 2017, he widened the competitive field of finalists from thirty-two to forty-eight teams.

The skeptical observer might think that this maneuver was an attempt to distract world football fans from FIFA's problems and political corruption. How did things get so out of hand in football's global governing organization?

Prior to Havelange taking over FIFA in 1974, the organization had been headed by Rous (1961–1974), the somewhat arrogant and fiscally conservative English official whose career was covered in brief above. As we saw, Rous was unable to appreciate or accommodate the growing influence or desires of African and Asian nations in the post-1945 era of decolonization and post-imperialism. As the number of non-European and non-South American football-playing nations grew in the 1950s, '60s, and early '70s,

Gianni Infantino and Vladimir Putin, 2017 (*Wikimedia Commons, soccer0010.com*)

they naturally wanted a bigger stake in FIFA, international competitions, and the World Cup. Rous did not appreciate the changing nature of global politics. Havelange did. The latter, a successful businessman, had learned the art of political cajoling, deal-making, networking, and flattery in the federal system of the Brazilian Football Association (Confederação Brasileira de Futebol, CBF), in which smaller states' votes were equal to those of larger ones. Havelange learned how to manipulate that system of administration in the 1960s, and it served him well in the early 1970s as he campaigned openly for the presidency of FIFA. He visited dozens of African and Asian nations and made it clear that he planned to give them a bigger role in the governing body of world football and in global tournaments, including the World Cup.

After his extensive efforts to cultivate FIFA member states, especially in Africa, Asia, and the Caribbean, it was little wonder that Havelange was elected its head in 1974. He would stay as president until 1998 and set a pattern of governance and largesse that has become the FIFA standard ever since. He was not afraid to bribe officials, reward friends, or punish enemies. He drove out of FIFA those bureaucrats left over from the Rous years, who still hoped to run it on a fiscally conservative basis. Under Havelange's administration, FIFA would generate much revenue and the World Cup would continue to grow as football's most important event, but it would also spend large sums of money and become known for its political and economic corruption. Havelange was able to leverage the World Cup into a money-generating vehicle that was unparalleled in sports history.[3]

Working with a number of close associates, including Horst Dassler of the Adidas sporting empire and the sports marketer Patrick Nally, Havelange realized that the broadcasting rights to matches and the advertising that went along with them could be exploited to enrich FIFA's coffers and add to its global sponsors. In the 1960s and '70s, television was transforming the way the game was watched and offered an obvious marketing tool for those willing to use it. Soon, multinational companies such as Coca-Cola would sign on for advertising rights to the World Cup. Havelange and his inner circle struck on the formula of only allowing one major international sponsor for each product or service area. Thus, when Coca-Cola signed on to promote the World Cup, it meant that no other distributor of soft drinks would have access to the global advertising opportunities offered by the tournament.

Throughout the 1980s and '90s, Havelange was able to grow the "brand" of World Cup football and to bring it to more and more households around the world as global television audiences expanded. In the bargain, he remade FIFA, from a relatively small and benign operation in the years before his administration, to a large bureaucratic and venal organization. He did not forget to make himself the most influential man in the game or to profit directly from the economic gains of the era. FIFA was quite a different creature by 1998, when Havelange retired, than it had been in the years from 1904 to 1974. However, so was the game of football itself, because he had helped introduce the Women's World Cup, the Confederations' Cup, the Indoor World Cup, and several youth tournaments. The men's World Cup had expanded from sixteen to twenty-four teams in 1982 and to thirty-two in 1998. On more than one occasion, Havelange referred to himself as the near emperor of the game and likened himself to the pope in Rome.[4]

What Havelange created as a model for FIFA, Blatter raised to the level of an art form. Under his direction (1998–2015), the organization set new marks for the selling of the game. Football's brand worldwide continued to generate huge amounts of income. The popularity of the game also continued to grow, especially in places like Africa, East Asia, and North America. Television broadcasts, digital channels, and the advent of the Internet have continued to shape and change the way football is watched. They have all contributed to expanding the popularity of the game. The World Cup is, after all, the most watched sporting event in the world. But Blatter and the associates and lieutenants he gathered around himself did much to sully football's brand and use it as a bargaining chip in their political machinations. He learned from Havelange how to muster and manipulate support from far-flung national associations to win elections and votes and to generate vast sums of money. He withstood a challenge to his power in 2002 from European organizations and officials by reaching out and influencing Asian, African, and Caribbean national associations, the same constituencies that had put him into power, to back him in his hour of need. FIFA's budgetary operations were almost completely hidden from public scrutiny throughout the Blatter years. When calls came to investigate some of the corrupt and Byzantine practices of FIFA, Blatter initially appointed some of his most loyal cronies to do the digging. By 2015, the mounting evidence of FIFA's corruption finally forced him out, and he was eventually banned from the game he had ruled over for nearly two decades.

Perhaps nothing stands out more clearly in the long history of influence-peddling in football than the awarding of the World Cup to Qatar for 2022. For public consumption, Blatter and FIFA claimed that this was a historic moment for world football—the cup would be held for the very first time in a Middle Eastern nation. On the surface of things, this could be defended as part of the global expansion of the game, another in a long line of firsts—in 1994, the cup had been held for the first time in the United States; in 2002, for the first time in east Asia (South Korea/Japan); in 2010 for the first time in Africa (South Africa). In 2018, the tournament was played in Russia, the first time the cup was contested in an eastern European country. There is an admirable, democratic, and defensible quality about making the world's

FIFA Headquarters (*Wikimedia Commons, albinfo*)

game reflect its global reach by staging the cup in as many non-European and non–South American settings as possible. Qatar, however, had and has no World Cup history and not much affiliation with football as such. At the time the decision was made to play the tournament there, the country possessed no adequate stadia. They all have to be constructed, and labor conditions in the country are abysmal. Charges of human rights abuses are common among laborers doing construction work in Qatar.[5]

Moreover, average summertime temperatures in the region would make it nearly impossible for players to compete at their highest levels or at all. In response, officials and members of the Qatar organizing committee decided to move the competition to late November and December, when there are more favorable weather conditions. Of course, a tournament in the winter will play havoc with the schedules of many leading domestic leagues, such as the Premier League in England, La Liga in Spain, and Serie A in Italy. Details on scheduling conflicts will have to be worked out in advance of 2022. Qatar's stadia are also being equipped with cooling technology to help fans viewing the games. Some political commentators originally suggested that the matches might be shared with other Muslim countries in the region, such as the United Arab Emirates and Saudi Arabia. This idea, however, never gained any traction and seems out of the question in light of the growing political tension between Qatar and its neighbors in the summer of 2017 and beyond. The country has become a flashpoint in political disagreements on the Arabian Peninsula. All of the public discussion and maneuvering in regard to Qatar as a site for the World Cup could not hide one basic fact: the decision had allegedly been heavily influenced by monetary bribes and political manipulation, the full dimensions of which will likely only come out in time. Already, however, enough accusations about the inner workings of FIFA and its decision-making process have been made that the awarding of the 2022 tournament to Qatar may go down as one of the most corrupt sporting decisions in world history.[6]

It is also not clear what Blatter's final fate will be. In moves reminiscent of a political chameleon, he resigned his position and then tried to move back into FIFA leadership positions. He was later served with a FIFA ban as the investigations into his tenure as its head continued. He has been replaced by Infantino, who has tried to indicate that FIFA is reforming itself. This has been a tough sell as many of Blatter's appointments to the organization are still involved in it and Blatter himself seems to be hovering in the wings, perhaps hoping, however improbably, for a chance to reclaim, eventually, a role in football's largest and most important governing body.

FIFA's plan to expand the World Cup to forty-eight teams from the current thirty-two-team format has also met with criticism. Precisely how the additional sixteen teams in the tournament will qualify for and play in the final rounds of the tournament is currently being discussed and determined. In many circles, the plan has been read as a further attempt at strengthening FIFA's hand, once again, with the non-European and non–South American national associations, which still do not have enough teams represented at or reap enough of the economic benefits from the competition. The plan may be a public relations gesture, but it will be fascinating to see how the political relationships between FIFA, its highest officials, national football associations, and the World Cup develop over the next few years as it is rolled out. The first tournament with forty-eight teams will be in 2026.[7] The site for that competition has officially been determined; it will be jointly hosted by Canada, Mexico, and the United States.

THE POLITICS OF INDIVIDUAL WORLD CUPS: THE 1930s

The 1930 World Cup in Uruguay set many of the modern political models that one associates with global sport. Although football had grown exponentially in the first decades of the twentieth century and was quite popular at the 1928 Olympic Games in Amsterdam, it was still not clear who could be recruited to host and attend the inaugural version of football's championship. The tumultuous politics of the 1930s and cost of traveling to South America persuaded most European nations to pass on the opportunity. When Uruguay finally agreed to stage the competition, it had several political motivations to do so. In 1930, it celebrated its one-hundred-year anniversary of political independence. The country also wanted to prove its position in South America to its bigger and stronger immediate neighbors, Argentina and Brazil. The development of the sport in the region also clearly played a role in Uruguay hosting the first World Cup. South America had become a global leader in staging football competitions in the late 1910s and into the 1920s. Several major European club teams had made successful tours to South America, especially to the River Plate region, and had become aware of the high quality of the game being played there. Finally, Uruguay's back-to-back Olympic titles in Paris in 1924 and in Amsterdam in 1928 meant that the South Americans were anxious to continue to prove themselves in an international competition.[8] Uruguay was perhaps not the obvious choice to stage football's first World Cup, but its position as two-time defending Olympic champion did give it political leverage.

However, European nations by and large stayed away from Uruguay in 1930. They worried about the costs associated with cross-Atlantic travel and being so far from their home base and fans. In response, Uruguay agreed to pay most of the on-site costs for the teams attending the competition. Nevertheless, only four European teams—France, Romania, Belgium, and Yugoslavia—made the trip to Montevideo, the capital of Uruguay, which staged all of the matches that year. Jules Rimet, who was then one of the driving forces behind FIFA, persuaded France to go. Belgium participated largely because of the influence of Rodolphe Seeldrayers, the German-Belgian vice president of FIFA. Romania went largely as a result of the direct intervention of its king, Carol II. The Yugoslavian team appeared to be the most eager European side to participate in Uruguay in 1930. All of the British teams that might have made the trip declined the offer. The English Football Association (FA) believed that football in Britain was superior to anywhere in the world and therefore sent a brief note stating simply that it would not be sending a team to the first World Cup. This was a blunder that would haunt the home nation of football for the next generation. The world's game had in many ways caught up to the British and surpassed them, something that they would learn in 1950 when they finally agreed to join the global tournament.

Thus, the bulk of the 1930 teams came from South America and the United States. The central rivalry of the tournament was Argentina versus Uruguay, both of which made it to the final match. In scenes that would become standard at World Cup finals, the demand for tickets to get into the Centenario, the newly completed stadium, exceeded the seats available. In Buenos Aires, people did not go to work; they gathered around newspaper offices to hear news of the game and filled public spaces to learn of the progress of the game via loudspeakers. The passion for the game was such that players in the final received threats against their lives. The referee, John Langenus from Belgium, asked for police protection after the match and for a boat to be ready to take him away as soon as the game concluded. Uruguay won the final, 4–2, and cemented its reputation as one of the leading footballing nations of the day, even if most of the major European nations had stayed away from the first World Cup. Unfortunately, it would not get an opportunity to defend its title four years later in Italy. The Uruguayan football authorities, citing very real financial difficulties and still stinging from the lack of European participation in the 1930 cup, decided not to show up when the competition was staged in a European nation four years later. Obviously, it would take time for the tournament to overcome its political growing pains and transform itself into the world's foremost global sporting competition.[9]

The inaugural World Cup in Uruguay established a number of key political and sporting contexts for the future. Sporting rivalries were set and a political tug-of-war between Europe and South America had been established. The threat of aggressive behavior and even violence hovered around the game, and its outcome triggered strong popular reactions in both the victor and vanquished nations. All of these dimensions of the game would be more or less in play at future competitions. Moreover, the desire or thirst for communications, information, and the ability to follow the matches would grow exponentially over the years, so that the competition could eventually be followed live globally. Most of that last development is better analyzed in the chapter on the economics of the World Cup.

The 1934 tournament presented the world with a serious political challenge: fascism. That tournament was held in Benito Mussolini's Italy, which was far advanced in his fascist remaking of the country. European fascism in the interwar years was a populist set of movements that was ultra-nationalistic and anti-communist in its orientation. It also was a worldview that had set notions about how societies and cultures should work, including highly conservative ideas about women and marriage, education and youth, and the popular and high arts. In the 1930s, fascist movements developed not only in Italy but also in a number of other European countries, most famously Adolf Hitler's Nazi Germany. Mussolini and Hitler both learned to use sports as part of their fascist propaganda about the regeneration of their respective societies. Hitler would get his opportunity with the famed 1936 Berlin Olympics. Mussolini's chance to use the increasing global popularity of football as a political vehicle came with the 1934 World Cup.[10]

Italy 1934 was a major expansion over Uruguay 1930. Whereas only thirteen teams had shown up to play in one city, Montevideo, in the first competition, now sixteen nations came to play. It had been especially difficult to persuade European countries to make the trek to South America in 1930. Now, many of them took part in a qualification in order to play in Italy in 1934. The World Cup was growing in political and sporting significance. Most Europeans assumed that they represented the best in footballing traditions and level of play, an attitude that did not match the results of the Olympic competitions of 1924 or 1928 and one that they had not much bothered to test in 1930 (all won by Uruguay). Italy 1934 would be different. The participants were Argentina, Austria, Belgium, Brazil, Czechoslovakia, Egypt, France, Germany, Hungary, Italy, Netherlands, Romania, Spain, Sweden, Switzerland, and the United States. The second World Cup also featured more playing sites in the host country, which gave more fans the opportunity to watch the matches in person and to join the nationalistic displays surrounding the games. Turin (in the Stadio Benito Mussolini, no less), Milan, Genoa, Florence, Bologna, Trieste, Rome, and Naples all hosted matches.

Perhaps most importantly, the fascist government would use the competition as a measure for and defense of its political and social makeover of Italy and as an international sporting yardstick. In this context, one must remember that the 1920s and '30s saw a global boom in sport. Participation in a wide variety of activities—tennis, swimming, cycling, track and field, etc.—skyrocketed in this period. Moreover, competitive sports were becoming big business, as they were watched and consumed by a wider and wider public. This was part of the overall interwar growth in leisure-time pursuits, such as cinema, outdoor activities, hiking, mountaineering, and touring. Increasingly, governments recognized the possibility of directing and using this boom in leisure activities and sports to reinforce their political agendas. This was certainly true of Mussolini's Italy and even more so of Hitler's Germany. By the 1930s, politics, culture, and sports were becoming increasingly intertwined.

The 1934 competition took on, therefore, serious and curious political overtones. Mussolini used the international platform provided by football to advertise himself and his movement incessantly. As in 1930 in Uruguay, the government covered some of the costs associated with teams traveling to the tournament site. The fascist regime, however, went much further. It also paid many of the traveling costs for international *fans* to come to Italy.[11] New stadia from the 1920s and '30s provided intriguing sites for the matches to be played. Further, the government issued commemorative stamps and numerous copies of the tournament's official poster for public consumption. The World Cup was packaged in new and innovative ways that helped communicate the political messages of Mussolini and the fascists.[12]

Politics and economic considerations also shaped the actual sporting competition. Once again, British teams rejected invitations to play at the World

Cup. Uruguay, the defending champion, was feeling the effects of the global depression that had set in, beginning in 1929, and did not send a team to Italy. The country's leaders and sports functionaries were also unhappy that many European teams had not traveled to Uruguay in 1930. Argentina, runner-up in 1930, did send a team, but it was severely weakened because some of its best players had been recruited to play for Italy. As migration between the two countries had been substantial for several decades, it did not prove too difficult to naturalize many of the Argentinian players in time to compete for Italy. For example, Luis Monti, Raimondo Orsi, and Enrico Guaita, all of whom had played for the Argentinian national team, appeared in the winning Italian team in 1934.

Several excellent European sides, including the Austrians and the Czechs, also took part in the tournament. They would reach the semifinal and final matches, respectively. They represented what was called a "Danubian" form of football in the interwar period and were noted for their skill and intellectual approach to the game. Austria fielded the so-called wonder team (*Wunderteam*), which had gone undefeated for many games in the early 1930s. Along with the Hungarians, the Austrians and Czechs formed another center of footballing excellence in the 1920s and '30s. Professionalism, club competitions, and national encounters had all worked to strengthen interwar Central European football. Unfortunately, all three of these nations were also under considerable political stress in the 1930s, which almost certainly affected their football-playing fortunes. Austria, for example, not only had to contend with Mussolini's ambitions to the south and Hitler's to the north but also with serious political domestic riffs that pitted home-grown fascists, Social Democrats, communists, and liberal democrats against each other. Open revolts broke out in several major cities. Austria was annexed by Nazi Germany in 1938, but the political situation in the country was already beginning to fall apart in 1934, when its *Wunderteam* made its way to Italy.[13]

For Mussolini, however, there were no political excuses to be made. He and his fascist movement rejoiced that the Italian side dispatched the Austrians in the semifinal match and the Czechoslovaks in the final in 1934. Many observers thought that the Italians played inelegant and even brutal football, with frequent fouling, and possibly won the final with the aid of the referee. Mussolini thought such charges were bogus and immaterial. A world championship was worth its weight in gold in terms of international propaganda and as confirmation of Italy's political, social, and cultural movement. To what extent the sporting triumph of 1934 buoyed the Italian fascists' political aspirations is difficult to know. In relatively short order, however, the Italians moved aggressively into overseas military campaigning in modern-day Ethiopia in 1935 and supported the authoritarian nationalist Francisco Franco in the Spanish Civil War beginning in 1936. One should be careful not to draw direct lines of connection between athletic competitions and political developments. One might say, nevertheless, that the confidence of post–World Cup Italy was high and might have contributed to its subsequent aggressive political and military moves.

Italy also won the 1938 tournament, which confirmed its place in the world's game. It marked the end of the most successful period in Italian football history. The Italians had also managed to win the Olympic football title in Berlin in 1936. Unfortunately, the competition in France was almost completely overshadowed by political developments. For example, the Austrian team, which had been so dominant in the early 1930s, ceased to exist as it was folded into an all-German team after the Nazi annexation of its southern neighbor in March 1938. The spliced-together German-Austrian team, which should have been a favorite to win the competition, did not function well and made a poor showing in France. It lost early on to Switzerland. Moreover, the competition on the pitch would soon be sacrificed to war in the field as Europe descended into military conflict on September 1, 1939. The world war and its immediate aftermath made it impossible for FIFA and the national football associations to stage a World Cup in 1942 or 1946.

Table 2.2.   Men's World Cup of Football, 1930–2018

Year	Place	Winner	Runner-Up
1930	Uruguay	Uruguay	Argentina
1934	Italy	Italy	Czechoslovakia
1938	France	Italy	Hungary
1950	Brazil	Uruguay	Brazil
1954	Switzerland	West Germany	Hungary
1958	Sweden	Brazil	Sweden
1962	Chile	Brazil	Czechoslovakia
1966	England	England	West Germany
1970	Mexico	Brazil	Italy
1974	West Germany	West Germany	Netherlands
1978	Argentina	Argentina	Netherlands
1982	Spain	Italy	West Germany
1986	Mexico	Argentina	West Germany
1990	Italy	West Germany	Argentina
1994	United States	Brazil	Italy
1998	France	France	Brazil
2002	South Korea/Japan	Brazil	Germany
2006	Germany	Italy	France
2010	South Africa	Spain	Netherlands
2014	Brazil	Germany	Argentina
2018	Russia	France	Croatia

Source: FIFA.com.

THE WORLD CUP IN THE POST–SECOND
WORLD WAR ERA: 1945–1970s

When the Second World War ended in 1945, there was still much global military conflict. For example, fighting continued for several years in parts of eastern Europe, which fell under the sway of the Soviet Union. A civil war broke out in China in 1949. In much of Europe and Asia, and soon enough in Africa and Latin America, too, an ideological and cultural struggle broke out that diplomatic, political, and world historians refer to as the Cold War. The name is not really appropriate. Open warfare between the two main global military powers—the United States and its North Atlantic Treaty Organization allies on the one hand and the Soviet Union and its Warsaw Pact members on the other—never broke out. There were, nevertheless, plenty of "hot" wars and global conflicts in the era. The Korean War, for example, broke out within days of the start of the 1950 World Cup. The Vietnam War, a war of ideology, nationalism, and anti-colonialism, raged for several decades, as indigenous Vietnamese forces, aided by communist governments in China and the Soviet Union, fought in turn against Japanese, French, and US forces. Moreover, many of the emerging states of Africa and Asia, which were going through a difficult process of decolonization, found themselves caught up willingly and often unwillingly in the politics and military conflicts of the Cold War.

Nevertheless, there was enough global political stability throughout the post-1945 period to allow FIFA, once it had regained its organizational and financial footing, to sponsor and stage a global tournament every four years beginning in 1950. Political conditions and contexts would shape all of the post-1945 competitions greatly. Brazil, the largest South American country and a nation wishing to prove itself not only in the footballing world but politically, economically, and culturally, held the 1950 cup. Moreover, Brazil had adopted the game as its national sport soon after it had been brought to the region. It saw itself as one of the world's footballing powers and was eager to host, and hopefully win, the 1950 tournament. To that end, the government in Brazil, along with its football federation, made elaborate plans and preparations for its team and the competition. Another new cathedral to the sport, the Maracanã, was constructed in Rio de Janeiro to host several of the key matches. One of the largest stadia in the world, it was a testament to the growing significance of Brazil globally, even if the country lacked the political and economic power of European or North American countries. Brazil's investment in tournament infrastructure involved political backing, economic wherewithal, and psychological and cultural support. In many ways, Brazil 1950 marked a new era in football history because of the country's massive commitment to and celebration of the game.[14] As Garry Jenkins writes, "When the Korean War broke out in 1950 it took a back seat to a front-page report on the World Cup. (Why not? To Brazilians that was equally life and death)."[15]

Despite its near-fanatical support, the Brazilian team was unable to win the actual competition on the field. After several brilliant early matches, in which the team looked and often acted superior to every other side, the Brazilians lost their final game to Uruguay, 2–1, in the Maracanã before an estimated 200,000 fans. The unusual format of the 1950 tournament, two sets of round-robin games with no actual championship match, meant that that result secured the title for Uruguay. There would be no final game.[16] Uruguay's team had entered the competition with little confidence and few expectations, which seemed to match the country's political and economic slide from the 1920s and '30s. Far from being the confident country that had campaigned to host the first World Cup, Uruguay had lost importance on the South American scene. As if to add sporting insult to national injury, its best players often left the country to play elsewhere in the 1930s and '40s.

The stunning result left Brazil looking for answers. With so much national preparation and investment, what had gone wrong? The answer to such a question could, of course, have been answered in many ways and on many levels, but seemingly the most convincing response was the one that would hurt Brazilian football and society for the next several years: race. Blame for the team's failure, which had taken a while to be digested, fell in the popular mind most frequently on the players of African descent on the team and most especially upon the goalkeeper, Moacir Barbosa. He was supposedly out of position on Uruguay's decisive second goal. Racial thinking and stereotypes, which Brazil had been dealing with and combating for decades, reemerged forcefully in the aftermath of the 1950 World Cup defeat on home soil. Questions about the black players' intelligence, commitment to the game, and personal resolve were aired publicly. Brazil, like many other countries in the 1950s, had to grapple with racism and its legacy both in football and society. Some observers of Brazilian football have pointed out that it would be several decades before a player of African descent was chosen to play goalkeeper for the national side.[17]

The Brazilian team and football association attempted to put the Maracanã defeat and humiliation behind themselves, symbolically and permanently. After 1950, the players on the national side would never wear the white jerseys of the earlier era again. They switched to their now famous yellow, green, and blue kit, which incorporates the colors of Brazil's national flag. Fortunately for the country, a largely new generation of footballing greats—many of whom were of African or mixed ancestry—was on the horizon and, wearing the new colors, would win championships in 1958, 1962, and 1970, in the longest stretch of football success in the history of the World Cup.[18]

After the Second World War, the World Cup organizers followed loosely for several decades the pattern of holding the tournament in rotation between South America and European countries every four years. After Brazil 1950, the competition returned to Europe and was held in Switzerland in 1954. Again, political and economic considerations played a primary role in the choice of site. After the destructive war years in Europe, FIFA, national organizations, and popular opinion were in favor of holding the cup in a neutral country, such as Switzerland. In the early 1950s, much of the rest of continental Europe was still recovering from the military conflict. Similarly, the 1958 cup was held in Sweden primarily because it, too, had survived the war years unscathed, had remained neutral during the conflict, and had produced a strong economy in the 1950s. Chile hosted the 1962 cup, which was a sign of the strength of football throughout South America, and somewhat of a shock because many observers might have thought the competition would go to Argentina, which had a longer and deeper history of football than its neighbor to the west.[19]

The next competition in 1966 brought the cup to England, where the rules for the modern game of football had been codified and from where the game had been exported to much of the rest of Europe and throughout the world. The English had joined the World Cup in 1950. The pattern of alternating the competition between South America and Europe would continue for the next two decades: 1970 Mexico; 1974 West Germany; 1978 Argentina; 1982 Spain; 1986 Mexico; and 1990 Italy. The 1974 competition held throughout West Germany followed the Munich Olympic Games of 1972. Together, these two global sporting events signaled how far political rehabilitation had come to the country that had brought Adolf Hitler to power in the 1930s and was responsible for much of the conflict and many of the atrocities of the Second World War.

While all of these competitions have interesting political contexts, let us focus our discussion on the 1966 World Cup held in England, which was the only one not won by the Brazilians in the twelve years between 1958 and 1970. England prevailed in a competition that politically represented much that had changed about world football and much that had not. First, the host country had refused to participate in the early tournaments. British teams had stayed away out of a mixture of sporting conceit, economic considerations, and political complications. When they joined in the World Cup matches beginning in 1950, they quickly learned that they were not at the top of the football world as they had so blithely assumed throughout the 1930 and '40s. Indeed, British teams made a rather poor showing at the tournaments prior to the 1966 competition. The English intended to change all of that by winning the first and thus far only World Cup held in Britain. Their preparations for the tournament were meticulous. They put together a team that was supposed to reflect British political and cultural values: hardworking, competitive, and with enough scoring options to win matches. Whereas the spectacular Pelé was the leading player in Brazilian football in the 1960s, Bobby Moore, a rock-solid defender, captained the English team. The competition in England was also a commercial success, as large television audiences viewed the games live for the first time.[20]

On the other hand, the 1966 Cup could not mask many of the political tensions of the day. African nations boycotted the competition because the entire continent was offered only one slot for the final round, and that had to be won through a playoff with the Asian champion. They felt justifiably slighted and would soon seek a larger role within FIFA and world football. Latin American countries, who were represented in good numbers in England, believed that a European bias existed against them that made it hard for them to compete on a level playing surface. As evidence, they cited the rough and mostly unpunished tactics various teams used against Pelé of Brazil. The Argentines, who played a brutal match against England, thought that they were also not treated fairly by the British press, sporting officials, or the public. The England coach, Alf Ramsey, dismissed their playing style as unnecessarily rough and reportedly referred to them as "animals."[21]

Fans of all the teams involved could, of course, hold various opinions about the 1966 matches. To this day, the Germans, whose team lost to England in the final, believe that they were undone by shoddy refereeing. As always, the World Cup competition could become an arena in which global, regional, and even local political tensions could be displaced and displayed. Throughout the history of football's foremost global event, the question was whether the game had the ability to ameliorate some of these tensions and play a constructive political role. Or, on the other hand, did the football matches tend to exacerbate existing political problems? For the period under discussion here, 1930 to 2018, the answer to that question would be decidedly mixed. Sports and the outcomes of their competitions have the ability to cut in many different directions. They can be used to integrate people across political and cultural divides, and they can sometimes lay those divides bare and show how raw they can be.

The competition in England in 1966 was perhaps a good example of political and cultural wrangling that led to changes in FIFA. After it was over, Latin American and African nations felt aggrieved by the outcome of the cup and its organization and would maneuver to play a stronger role in world football. Havelange, a leader in Brazilian sports, would launch his campaign to become president of FIFA. At the center of that campaign was his ability to cultivate political support for his candidacy in African and Asian countries and to nurture South American grievances. Havelange's ascendancy to the head of FIFA in 1974 marked a new and decisive political era. His rise to football's preeminent global administrative position is only understandable, however, against the political background of the 1960s World Cup competitions. African, Asian, and especially Latin American football associations felt underrepresented, slighted, and sometimes ignored in global football competitions. They reacted by helping to elect a non-European, Havelange, to head FIFA and hoped that he would address their grievances.

Another example of the highly charged political environment of the World Cup was the 1978 tournament in Argentina. Football was the national sport of the country, but it had not yet either hosted or won a World Cup. When FIFA awarded the competition to Argentina in 1964, there seemed to be plenty of time for the necessary preparations to stage the event. Not much was accomplished, however, even as the date for the competition drew near. When the country fell into political disarray in the mid-1970s and a military junta took over, the fate of the 1978 tournament seemed to be in jeopardy. The new government was brutal toward all real and imagined opposition, and many trade unionists, student radicals, and suspected leftists simply "disappeared" from Argentinian society. Despite international protests, FIFA stood firm in its commitment to host the competition in Argentina. Disregarding crushing financial burdens, the junta made the money available to build new and reconstruct old stadia and to provide the necessary transportation infrastructure for the competition. It did so while skimming off sizeable funds for itself, much to the long-term detriment of the country. Against a backdrop of economic corruption and open political brutality that included torture and murder, the 1978 World Cup would be played. The Argentinian government also made sustained and somewhat successful propaganda efforts to mask violence taking place in the country. When asked about the on-the-ground situation in the World Cup host country, Berti Vogts, captain of the West German squad, replied: "Argentina is a country where order reigns. I haven't seen any political prisoners." At the time, executions were being carried out in Buenos Aires.[22]

Argentina did emerge as victors of the competition, but the tournament has gone down as one of the most controversial ever played. Allegations have persisted that Peru capitulated in a match against the hosts so that they might go through to the final game and simultaneously exclude their South American rival, Brazil, from reaching it. Further, some commentators have maintained that the referees were heavily involved in determining the outcome of several matches. Brian Glanville, one of the longest-serving and best observers of the World Cup, commented on the 1978 tournament as follows:

Argentina was the worst. Won by the worst . . . in the worst and most unsatisfactory circumstances. Disfigured by negative football, ill temper, dreadful refereeing, spiteful players, and the wanton surrender of Peru.[23]

Despite this type of damning assessment, the junta in Buenos Aires tried to use the victory to legitimize its rule and to bring a fractured Argentinian society together. Short-term but very real celebrations could not, however, cover the very deep fissures that had been opened up by the trauma of torture, abuse, and killing of real and imagined political enemies.

The military leaders in Argentina would continue for the next several years to associate themselves with the national football team. In 1982, they overplayed their hand by challenging the British over control of the Falkland/Malvinas Islands and lost power. Britain's Margaret Thatcher, confronted with her own domestic problems, struck back by taking military action to reestablish administrative control over the mostly economically unimportant islands located deep in the South Atlantic Ocean. For Argentina, the end of the reign of the junta in 1983 exposed the degree to which economic problems and social issues had not been addressed despite the recent success of its football team.[24]

THE POLITICS OF RECENT WORLD CUPS

When the cup went back to Europe in 1982, Spain, the host nation, was just emerging from several decades of authoritarian rule under Francisco Franco. Football had embedded itself deeply into Spanish society and its economy—witness the top performances by the country's leading clubs, Real Madrid and FC Barcelona—but Spain itself had, as of the early 1980s, not been able to accomplish very much on the World Cup scene. It would not be able to win the competition on home soil in 1982 either. The next tournament, 1986, was originally scheduled to be held in Colombia. FIFA's decision to stage the cup there had been made as early as 1974, but Colombia backed out in 1982, citing financial reasons. Even as the cup was becoming financially more lucrative because of increased television and advertising revenue, it was not always clear that the host nation would benefit financially from staging football's most notable event. In a terse assessment of his country's economic situation, President Belisario Betancur announced: "The 1986 World Cup finals will not be held in Colombia. The golden rule whereby the championship would serve Colombia and not a group of multi-national companies was not observed. Here we have many other things to do and there is no time to attend to the extravagances of FIFA."[25] This was a tough but honest critique of the direction in which football was headed by the 1980s under the leadership of

Havelange and his lieutenants at the head of football's global organization. Still, it was a sting to Colombian pride not to host the 1986 cup. The country's domestic league and football culture were already dealing with the corrupting influence of drug money and the infamous cartels that went with it. Even in the early 1980s, narco-dollars were being laundered through Colombia's professional league. The situation would only get worse in the next decade, as bribery, match fixing, intimidation of officials, and violence became commonplace in Colombian football.[26]

FIFA was forced to decide quickly about the location for the 1986 competition and settled on Mexico as the substitute host. This kept the competition in the Americas, even if it meant sending it back to a country that had been the site for the tournament as recently as 1970. Moreover, an offer from the United States, in the person of none other than Henry Kissinger, the famous former secretary of state, to serve as surrogate host fell on deaf ears. For promoters of football in the United States, whose original bid for the 1986 competition had been denied, FIFA's choice to move the event to Mexico was a second body blow. Steve Ross, then head of Warner Brothers and the New York Cosmos of the North American Soccer League (NASL), was deeply angered. He said: "I will not put in another dime, I'm out, it's the end of football for me."[27] Ross and others were trying to grow interest in football in the United States and hoped that a successful staging of the 1986 tournament would solidify the game in the country and simultaneously help the fortunes of the domestic league.

Even a devastating earthquake that hit Mexico City in September 1985, however, did not derail the cup from being held in Mexico. Havelange, who held tight control over FIFA at the time, held firm in his decision to relocate the competition there. The tournament itself would turn out to be politically notable for a number of reasons. First, many of the knockout stage matches toward the end of the competition would feature South American versus European teams, with the latter prevailing. As the hosts Mexico faltered, and then the favored Brazilians lost, Argentina, a team not well regarded in 1986, became the only team left to represent South America. In succession, the side led by Diego Maradona defeated England, Belgium, and West Germany to take the cup.

The 1986 match between Argentina and England has become an important point of intersection between politics and sport. The contest came only a few years after the Falklands/Malvinas War (1982). Some newspapers and commentators even invoked military language and images in the run-up to the match. For the most part, the players did not buy into this narrative at the time. Maradona himself went so far as to say: "Look, the Argentina team doesn't carry rifles, nor arms, nor ammunition. We came here only to play football. . . . Look, we are in the World Cup, we have come here to play football not politics."[28] Later, his attitude toward the match and England would harden quite markedly and take on decidedly political overtones. The game featured two of the most discussed goals in football's history: Maradona's "hand-of-God goal," which he clearly achieved with the illegal use of his hand, and his quite stunning second goal, scored after dribbling more than half the length of the pitch and leaving several English defenders and the goalie sprawled on the pitch. It is universally acknowledged as one of the greatest goals in football history and cemented Maradona's place among the most spectacular, if flawed, players of the game, a topic that is discussed at greater length in chapter 5. In a matter of a few minutes, he had shown a willingness to use deceit and deception and sublime ability to score two goals that saw Argentina through to the semifinals, in which they bested Belgium. The final against West Germany seemed almost anticlimactic. For the second time in three tournaments, Argentina was champion. Despite their victories in 1978 and 1986, Argentina has not won the World Cup again in over thirty years. Nevertheless, Argentina continues to produce some of the world's top players, including Lionel Messi, who is often regarded as the best footballer of the present generation and as Maradona's successor.

In the 1990s, the cup was staged first in Italy (1990), then in the United States (1994), and finally in France (1998). The first and last locations seemed politically and economically logical—Italy and France both had hosted the cup before the Second World War, had long histories with the sport, and had professional leagues and stadia to support the competition. The choice to bring the tournament to the United States in 1994 was, however, controversial. The United States's experiment with a high-level professional league, the North American Soccer League (NASL), had ended with disastrous economic problems after a brief successful run in the mid-1970s. North American fans also did not seem to hold the sport in high regard, especially when one compared the game's followers to those of American football, basketball, and baseball. The US fan base for football (soccer) did not compare to its counterparts in South America, Europe, or even to parts of Africa and Asia.

Staging the 1994 World Cup in the United States was, therefore, a complicated political affair. As we have seen, US officials had hoped to land the 1986 cup in order to help save its struggling professional league, the once successful NASL. When that did not happen, the league went broke and folded, and the professional game in the United States was dealt a serious blow. The 1994 cup came too late to save the NASL, but it did provide a new set of opportunities to the host country. First, in the aftermath of the competition, a new professional league, Major League Soccer (MLS) was born that employed initially a very conservative financial model. The MLS has followed, until recently, a slow growth plan that has emphasized acquiring football-only stadia in the United States and Canada, where three teams (Vancouver, Toronto, and Montreal) have come to be based. MLS wants to win over fans gradually to an expanding league and its style of play. Thus far, the model has been relatively successful, as new teams have been added to it and the competition within it has improved. For the 2017 season, the league featured twenty-two teams. In addition, many of the desired stadia in places like Los Angeles, Chicago, and Houston have been built, and strong fan bases are in place in a number of North American cities. For example, a good rivalry has developed among the Pacific Northwest teams of Portland, Seattle, and Vancouver.[29]

MLS has also heavily recruited players from South and Central American countries to help attract fans in the United States who have migrated from these countries. In the last several years, the league has started to look somewhat like the old NASL as it has become a last port of call for aging global superstars such as David Beckham (England), Thierry Henry (France), David Villa (Spain), and Kaká (Brazil). Clubs sign these individuals as "designated players" whose compensation does not count against the league's salary cap. Whether this development ultimately helps to grow the league in terms of popularity and revenue or burdens it with hard-to-pay contracts is still open for debate, as is the level of play in the North American league itself. The former US men's national team head coach, Jürgen Klinsmann, a veteran player and coach of the German national team, questioned the quality of MLS competition and encouraged leading American players to look for opportunities to play abroad in European leagues. Some American players followed his advice and found clubs in Germany or England, for example. Others chose to stay and play in the MLS.

The 1994 tournament may have served as the catalyst for the establishment and growth of a new men's professional league in the United States, but it was also an important tournament politically for a number of other national teams. Teams from Romania and Bulgaria, which had just emerged from Soviet dominance, did very well and helped solidify the growing reputation of eastern European football. Star players such as Gheorghe Hagi of Romania and Hristo Stoichkov of Bulgaria shone very brightly during the tournament. Teams from South America endured varying fates. Colombia, a pre-tournament favorite based on a tremendous round of qualification, came up flat in the United States and exited the cup early. Several of its players were physically or verbally assaulted once they returned home, and Andrés Escobar, who had the great misfortune of scoring an own-goal in a match against the host, the United States, that Colombia needed to win, was tragically murdered in an altercation in Medellín. Argentina, led initially by an aging Diego Maradona, vowed to win the cup for their superstar after he had been caught with drugs in his system and was banned from the tournament. It came up short against Hagi's Romania, which won, 3–2.

After winning the tournament in the United States, Brazil should have returned to its role as the global leader of football. Overall, it was the country's fourth World Cup triumph, but it was their first since the great Pelé-led team of 1970. In 1994, Brazil did what none of its national teams had been able to do for almost a quarter of a century. There was, however, very little joy or political capital to be made in the outcome. The team played organized, defensive football, not the beautiful game that had become the calling card of Brazilian teams over the years. The final, won in penalties over Italy after 120 scoreless minutes, was a mostly dull and dismal game that did not energize the country's huge and rabid fan base. Instead, after celebrating the victory, many in Brazil did a post-mortem on the team to investigate what had gone wrong to rob it of its spirit, its playmaking verve, and its flair.

The next two World Cups, France 1998 and South Korea/Japan 2002, would provide opportunities to at least partially answer that question. Brazil finished second to the hosts in 1998 and won the latter over Germany in 2002. It was the country's fifth World Cup victory, more than any other nation to date. Moreover, the 2002 team, which featured Ronaldo, Rivaldo, and Ronaldinho, was more typical of the attacking, attractive sides that Brazilian fans had come to expect. The French side that had prevailed over Brazil in the 1998 competition was one of the most ethnically diverse in the history of the tournament. It was, in many respects, a product of the changed social composition of a post-colonial society in the last decade of the twentieth century.[30]

Italy won the 2006 competition, which was held in Germany. By the time of the tournament, Germany had had sixteen years to digest the consequences of political reunification after the collapse of the Berlin Wall and the end of the Cold War (1989–1991). The country had struggled to integrate its new eastern citizens into a federal republic dedicated to modern market capitalism. At the same time, Germany was emerging as the economic and political leader of the European Union (EU), which had gradually grown more financially integrated over the course of the 1990s and introduced a common currency, the euro, on January 1, 2002. German influence and prestige were, therefore, growing in the run-up to the 2006 World Cup, but all of the rapid political and economic transformations of the previous decade and a half had shaken the country. The competition was an opportunity to show how well the nation was adapting to all of the political and economic changes. Unfortunately for the Germans, they could not win the tournament played on home soil. In fact, they did not even make the final, which Italy won over France in penalty kicks.

The 2010 competition in South Africa was the first time the World Cup was staged on the African continent. Other African nations—Nigeria, Ghana, Cameroon, and Ivory Coast—might have laid claim to longer or deeper footballing traditions than South Africa. The last, however, seemed to possess more economic wherewithal to host the cup. Moreover, it was the country in which apartheid, the brutal system of race segregation and discrimination, had been disbanded and majority black rule established, most famously under the presidency of Nelson Mandela. It was, therefore, a global political statement to bring the cup to South Africa in 2010. The tournament was won by Spain, which returned home with its first, and thus far only, World Cup trophy.

In 2014, after a twenty-eight-year hiatus, the World Cup returned to South America, as Brazil played host for the second time in the history of the competition. It was supposed to be a historic opportunity for the country to rid itself of the specter that still hung over it from its 1950 loss in the Maracanã to Uruguay. The Brazilians would not make it back to the fabled and renovated stadium in Rio de Janeiro for the 2014 final. They lost 7–1 in one of the semifinal matches to a talented and in-form German team. Sporting commentators and many fans considered the game a total collapse on the part of the Brazilians, who looked unable to deal with the pressure of having to live up to national expectations. In a stunning match, the Germans scored goal after goal in the first half of the game, which was all but over by halftime. Brazil may have coveted staging the tournament in 2014 to bookend with its hosting the Olympic Games in Rio in 2016, but there was plenty of domestic criticism of the money spent in hosting both, and the price of constructing and updating new stadia came under scrutiny. The nation that has won more World Cups—five—than any other country but never triumphed on home soil may itself desire a long break before being named the site for another global competition.

CONCLUSION

Political considerations were a part of every World Cup played between 1930 and 2018. In 1930, Uruguay hoped to announce itself as a world economic contender. In 1934, Mussolini wanted to invigorate his fascist project in Italy. Brazil planned to prove itself *the* South American footballing power in 1950. England, the home of the modern game of football, finally overcame decades of hubris and poor international teams to win the cup it hosted in 1966. The Argentinian junta used the 1978 cup to mask the political torture and murder going on not far from its stadia and to project a state of economic stability that simply was not there. Havelange and his circle used the 1982 tournament for their own political and financial gain. Colombia was wracked with internal political and economic problems that prevented it from hosting the cup in 1986. The United States finally got its opportunity to prove how well it could stage the global competition in 1994, which may have proved to be a turning point in the growth of the game domestically. France, which had for generations fielded ethnically diverse teams but had never won a World Cup, finally broke through in 1998, which prompted a national discussion and debate on immigration, empire, and post-colonialism. The 2014 tournament in Brazil was supposed to be the host country's opportunity to rid itself of the ghosts of 1950. It turned out to be an international disaster witnessed by hundreds of millions of fans around the world. The 2018 cup in Russia was firmly in the hands of Vladimir Putin, the former KGB officer and current political strongman. It was in most respects a sporting and propaganda success for the host country. There were many exciting matches during the 2018 competition, which came off without any fundamental problems and generally favorable media coverage.[31] Finally, one can only speculate about the full range of political outcomes from the 2022 matches in Qatar, which has been mired in conflict since the decision to stage the tournament in the gulf state was made.

One must also attempt to measure the political significance and importance of the World Cup through the lens of its critics. Some of the sport's fiercest critiques have stated that it is part of a modern complex of "bread and circuses," a very old classical phrase that refers to the idea of distracting and placating the masses so that they will not be politically aware or active. As the saying implies, if one gives people enough to eat (bread) and enough to entertain themselves (circuses), they will be content enough not to worry about the political state of the world, their country, or their community. According to this critical view, football, along with many other contemporary global sports, is part of a vast array of spectacles that ultimately distracts people from playing essential political roles and even deadens them to political activity altogether. Why worry about the political direction of your country under current conditions when it is seemingly so much easier to be fanatical about the outcome of your favorite game? This kind of interpretation is especially important when it comes to something like the World Cup or the Olympics, sporting events that can stand in as surrogates for national identity. This type of political analysis attempts to get at the heart of political and psychological aspects of sports and how individuals experience them.[32]

The "bread and circuses" critique, which has been rendered in very serious and sophisticated critical theory, may be valid in some respects and must be taken into account by anyone seeking to come to grips with the political interpretation of sports in the modern world. It still, however, does not and ultimately cannot capture the whole range of political responses and reactions individuals and societies may have to sporting events. Although it is quite possible to watch a football match and have one's political instincts dulled and even deadened, it is also possible that one's interest might be piqued to ask further questions of one's nation and world. For every team, every coach, and every player may throw up political issues that individual fans or communities or even nation-states choose to discuss and attempt to digest in some fashion or another. The political outcomes of these discussions and episodes of political awareness are again difficult to determine or analyze precisely, but they can and do have real consequences. For example, the great Brazil teams of the 1958 to 1970 era were a study in the possibility of racial integration and advancement. The emergence of a women's World Cup in the early 1990s was a sign of the global growth of female sports and a boon to their further expansion. Individual players, such as Lilian Thuram of France, might choose to use their success—he starred on the 1998 French national team that won the tournament—as a platform for a discussion of race, identity, and politics in their home country. Thus, the impact of sport, in this case of the World Cup, upon the political psyche of an individual, community, or nation is impossible to measure precisely and is of a very mixed nature. Sports may work to deaden, dull, and even rob people of their political instincts *or* they may create political awareness in the individual or nation. In many instances, sports do both and at the same time, making their political impact very difficult to analyze. Scholars and students of sports and world history, therefore, need to be aware of the complicated political legacy of football and other athletic endeavors when they try to make sense of the overall impact of such activities.

One can bring another overarching interpretation to the World Cup of football. The mere fact that it has been played every four years—with the exception of the Second World War era—is a hopeful political sign. Its growth to incorporate many countries around the world points to its relatively progressive nature and to its inclusive format. Of course, it has taken decades for the competition to open up to include countries from Africa and Asia on a somewhat fairer basis. Europeans also still dominate too much of the actual running and working of FIFA. Moreover, the internal workings of the organization are almost always messy and frequently corrupt. Nevertheless, there is a current of egalitarianism in a sporting tournament that truly can be said to be global in nature and that occupies the attentions of millions worldwide. Over the years, teams from Ghana and Senegal, Uruguay and Colombia, South Korea and Japan, Saudi Arabia and Iran have captured the attention of football fans everywhere during certain matches and tournaments. What happens precisely with the political and cultural images generated from these sporting events is impossible to say, but athletic matches can send out as many positive as negative messages. At the very least, one would have to conclude that the political legacy of football's World Cup is very mixed indeed. For every political conflict or situation perhaps hidden or obscured by the competition (Italy 1934 or Argentina 1978), one can hope for political or cultural or at least sporting progress in the outcome or aftermath of a tournament—South Korea/Japan in 2002 or South Africa in 2010.

Whatever critique or interpretation one brings to the politics of the World Cup, it is clearly in many respects a direct reflection of world historical developments over the last century. Globalizing trends have been much on display in the evolution and development of football since the inception of the tournament in 1930. World historians should, of course, remind themselves that globalization has been going on for centuries, and indeed millennia, and that association soccer—football—the basis of the World Cup, reveals much about the most recent iteration of that complex phenomenon, globalization. On the other hand, sports historians should appreciate how the games and leisure-time activities they research intersect closely with global themes and analytical contexts that have fascinated and engaged world historians for the past several decades. A political discussion of the World Cup is a good point of intersection between the concerns of world and sports historians.[33]

The history of immigration and empire are, for example, clearly linked to the development of the World Cup. From small beginnings in 1904 and into the 1920s and '30s, FIFA struggled initially to sponsor a global tournament. By the 1950s and '60s, however, there was increasing demand for more countries to have access to the final rounds of the competition than there were allotted slots. In part, this was because of the increasing popularity of the tournament in Europe and South America, where football associations had been founded early in the twentieth century and had driven the rapid organization and growth of the sport. The increased demand to be allowed into global competitions also owed much, however, to the process of de-colonization that began in earnest after the Second World War. As numerous countries reemerged or created themselves out of retreating European empires, the former founded their own football associations and sought entry into FIFA and the tournaments it sponsored. The process of opening up the World Cup to Asian and African nations has been gradual, complicated, contested, and incomplete. Important steps were taken in the 1970s, '80s, and '90s, in particular. Staging the competition in South Africa in 2010 was but one step in a long-term political process that had begun several decades earlier. The fact that FIFA's first World Cup in an African nation was held in the republic that had sponsored institutional racism—apartheid, from the late 1940s to the early 1990s—was not lost on the global footballing community or political observers or activists. At the same time, all involved in world football understood that much more would have to be done before the game was free of institutional and casual racism. Moreover, African and Asian nations are still underrepresented in the World Cup compared to their European counterparts. For Russia 2018, for example, fourteen European as opposed to five Asian and five African nations qualified for the final tournament.

FIFA's membership has continued to grow to the point that it now outnumbers countries represented in the United Nations (211 football associations compared to 193 nations). And, unlike the UN, football's governing body has no Security Council to veto political measures and moves unpopular with the most powerful and populous nations on earth. Thus, FIFA has, on the one hand, developed a structure that gives as much political weight and voting power to the smallest, least powerful, and least populated countries as it does to traditional European, South American, North American, or Asian powers. However, strong activist presidents such as Havelange and Blatter have exploited this structure to create a self-serving, secretive, and ultimately corrupt bureaucracy that has guided world football into questionable situations. For example, FIFA gave the 2022 World Cup to Qatar, a country seemingly unprepared to hold such an event. Moreover, the massive amounts of money that flow into and around global tournaments because of television, advertising, and merchandising revenue have influenced the political functioning of FIFA and consequently of the World Cup which it sponsors (see chapter 3).

FIFA's current political position may be unique in world sports, but the World Cup has always been an arena in which local, regional, national, and international encounters and confrontations have played themselves out. Moreover, the political impact and meaning of the World Cup often depends on what level of the competition one is viewing and analyzing. For example, the tournaments held every four years have frequently been important for negotiating relations and tensions between European and South American nations, which have most often played host to the competition. Most of the foremost European football-playing nations did not show up for the inaugural cup in Uruguay, a state of affairs that angered the hosts. A system of moving or sharing the cup between the two continents—Europe on the one hand and South America plus Mexico on the other—was worked out, then held in place until 1994, when the cup moved to the United States to take advantage of the commercial opportunities there. Since 1994, the cup has been held in Asia (South Korea/Japan in 2002) and in Africa (South Africa, 2010). The global growth of the game has been reflected in the sites chosen to host the tournament. Modern football, therefore, has numerous political dimensions. The processes of globalization, post-colonialism, and immigration have affected the game dramatically. Organizing and staging the global quadrennial competitions are in and of themselves extremely political undertakings. Finally, the outcome of matches and the legacies they create are important for individual countries, regional neighbors, and even the global community.

DOCUMENTS AND ARTIFACTS RELATED TO THE POLITICS OF THE WORLD CUP

A. 1934 World Cup Programme, in David Goldblatt and Jean Williams, *A History of the World Cup in 24 Objects*. De Montfort University, Leicester, UK. https://www.dmu.ac.uk/documents/world-cup-2014/world-cup-24-objects.pdf

   1. What does the design of this program tell one about the political aspirations of Italy in 1934?
   2. According to Goldblatt and Williams, in what other ways did Italy use art and design to promote its fascist vision at the 1934 World Cup? Research some of the other uses of art and architecture in 1934.

B. FIFA, "World Championship—Jules Rimet Cup 1966: Final Competition, Technical Study." https://resources.fifa.com/image/upload/world-cup-1966-500971.pdf?cloudid=mum7m7twoxdrbcwvfks8

   1. How does the technical report's section on refereeing (uniform application of rules) help us to understand the politics of football in 1966?
   2. How does the technical report's sections on Preliminary and Final Competition help us to understand the politics of football in 1966?

C. Gavin McOwan, "João Havelange Obituary," *The Guardian*, August 16, 2016. https://www.theguardian.com/football/2016/aug/16/joao-havelange-obituary

   1. In what ways did Havelange as president shape FIFA as a political organization?
   2. In your estimation, what will be Havelange's political legacy to world football?

D. Spain 1982 World Cup Poster by Joan Miró, in David Goldblatt and Jean Williams, *A History of the World Cup in 24 Objects*. De Montfort University, Leicester, UK. https://www.dmu.ac.uk/documents/world-cup-2014/world-cup-24-objects.pdf

   1. What does the poster by Miró tell us about the relationship between football, politics, and art in 1982?
   2. According to Goldblatt and Williams, how was regional identity also represented in the programs and posters for the 1982 World Cup?

E. Tony Karon, "The Hidden (and Not So Hidden) Politics of the 2018 World Cup," *New York Times*, July 18, 2018, sec. Opinion. https://www.nytimes .com/2018/07/17/opinion/2018-world-cup-russia-politics.html.

1. What arguments does this article make about the politics of the 2018 World Cup?
2. From your reading of this piece, what does the World Cup of football help us understand about globalization and nationalism in 2018?

SUGGESTIONS FOR FURTHER READING AND RESEARCH

Akpabot, Samuel Ekpe. *Football in Nigeria*. London: Macmillan, 1985.

Alegi, Peter. "Football and Apartheid Society: The South African Soccer League, 1960–66." In *Football in Africa*, edited by Gary Armstrong and Richard Giulianotti. London: Palgrave, 2004.

Arbena, Joseph L., ed. *Sport and Society in Latin America: Diffusion, Dependency, and the Rise of Mass Culture*. Westport, CT: Greenwood, 1988.

Armstrong, Gary, and Richard Giulianotti, eds. *Fear and Loathing in World Football*. Oxford: Berg, 2001.

———. *Football in Africa: Conflict, Conciliation and Community*. London: Palgrave, 2004.

Bottenburg, Maartan van. *Global Games*. Urbana: University of Illinois Press, 2001.

Ciria, Alberto. "From Soccer to War in Argentina: Preliminary Notes on Sports-as-Politics under a Military Regime, 1976–1982." In *Latin America and the Caribbean*, edited by A. R. M. Ritter. Ottawa: Canadian Association for Latin American and Caribbean Studies, 1984.

Dimeo, Paul, and James Mills, eds. *Soccer in South Asia: Empire, Nation, and Diaspora*. London: Frank Cass, 2001.

Finn, Gerry, and Richard Giulianotti, eds. *Football Culture: Local Contests, Global Visions*. London: Frank Cass, 2000.

Foulds, Sam, and Paul Harris. *America's Soccer Heritage: A History of the Game*. Manhattan Beach, CA: Soccer for Americans, 1979.

Gardner, Paul. *The Simplest Game: The Intelligent Fan's Guide to the World of Soccer*. New York: Collier Books, 1994.

Guttmann, Allen. *Games and Empires: Modern Sports and Cultural Imperialism*. New York: Columbia University Press, 1994.

Held, David. *Global Transformations: Politics, Economics and Culture*. Cambridge, UK: Polity, 1999.

Horne, John, and Wolfram Manzenreiter, eds. *Japan, Korea, and the 2002 World Cup*. London: Routledge, 2002.

Jose, Colin, and William F. Rannie. *The Story of Soccer in Canada*. Lincoln, ON: W. F. Rannie, 1982.

Kuper, Simon. *Football against the Enemy*. London: Orion, 1994.

Mangan, J. A. *Tribal Identities: Nationalism, Europe, and Sport*. London: Frank Cass, 1996.

Markowitz, Andrei, and Steven Hellerman. *Offside: Soccer and American Exceptionalism*. Princeton, NJ: Princeton University Press, 2001.

Martin, Simon. *Football and Fascism: The National Game under Mussolini*. Oxford: Berg, 2004.

Moffett, Sebastien. *Japanese Rules: Why the Japanese Needed Football and How They Got It*. London: Yellow Jersey Press, 2002.

Sugden, John Peter, and Alan Tomlinson. *FIFA and the Contest for World Football: Who Rules the Peoples' Game?* Cambridge, UK: Polity, 1998.

Tomlinson, Alan, and Christopher Young. *National Identity and Global Sports Events: Culture, Politics, and Spectacle in the Olympics and the Football World Cup*. Albany: The State University of New York Press, 2005.

Williams, John, and Richard Giulianotti, eds. *Games without Frontiers: Football, Identity, and Modernity*. Aldershot, UK: Arena, 1994.

NOTES

1. There is a rich bibliography on the politics of football. See, for example, Tamir Bar-On, *The World Through Soccer: The Cultural Impact of a Global Sport* (Lanham, MD: Rowman & Littlefield, 2014); Bar-On, *Beyond Soccer: International Relations and Politics as Seen through the Beautiful Game* (Lanham, MD: Rowman & Littlefield, 2017); James Dorsey, *The Turbulent World of Middle East Soccer* (Oxford: Oxford University Press, 2016); Nigel Boyle, "Teaching History and Political Economy through Soccer," *Soccer and Society* 18, nos. 2–3 (2017): 407–17; Brenda Elsey, "Breaking the Machine: The Politics of South American Football," in *Global Latin America*, eds. Matthew C. Gutmann and Jeffrey Lesser (Berkeley: University of California Press, 2016); and Jennifer Doyle's blog, "From a Left Wing," which she maintained from 2007 to 2013.

2. Laurent Dubois, *Soccer Empire: The World Cup and the Future of France* (Berkeley: University of California Press, 2010), 25–28.

3. David A. Yallop, *How They Stole the Game* (London: Poetic, 1999). The introduction of the Champions League for European club teams in 1955, which was substantially rebranded and repackaged in 1992, has also created extraordinary streams of money.

4. Richard Goldstein, "João Havelange, Who Built and Ruled World Soccer with Firm Hand, Dies at 100," *New York Times*, August 16, 2016.

5. Owen Gibson, "FIFA Faces 'Tough Decision' over Qatar World Cup If Human Rights Abuses Continue," *The Guardian*, April 14, 2016, https://www.theguardian.com/football/2016/apr/14/fifa-qatar-world-cup-report-human-rights.

6. There are numerous newspapers following and documenting the ongoing scandals and problems of the World Cup scheduled for 2022 in Qatar. See, for example, Oliver Laughland, "FIFA Official Took Bribes to Back Qatar's 2022 World Cup Bid, Court Hears," *The Guardian*, November 14, 2017; and Noor Nanji, "New Qatar

World Cup Corruption Scandal over 'Secret $100 Million Deal between FIFA and beIN,'" *The National*, January 21, 2018, https://www.thenational.ae/sport/football/new-qatar-world-cup-corruption-scandal-over-secret-100m-deal-between-fifa-and-bein-1.697343.

7. There has been very recent discussion of speeding up the process for expanding the tournament to forty-eight teams in Qatar in 2022. See David Conn, "World Cup Expansion to 48 Teams Could Happen at Qatar 2022, Says FIFA," *The Guardian*, October 31, 2018, https://www.theguardian.com/football/2018/oct/31/fifa-world-cup-expansion-2022-qatar-infantino; CNA, "Football: FIFA Discussing 48-Team Qatar World Cup, Confirms Infantino," January 18, 2019, channelnews asia.com. As of May 2019, however, the proposal seems to have been dropped for good. See Samuel Lovett, "FIFA Abandons Plans to Expand 2022 World Cup to 48 Teams," *Independent*, May 22, 2019, https://www.independent.co.uk/sport/football/international/2022-world-cup-fifa-48-teams-latest-qatar-a8926266.html.

8. Brian Glanville, *The Story of the World Cup* (London: Faber and Faber, 2014), 15–16.

9. Glanville, *Story of the World Cup*, 25–26.

10. On the 1936 Olympic Games, see David Clay Large, *Nazi Games: The Olympics of 1936* (New York: Norton, 2007). On the 1934 World Cup and Mussolini, see Simon Martin, *Football and Fascism: The National Game under Mussolini* (Oxford: Berg, 2005).

11. As far as I know, no statistics exist to confirm how many fans might have made use of the Italian government's offer to pay their traveling costs to the 1934 World Cup.

12. On propaganda and popular opinion in 1930s Italy, see Paul Corner, *The Fascist Party and Popular Opinion in Mussolini's Italy* (Oxford: Oxford University Press, 2012).

13. Steven Beller, *A Concise History of Austria* (Cambridge: Cambridge University Press, 2006), 197–231.

14. David Goldblatt, *The Ball Is Round: A Global History of Soccer* (New York: Riverhead Books, 2008), 288–94.

15. Gary Jenkins, *The Beautiful Team: In Search of Pelé and the 1970 Brazilians* (London: Simon and Schuster, 1999), 170.

16. In 1934 and 1938, the World Cup had used a straight knockout format; teams were matched against one another and the loser of each game was out. In 1950, the Brazilian organizers convinced FIFA to use a round-robin format, in which teams were pooled in groups and played each other to advance. This was done to guarantee more games were played and that every participating team, especially those coming from Europe, had at least three matches at the 1950 tournament. The winners of the first round of pool play were then grouped together to play each other in a round-robin fashion. The winner of that final group play, Uruguay, was the World Cup champion. In later World Cup tournaments, FIFA used round-robin competition for initial pool play with teams from those groups advancing to knockout stages. This revised format meant that after 1950 every World Cup featured a final or championship game.

17. Goldblatt, *The Ball Is Round*, 291–94.

18. For more on the Brazilian teams of the 1950s and '60s, see chapter 4.

19. For an overview of the development of football in Chile, see Brenda Elsey, *Citizens and Sportsmen: Fútbol and Politics in Twentieth-Century Chile* (Austin: University of Texas Press, 2011).

20. The economic evolution of World Cup competitions will be examined more thoroughly in chapter 3 of *The World Cup as World History*.

21. As cited in Hugh McIlvanney, ed., *World Cup '66* (London: Eyre & Spottiswoode, 1966), 117.

22. As quoted in Eduardo Galeano, *Soccer in Sun and Shadow*, trans. Mark Fried (London: Verso, 1998), 153–54.

23. As quoted in *World Soccer*, August 1978, 10.

24. Amnesty International, *Argentina: The Military Juntas and Human Rights* (London: Amnesty International, 1987).

25. As quoted in Andreas Campomar, *Golazo! The Beautiful Game from the Aztecs to the World Cup: The Complete History of How Soccer Shaped Latin America* (New York: Riverhead Books, 2014), 370.

26. Campomar, *Golazo!*, 397–404.

27. As quoted in Jenkins, *The Beautiful Team,* 73–74.

28. As quoted in Neil Clack, *Animals! Argentina vs. England* (Studley, UK: Know the Score Books, 2010), 159–60.

29. Beau Dure, *Long-Range Goals: The Success Story of Major League Soccer* (Washington, DC: Potomac Books, 2010).

30. The racial and ethnic composition of the French team is analyzed in detail in chapter 4.

31. FIFA, "2018 FIFA World Cup Russia," https://www.fifa.com/worldcup.

32. See, for example, Marc Perelman, *Barbaric Sport: A Global Plague* (London: Verso, 2012).

33. For more on the politics of the World Cup in the modern era, one might usefully consult Goldblatt, *The Ball Is Round*; Bar-On, *Beyond Soccer* and *The World through Soccer*; and Dubois, *Soccer Empire*.

Chapter 3

The Economics of the World Cup

There are numerous ways to gauge the economic impact of the World Cup of football. This chapter will first focus on attendance at matches before turning to the economic revolution around the tournament that João Havelange and his lieutenants ushered in beginning in the 1970s. Further, it will examine the commercialization of the draw to place teams in groups for the final round of the competition and investigate the ways qualifying rounds for the tournament have become economic vehicles for world football. The chapter also looks at the communications transformation caused by the advent of television and the hugely important shifts in advertising culture that came with it as part of the economic changes in global football. Players' salaries, bonuses, and prize money are also discussed in an analysis of the economics of the World Cup.

WORLD CUP ATTENDANCE

Attendance figures are one primary indication of the growth of football's World Cup. As the popularity of the game has spread, the number of people witnessing matches has certainly increased, allowing for more money to be generated through ticket receipts and on-site sales of football-related gear and memorabilia. In addition, attending the tournament has become a way for tourists to spend several weeks abroad and to add financial resources to the host country's economy.[1] There is considerable question, however, as to how much direct benefit—new jobs and hotel stays, for example—this type of financial exchange generates for a local economy. Hosting a tournament also involves a large number of direct costs, such as construction, infrastructure renovations, and paying for hotels and transportation for football officials, players, and referees. Indeed, most sports economists have concluded that when all the costs are subtracted from increased revenues generated, there are few, if any, direct economic benefits to hosting a World Cup.[2] It is, however, clear that the spectacle of World Cup matches as broadcast throughout the globe has considerable economic effects and has become part of the culture of football. The dramatic financial reach of football's quadrennial competition, and its ability to raise money, has come in the age of television and technology, and the amounts of money it generates are linked most closely to the sale of broadcast rights, advertising, merchandising, and multinational corporations' sponsorship, and not to hosting the tournament as such. Nevertheless, it is important to consider the attendance of actual matches briefly (table 3.1) to see what they indicate about the growth of the game and its economic impact.

The attendance table allows us to draw a few clear conclusions about football's most important global event. Before the Second World War, the World Cup was a relatively modest undertaking, with sixteen or fewer teams participating. In 1930 and 1950, only thirteen teams played in the final rounds of the tournament. As noted elsewhere, Austria would have been the sixteenth team

Table 3.1.   World Cup Attendance

Year	Place	Teams	Matches	Attendance (total)	Average/Match
1930	Uruguay	13	18	590,549	32,808
1934	Italy	16	17	363,000	21,353
1938	France	15	18	375,700	20,872
1950	Brazil	13	22	1,045,246	47,511
1954	Switzerland	16	26	768,607	29,562
1958	Sweden	16	35	819,810	23,423
1962	Chile	16	32	893,172	27,912
1966	England	16	32	1,563,135	48,848
1970	Mexico	16	32	1,603,975	50,124
1974	West Germany	16	38	1,865,753	49,099
1978	Argentina	16	38	1,545,791	40,679
1982	Spain	24	52	2,109,723	40,572
1986	Mexico	24	52	2,394,031	46,039
1990	Italy	24	52	2,516,215	48,389
1994	USA	24	52	3,587,538	68,991
1998	France	32	64	2,785,100	43,517
2002	South Korea/Japan	32	64	2,705,197	42,269
2006	Germany	32	64	3,359,439	52,491
2010	South Africa	32	64	3,178,856	49,670
2014	Brazil	32	64	3,386,810	52,919
2018	Russia	32	64	3,031,768	47,371
Total			**900**	**40,489,415**	**44,988**

Source: FIFA.com.

at the 1938 competition, but it was annexed by Nazi Germany and ceased to exist politically, for all practical purposes, after March 1938. Its best players were folded into an all-German team. For economic considerations, what is perhaps most important about these pre-WWII tournaments is the relatively small number of matches that were played at each of them: eighteen games in 1930, seventeen in 1934, and eighteen in 1938. This was an obvious by-product of the limited number of teams vying to determine football's world champions in these years. Thus, the on-the-ground and in-the-stadium economic impact of these competitions was limited by the number of teams participating and the relatively few games they played against each other. Average attendance at these matches was still reasonably healthy, ranging from a low of 20,872 in 1938 France to a high of 32,808 in 1930 Uruguay. These numbers show that the World Cup was still establishing itself as a sporting event and as an economic engine in the interwar years. A clear base as a global tournament was being set up that created the conditions for the dramatic growth of the competition after 1945, but the overall economic impact of these early tournaments was limited compared to their post-war counterparts. Economic growth was especially clear after the age of widespread television and broadcasting took hold in the 1960s and '70s.[3]

Beginning in 1950 in Brazil, the number of games played as part of the tournament grew, which obviously expanded the number of fans who could witness a match in person and spend their money in a host country. As the number of teams at the World Cup finals increased from sixteen in Switzerland in 1954, to twenty-four in Spain in 1982, to thirty-two in France in 1998, the number of games played as part of the tournament also increased: from thirty-two in 1962, to fifty-two in 1982, to sixty-four in 1998. The number of fans at live matches has obviously kept pace. Let us highlight a few elements in this development. With only sixteen teams in the tournament, football matches in England in 1966 still managed to draw a total of 1,563,135 fans. This was the first time that overall attendance for a tournament had topped the one million mark. Average attendance at each of those matches was 48,848. Thereafter, average attendance at each of the tournaments, up to and including Russia in 2018, has always been above the forty-thousand-person threshold, with several tournaments (Mexico 1970; Germany 2006; and Brazil 2014) achieving average attendance numbers in excess of fifty thousand. The average attendance for matches in the most recently completed World Cup was 47,371.

The record for average attendance at World Cup matches is held by the United States. In 1994, 68,991 fans per match turned out for each of the fifty-two scheduled games, for a total attendance of 3,587,538. These numbers might seem surprising given that the United States had no strong domestic league at the time, and football clearly was not at the top of the pecking order of sports in the country. On the other hand, the United States had a highly developed infrastructure of large stadia, a huge population from which to draw fans, and substantial immigrant communities that supported their "home" teams at matches across the country.

To date, official FIFA statistics have shown that over forty million individuals have witnessed World Cup matches in person.[4] These fans' economic impact is delivered in a number of different ways but is hard to measure. They generate financial activity at tournament sites through the purchase of tickets and game souvenirs, booking of hotels and rooms for rent, and the consumption of food and drink, including a fair amount of alcohol. They may also contribute to economic activity at a local, regional, or even national level, through using long-distance and ground transportation, paying parking and similar fees, and purchasing a large number of incidental items. Sports economists claim, however, that the aggregate effect of this spending does not usually or directly benefit a host country or a given locale hosting a tournament. Scholars have shown that increased travel and hotel bookings in a country, for example, might be matched by drops in other types of travelers who are trying to stay away from the sporting spectacle and all that it brings with it. The competition clearly generates much financial activity on the ground (attendance, transportation, consumption), but the overall net economic effect of a tournament remains quite muted. In 2006, for example, Germany spent more in preparation for staging the World Cup than it earned from money spent by visitors to the tournament. The competition in the United States in 1994 did not bring much, if any, financial advantage to the cities that hosted matches.[5] South Africa 2010 was a sporting success on the pitch, but the country did not seem to benefit economically overall from hosting the event. The three billion dollars invested in new stadia and road construction did not generate much interest in football after the tournament ended.[6]

THE HAVELANGE ECONOMIC REVOLUTION

A key moment in the economic development of the World Cup came with the ascension to power of João Havelange within the ranks of FIFA. In chapter 2, we investigated the political wrangling and jockeying that culminated in his takeover of football's world governing body in the mid-1970s. Among the most significant events of the early Havelange era was the heavy accent on the commercialization of the tournament. He reached out and found a number of willing partners to help him in his quest to turn the competition into truly big business and to earn large amounts of money for FIFA. He joined with

Horst Dassler, whose family had helped create Adidas, the German sports apparel conglomerate, and Patrick Nally, a British-based sports marketer, to form what David Goldblatt has called an economic "troika," to manage the economic arrangements concerning the World Cup. The three established a number of rules for how football could take advantage of its immense global popularity, the rise and spread of television and sports broadcasting, and the potential of corporate sponsorships. The game had already shown in the 1950s and '60s that it could produce revenue, but what Havelange, Dassler, Nally, and their associates had in mind was the massive commercial exploitation of the competition.[7]

The general outline of their plan was relatively straightforward and very effective. First, they determined that only multinational companies that had genuine global reach and could therefore take advantage of the vast television markets for football would be suitable sponsors. Second, they sought to make sponsorship more desirable by allowing only one product or service in a given commercial branch—soft drinks, alcohol, electronics, etc.—to be the official sponsor of the World Cup at any given time. Thus, advertisers could claim that their companies held the exclusive rights to be associated directly with the tournament. These companies, many of which are listed in table 3.2, were the "official sponsors of the World Cup." Third, the troika moved to make sure that FIFA had economic control over the tournament. Television rights, stadium seating, and advertising would all be under FIFA's financial wing, and many local commercial arrangements within a host country would have to be sacrificed or coordinated so that the global governing body's financial partners and sponsors would have exclusive advertising and marketing rights. As Havelange later commented: "Soccer is a commercial product that must be sold as wisely as possible. . . . You have to pay a lot of attention to the packaging."[8] Finally, the three decided that FIFA itself would not handle all of the work of cutting marketing, advertising, and television deals. These would be handled by individuals and companies that had contracted with football's governing body for the economic rights. In practice, this meant that Dassler and Nally and their sports-marketing companies would handle the details of marketing the World Cup and selling rights to it. It was a convenient arrangement that allowed for a lot of economic power to be concentrated in the hands of a few individuals. It also lent itself to the possibility of financial corruption.[9]

Throughout the late 1970s and especially into the early 1980s, the economic potential of the World Cup grew and FIFA's ability to leverage that potential expanded. Havelange and his circle were able to use some of the money flowing in and around football's premier event to expand their base of political support in Africa, Asia, and the Caribbean. They did so by help-

Table 3.2. Official FIFA World Cup Partners and Sponsors since 1982 (excluding national or regional sponsors)

Company	World Cup Tournaments
Adidas	1998–2018
Anheuser-Busch	1986, 1990, 1998–2018
Avaya	2002, 2006
Canon	1982–1998
Castrol	2010, 2014
Coca-Cola	1982–2018
Emirates	2006–2014
Fujifilm	1982–2006
Gazprom	2018
Gillette	1982–2006
Hisense	2018
Hyundai-Kia	2002–2018
JVC	1982–2002
Mastercard	1994–2006
McDonald's	1994–2018
Mengniu Group	2018
Opel	1986, 1994, 1998
Philips	1986–2006
Qatar Airways	2018
R. J. Reynolds	1982, 1986
Seiko	1982, 1986
Snickers	1990–1998
Sony	2010, 2014
Toshiba	2002, 2006
Visa	2010–2018
Vivo	2018
Wanda	2018
Yahoo!	2002, 2006

Source: FIFA.com.

ing to build new facilities and sponsor new tournaments in those places. An exact economic accounting of all of these moves is impossible, because FIFA and its surrogates also demanded commercial secrecy agreements in their corporate sponsorship contracts. It was, therefore, difficult to follow the flow of funds in world football in the Havelange era. It would prove no easier once his protégé, Sepp Blatter, took over in 1998.[10]

The growing economic base of football and the accession to power of a FIFA president whose reach was increasingly global in nature were two reasons that the number of teams in the tournament expanded from sixteen to twenty-four for the 1982 tournament in Spain. On the one hand, the extra teams were going to mean added expenses for staging the competition. These costs were largely covered by selling television and marketing rights for the next two competitions in Mexico (1986) and Italy (1990) and by the host country. On the other hand, the expanded field meant that Havelange could claim to have delivered on his promise to make the tournament more global in nature and to bring in more non-European and non–South American teams. Algeria, Cameroon, Honduras, Kuwait, and New Zealand all competed in a World Cup final for the first time in 1982. Further, the plan was that the larger field of nations would create more worldwide interest in the tournament, which in turn would create greater economic opportunities for marketing, advertising, and television going forward. The World Cup, as a vehicle for financial gain, was taking on new and self-sustaining dimensions. In the last several decades, every discussion of and move to expand the tournament, first to thirty-two teams in 1998 and then to forty-eight participants in 2026, has been largely based on the economic model that Havelange, Dassler, and Nally established in the 1970s and '80s, and that their FIFA successors and corporate associates in many corners of the globe elaborated.

After the Havelange economic revolution, the World Cup became more systematically commercialized and acquired a large number of "official" (FIFA-recognized) corporate sponsors. These companies were in many ways a reflection of the global nature of the competition, but they also were responsible for taking football's brand into new territories and to new levels of society around the world. In recent years, select major multinational companies have been brought into the status of corporate "partner" of the World Cup, with extra marketing privileges.[11] Thus, a type of economic pyramid— partners and sponsors—has been set up that establishes a hierarchy among the financial giants that want to associate themselves with football's most significant event for advertising and merchandising purposes. One is not surprised by the list of companies that have been partners or sponsors over the course of the last several decades. Coca-Cola became involved in promoting itself through an economic arrangement with FIFA as early as the 1982 World Cup in Spain. It has remained a sponsor of the tournament through 2018 and currently enjoys partnership status among the game's leading backers. Gillette and Fujifilm were official financial sponsors of the cup from 1982 to the competition in 2006 in Germany. From 1994 to 2006, Mastercard was a recognized or official sponsor of the tournament, but Visa has since taken its place, serving as a partner of the 2010, 2014, and 2018 tournaments in South Africa, Brazil, and Russia, respectively. This development follows, of course, the financial plan set up by Havelange and his closest advisors, Dassler and Nally, whereby only one economic branch from one major corporation at a time—in this case financial institutions and credit card companies—would be allowed to serve as an official sponsor or partner.[12] The idea was to leverage the World Cup name, image, and brand for maximum economic benefit for FIFA and its associates on the one hand and the designated corporate sponsor on the other. The latter could then, for example, claim to be the "official" financial company or sports apparel conglomerate of the World Cup.

For the 2014 tournament in Brazil, Emirates, the international airline that has made a big push into sponsoring club teams, Hyundai-Kia Motors, and Sony, the electronics giant, served as official partners of the competition. Emirates had begun its economic relationship with the competition in 2006; Hyundai had first become involved in 2002, when the tournament was played jointly in South Korea and Japan; and Sony had only been added to the corporate mix in 2010. In previous competitions, other multinational corporations had been part of the FIFA sponsorship team: JVC, an electronics corporation, for example, was involved from 1982 (Spain) to 2002 (South Korea/Japan); Canon, the electronics and photography giant, from 1982 to 1998 (France); and Philips, the electronics manufacturer, from 1986 (Mexico) to 2006 (Italy). Two other major American companies, Anheuser Busch, the beer distributor, and McDonald's, the fast-food giant, have been financial backers of the World Cup for quite some time. The former was an official sponsor for the 1986, 1990, 1998, 2002, 2006, 2010, 2014, and 2018 competitions. The latter has been a sponsor continuously from 1994 (United States) to 2018 (Russia). For the last competition, however, neither Anheuser Busch nor McDonald's rose to the role of full-blown economic "partner" of the World Cup. In 2018, several new companies based in China (Wanda, Hisense, Mengniu Group), Russia (Gazprom), and Qatar (Qatar Airways) became FIFA sponsors for the first time. These Asian-based companies' financial commitments helped make up for the decline in sponsorship monies from US and European companies, which had reduced their advertising dollars in the aftermath of the FIFA scandals. As part of its corporate arrangements, FIFA also often contracts with several "national or regional sponsors" for tournaments. These national sponsors rotate based on where the tournaments are being held.[13]

BIDDING, STAGING, QUALIFYING, AND THE WORLD CUP DRAW

Other mechanisms by which FIFA raises revenue from the World Cup are through the bidding process, the commercialization of the draw for the final competition, and by staging numerous qualifying matches. From the point of generating income, it is ideal for FIFA to have several countries competing for the rights to stage the global tournament, which drives up the cost of hosting the event. Such was the case in the race for staging the 2018 and 2022 cups, whose rights were handed out by FIFA jointly in 2009. Several countries representing seven bids—Australia, Belgium and the Netherlands (as co-hosts), England, Japan, Russia, Spain and Portugal (as co-hosts), and the United States—put in to host either competition. In addition, Indonesia, South Korea, and Qatar put in to stage the 2022 tournament only. At the end of the process, Russia and Qatar emerged victorious. As we have seen above, these decisions have been embroiled in controversy for political and economic reasons.[14]

Given the obvious costs to host the World Cup, what are the real or perceived financial benefits to the country bidding to sponsor the competition? Of course, national pride and prestige, alongside other political and cultural motivations, play a major role in nations competing with each other to sponsor the tournament. We analyzed the major political dimensions of the process in the preceding chapter. Financial considerations, too, have always been part of the decision to bid to host the tournament. Countries hope to reap direct or indirect economic benefit from staging football's global centerpiece.[15] Nevertheless, sports economists in recent decades have been highly skeptical of the long- and short-term financial benefits of hosting a World Cup. They find it difficult to correlate direct improvements in numbers, such as gross domestic product (GDP) or unemployment and wages, to staging a global tournament. National boosters have often claimed that bringing the tournament to their countries will automatically bring an economic windfall to their homelands. Sports economists are far less certain. They do agree, however, that hosting the cup can bring several possible indirect economic benefits to the sponsoring nation. For example, secondary industries, such as breweries or hotels, may do better business during the months when the tournament is being played. But even some of these benefits may not be as considerable or certain as the boosters hope or claim.[16]

Countries might benefit economically from staging the World Cup if the money spent on hosting the tournament contributes to the overall welfare of the nation. For example, improvements in infrastructure, such as transportation networks, roads, mass transit, etc., and the continued use of stadia built to host the tournament as sporting sites, or their creative repurposing, could be seen as economic investments for a hosting country. Even this type of benefit, however, can be called into question when money spent for a sporting event does not lead to overall economic improvements for a country's population, or even for the people living close to sites at which stadia have been built or roads improved.

The 2014 tournament in Brazil is a case in point. On the one hand, Brazil, as one of the most famous and successful footballing nations in the world, was keen to host the 2014 competition. As the only five-time champion of the tournament, Brazil hoped that the national team would finally win a cup at home. It fell short, of course, losing decisively to Germany, 7–1, in the semifinal match. Before the tournament began, while it was underway, and certainly after it had concluded, there was much discussion in Brazil about the overall economic impact to the host country. Many individuals pointed out that the country needed much more investment in education, medicine, and housing than in rebuilding or constructing stadia, even if one of the playing sites to be refurbished was the legendary Maracanã in Rio de Janeiro. The choice to play games in Manaus, in particular, generated controversy. The city was on the edge of the Brazilian rain forest, far from the other cities designated to host matches. The new stadium there cost at least $270 million to construct, and it was not certain that it would have any useful purpose at the conclusion of the cup. Nevertheless, construction went on and the stadium was used for only four games. Since 2014, the stadium has been used primarily for its parking lot, which functions as an informal bus terminal and parking lot. A few early rounds of football were played in Manaus as part of the 2016 Olympic Games. Overall, however, the stadium has been greatly underused since its construction for the 2014 competition.[17]

Advanced economic models have called into question the direct benefits of staging global sporting events in terms of gains in gross domestic product or in increased employment or wage numbers. Further, many scholars have doubted that even indirect economic benefits—improved infrastructure and the like—can be linked to the World Cup. These sophisticated economic models are based primarily on recent tournaments, 1994 and beyond, when more economic data has been available.[18] It is harder to estimate the overall impact of earlier competitions upon their hosts' gross national product, employment numbers, and other direct or indirect economic indicators.

On the other hand, there is a growing consensus among sports economists that "feel-good factors" and "happiness" measures should also be included in the final financial assessments of global sporting events. Citizens of a country often feel a residual sense of "happiness" for having played host to a tournament, and this psychological state of mind in and of itself may have economic benefits for two to four years after a tournament is concluded. This is true if a country does well in a competition it is hosting, but it also applies if the home team performs poorly. Unfortunately, the "happiness model" for hosting major sporting events only seems to hold for already economically advanced nations, in which basic material needs have been met for the bulk of the population. Poorer nations, such as South Africa in 2010, would almost certainly do better to invest the resources dedicated to hosting a World Cup into housing, medicine, and basic infrastructure.[19] However, the advanced economic models, which do not point to obvious or sustained financial gains on the part of a hosting country, have done little to dampen enthusiasm for seeking to stage the World Cup.

Another sign of the growing global impact of the World Cup has been the introduction of qualifying tournaments to winnow the field to a manageable number of final participants (sixteen, twenty-four, thirty-two, or forty-eight in 2026). The qualifying tournaments are organized by football's continental confederations: Confederation of African Football (CAF), Asian Football Association (AFC), Union of European Football Associations (UEFA), Confederation of North, Central American, and Caribbean Association Football (CONCACAF), Oceania Football Confederation (OFC), and Confederación Sudamericana de Fútbol (CONMEBOL). FIFA determines the number of teams from each federation for the World Cup finals at the start of the qualifying tournament. Over the years, the size of these competitions has increased markedly, making the playing run-up to the final round another opportunity for financial gain. In recent decades, qualifying for and possibly competing in the final round has become an affair that lasts two years or more. For example, qualifying games for Qatar will run from June 6, 2019, to March 2022. This cycle of games allows ample opportunity for generating interest in the competition and making it an almost constant source of considerable economic activity. The potential for generating revenue through television broadcasts, advertising, and marketing is considerable, even if it is difficult to be precise about the final financial numbers associated with all of these qualifying games.

Table 3.3. World Cup Qualifying

Year	Number of Teams	Qualifying Matches
1930	13	(no qualifying matches)
1934	32	27
1938	37	22
1950	34	26
1954	45	57
1958	55	89
1962	56	92
1966	74	127
1970	75	172
1974	99	226
1978	107	252
1982	109	306
1986	121	308
1990	116	314
1994	147	497
1998	174	643
2002	199	777
2006	198	847
2010	205	852
2014	203	820
2018	209	868

Source: FIFA.com, History of the FIFA World Cup Preliminary Competition (by year).

As far as can be established, no one has attempted to bring together aggregate economic data—for example, attendance figures and ticket sales, and broadcasting rights and advertising fees—for all of these qualifying matches. For Russia 2018, FIFA has published the following: 868 matches contested by 209 different teams. In addition, the qualifying matches took place over more than a two-year period, from March 12, 2015, until November 15, 2017.[20] Clearly, these qualifying matches show how the World Cup has grown over the last century into a global event that has potential financial impacts in a wide variety of places over sustained periods of time. From the modest beginnings of the 1930s to the most recent tournament in Russia, the number of countries attempting to reach the final rounds has grown at least sixfold. This growth is also dramatically represented in the number of matches played just to reach the end stage of the tournament: from twenty-seven games in 1934 to more than 800 for the last four competitions. Each of these qualifying games, whether they take place in Ecuador, Chile, Panama, Mexico, Portugal, Nigeria, Algeria, Cameroon, Kazakhstan, Japan, Australia, or dozens of other countries around the globe, represents a component to the overall economic effect of the World Cup. Each game offers opportunities for ticket sales, marketing merchandise, establishing local or national sponsorships, and, of course, broadcasting and advertising rights. These qualifying matches are important for both economic and sporting reasons. When England crashed out during the qualifying rounds for the 1994 tournament, the *Daily Mirror* published a bold, all-capital headline that simply read: THE END OF THE WORLD.[21]

The World Cup, therefore, has become much more than a month-long sporting festival held every four years. It is an ongoing event that can sustain the interest of fans and economic sponsors for years at a time. Indeed, star football players complain that between club competitions and qualifying for major global tournaments they are increasingly overstretched, unable to maintain peak performance, and prone to injuries. The players are almost certainly right about the state of modern global football. Given the amount of money to be made by everyone, from FIFA to club owners to local entrepreneurs, there is very little chance of this situation changing soon. If anything, the pressure on players, especially at the highest level of competition, is likely to continue to grow. The European Champions League, for example, has also become a huge economic juggernaut in recent decades. It matches the best club teams from throughout Europe in a year-long tournament. As many of the best players in the world currently play for European clubs, the burden upon them is great, especially when they also play for their national teams, which is often the case.[22]

The World Cup draw, which seeds teams into groups for round-robin play at the finals tournament, has over time also become a money-making proposition. In Uruguay in 1930, the draw for determining the precise order of play was more or less a formality. It was conducted on site right before the tournament began and was not much of a production. In 1934, when the first qualifying tournament was introduced, the draw for the final round of games in Italy was also conducted right before the competition began and was not seen as an important economic event. France 1938 represented the embryonic beginnings of what would become a major global spectacle and source of economic revenue in its own right: the World Cup draw. For the first time, the draw was held considerably in advance of the tournament (March 5, 1938) in Paris and was made by the grandson of Jules Rimet, the then president of FIFA. Football executives and promoters were beginning to understand that the tournament could be packaged in a number of different ways for consumption by the sporting fan and casual observer alike.

In the post-1945 era, the World Cup draw would become a major undertaking in its own right. In 1966, for example, it was televised for the first time. The broadcast emanated from the Royal Garden Hotel in London on January 6, 1966, several months in advance of the actual scheduled finals round. The intention was clear; the draw itself could generate interest and revenue and also add to the interest in matches in an extended run-up to the tournament. Increased tension and expectation could be built into the competition, which could also add to newspaper and television reporting, advertising and sponsorship opportunities, and an overall heightened state of anticipation about football's most important global event.

The 1970s and '80s would witness increased interest in the World Cup draw. The 1978 draw for the tournament in Argentina, for example, was held in the Teatro General San Martín in Buenos Aires. In 1986, it was broadcast from television studios in Mexico City. The extravagance and economic exploitation of the event was in many ways just getting started. The draw for Italy 1990 was held on December 9, 1989, from the Palazzo dello Sport in Rome. Sepp Blatter was the ringmaster for a show that included opera, rock music, and dance. The headliners were Luciano Pavarotti, the world-class tenor, and Sophia Loren, perhaps the most famous Italian actress of all time. In attendance were also some of football's luminaries, including Pelé from Brazil and Bobby Moore from England, both of whom were World Cup winners and icons of the game.[23] Clearly, football's executives and officials realized the crossover economic benefits of mixing well-known personalities from the entertainment and sporting worlds. This kind of production offered great advertising opportunities for corporate sponsors.

The draw for the tournament in the United States in 1994 was held in Las Vegas and featured the same kind of mix of show business personalities and sporting figures that had been on display in Italy four years earlier.[24] The draw had become big business. Not to be outdone, the French organizers of the 1998 competition held their draw for the first time in a stadium, the Stade Vélodrome in Marseille. Thirty-eight thousand people showed up to witness the event, which was also simultaneously broadcast to a global audience. Blatter was once again on hand, as was a whole array of football stars, including Franz Beckenbauer, Raymond Kopa, Jean-Pierre Papin, and, in a nod to the growing importance of women's football, Julie Foudy of the United States women's national team. Beckenbauer, of Germany, was at the time one of the legends of the game and a World Cup winner from 1974. Kopa (1952–1962) and Papin (1986–1995) represented two different glorious eras of French football.

The draw as a show and economic vehicle has continued to grow in recent years. For the 2002 competition, it was broadcast from Busan in South Korea to 130 countries globally. Germany 2006 represented not only an economic opportunity to feature the draw in the lead-up to the tournament but a chance to showcase the reunified political state. Held in Leipzig, a former East German city, it was broadcast to at least 150 countries worldwide. In attendance were Heidi Klum, the German supermodel; Pelé; Johan Cruyff, the Dutch footballing icon from the 1970s; and Goleo the Lion, who was the official mascot of the 2006 tournament. Over time, the broadcast, marketing, and advertising possibilities of the World Cup have continued to grow dramatically, and one sign of that growth has been the increasing interest in branding, selling, and promoting the draw in advance of the tournament.[25]

Another indicator of the overall economic impact of the World Cup has been the growth in the length of the tournament. As more teams have played in the final rounds of the tournament and more games have been scheduled, the competition has become decidedly longer over time. In the interwar period, when thirteen to sixteen teams were involved in the end phase of the cup, the entire affair could be conducted in fifteen to eighteen days. That is, tourists and fans, players, coaches, referees, newspaper reporters, and FIFA officials were in Uruguay, Italy, or France, respectively, for a little over two weeks. In the 1950s, '60s, and '70s, however, the tournament was played over the course of anywhere from nineteen to twenty-five days and was therefore regularly a three-week-long tournament. When the number of teams in the final round grew to twenty-four, in Spain in 1982, the end phase of the tournament grew correspondingly to its current month-long format.

The length of the tournament is linked directly to its economic effects; more games played over more dates provides increased opportunities for more revenue generated (ticket sales, parking, and same-day merchandise purchases) but also necessitates a longer stay in a host country, with greater expenditures for housing, transportation, and food. Estimating the total figures spent during any World Cup, regardless of its duration, is difficult, but it is clear that over time the conditions for greater financial activity in a host country have expanded remarkably. These direct sources of revenue, as we saw above, do not usually amount to a net economic benefit for the hosting nation and the locales where games are played. The extended World Cup tournament, however, does mean more matches played on more dates will be televised, which creates increased advertising and marketing possibilities. The tournament in Russia in 2018, for example, was played over thirty-two days (June 14–July 15) in twelve different venues in eleven cities. The 1930 tournament in Uruguay took just eighteen days and was played at three sites in just one city, Montevideo. The 2022 competition in Qatar is currently scheduled to be played from November 21 to December 18, a twenty-eight-day span of time in seven cities or municipalities. These playing dates cut across those of most of the domestic leagues in the world, including those from every major European country. How these 2022 scheduling conflicts will be worked out is still under discussion, especially as they have potentially massive economic effects. The Qatar World Cup could seriously damage the financial position of club football teams that generate considerable revenue from broadcasting domestic competitions in November and December of each year.

THE TELEVISION REVOLUTION

The overall economic growth and importance of the World Cup has been tied directly to the global and ongoing revolution in communications in the twentieth and early twenty-first centuries. The earliest World Cups of the 1930s were disseminated primarily through newspapers and radio broadcasts. Although they were important for helping to create the game's popularity and establishing the tournament as the sport's most significant event, their economic impact would not be as great, indeed would be dwarfed by the competitions held after the Second World War. This is especially true as the revolution in television took hold and transformed the way sports could be transmitted and consumed. As a product with global appeal, football became one of the leading and earliest vehicles for testing the economic power of new media.

There were several key moments in the process whereby global football wed itself to television. For example, the 1954 cup in Switzerland provided some of the earliest transmitted images of the game, although they were on tape and not viewed live. In the next several years, television broadcasts of matches would continue to grow, but the most important developments in making the World Cup a major television commodity came in the period from the 1960s to the 1980s. In 1966 in England, for example, the contracts to broadcast the games on television demanded and required that only stadia of a certain size be used to host the matches. Moreover, details were worked out on the precise positioning of cameras within the stadia in order to capture the best angles with which to film the games and send them out to a viewing public. In addition, 1966 saw the introduction of slow-motion replay to television broadcasts of Cup matches. This meant that a new appreciation of the game could be gained by a wide viewing public. All of these changes and innovations helped to transform the relationship between sport as commodity and the way it was packaged and sold to its consumers and fans. Of course, it did not hurt financially that the 1966 Cup was held in England, the birthplace of the game, and that the hosts won the tournament, albeit not without controversy.[26]

The revolution in communication technology continued and worked to shape the way football matches and the World Cup were shown. Color broadcasts had become the norm by the time of the 1970 competition in Mexico. Fans could see the Brazilians in their famous yellow shirts and blue shorts, the uniform that the team had adopted after the debacle of 1950 in Rio, in living color. At the same time, the number of games and the total number of hours of broadcasting football continued to grow. In addition, the countries of the world that had access to these broadcasts also expanded. Thus, the size of the overall viewing audience for the competition continued to expand, so that it reached into the hundreds of millions and finally topped the one billion mark. Of course, it is difficult to know the exact size of the television audience for matches. In some instances, whole families or groups of friends might be around one broadcast device to watch a match. It is also impossible to know how intently or for exactly how long any individual fan is engaged by the broadcast of a game, but it is clear that football's most important tournament stands alongside the Olympic Games and, in more recent years, the European Champions League—also a football competition—as one of the most viewed sporting activities on the face of the planet. For example, the 2006 World Cup in Germany was viewed by an estimated 3 billion people, 2010 South Africa by 3.2 billion, and 2014 Brazil by 3.2 billion. The corresponding figures for television rights for those tournaments were $1.4 billion in 2006, $2.4 billion in 2010, and $2.5 billion in 2014.[27]

The remarkable global involvement with and investment in viewing the games has only taken on new dimensions and possibilities in the age of cable broadcasting and the Internet. The number of channels and the type of platform or device through which one views football matches has continued to expand, especially in the last two decades. These developments, in turn, have made the game ever more accessible and popular, especially in areas of the world where domestic leagues and competitions by themselves might not generate as much interest in football.[28] Of course, broadcasting tournament games sometimes comes at a steep cost to the players. In Mexico 1986, many of the most important matches were played at noon so that they could be viewed on live television in the evening in Europe. Harald Schumacher, the West German goalkeeper that year, commented about the playing conditions that resulted from the early start times: "I sweat. My throat is dry. The grass is like dried shit: hard, strange, hostile. The sun shines straight down on the stadium and strikes us on the head. We cast no shadows. They say this is good for television."[29] The television revolution was undoubtedly good for expanding the viewing public, but it sometimes took a physical toll on the players.

The explosion in television coverage of World Cup matches has led to the equally dramatic growth in the revenue they can generate and to the model of exploiting this economic potential developed by Havelange, Dassler, and Nally. Perhaps no other sport in the world has taken advantage so directly of marketing opportunities as world football. The model they established of linking and integrating football as a product or commodity with television and broadcasting in all of its forms and then selling that product to major international corporations through exclusive advertising contracts created a financial base from which FIFA and national associations could benefit. Some of the money generated from this model was plowed back into the further development of the game, especially in places such as Africa and Asia and in youth tournaments. Some of it clearly has been used within the FIFA executive for private gain, bribery, and corruption.[30]

Giovanni (Gianni) Infantino, the new head of FIFA, has worked to expand the World Cup finals from thirty-two to forty-eight teams for the 2026 competition. The change fits a long-standing pattern of institutional and economic struggle within FIFA. The expansion of the final round of the tournament from sixteen to twenty-four and then to thirty-two teams over the course of the last several decades was greeted favorably in Africa, Asia, Oceania, and the Caribbean, where it was seen as a chance for greater participation by some of the less traditional football powers that have not won the World Cup competitions. In Europe, the expansions were accepted, sometimes grudgingly, but they are frequently accompanied by talk of "diluting" the tournament. Similar objections have already been raised to Infantino's expansion of the cup to forty-eight teams. Large-scale political and economic considerations are at the heart of these power struggles over control of the world's game.[31]

The growth in the number of teams and television audiences means that a large number of TV journalists are always on hand to follow and report on World Cup play. In 1994, for example, Bolivia was in the finals for the first time since 1950. Football games saturated its television stations throughout the tournament. Its journalists noted a huge demand and desire for information about the national team, the quality of other sides, and every detail of play.[32] Bolivia was unable to advance past the first round of play and finished last in its group. By then, the competition had captivated the country, which contributed to the tournament's overall viewership and economic impact.

The television revolution's impact upon the global game continued to grow in the following two decades. According to FIFA's final official figures, the 2014 tournament in Brazil reached a global television audience of 3.2 billion people.[33] Many of the competitions from Brazil were also shown quite late or in the early morning hours in Asian television markets, which are some of the largest in the world. FIFA further estimated that one billion people watched the 2014 final between Germany and Argentina. One could imagine that that number would have been even higher if Brazil, the host nation, had reached the final game. Finally, FIFA estimated that 280 million people had followed the tournament online or by using some type of mobile device. The total number of televised hours of matches and commentary for 2014 was a staggering 98,087, which was a 36 percent increase over 2010. The numbers for Russia 2018 were equally impressive; an estimated 3.57 billion people watched all of the matches on television or the Internet. The final was watched by approximately 1.2 billion viewers. Given these numbers, one wonders whether there is an upward limit when it comes to the global coverage of and reporting on the World Cup. Be that as it may, the market for the matches and the global appetite for information have clearly enhanced the economic importance of the tournament.[34] As we saw above, multinational corporations have long recognized the tournament's financial reach and have therefore invested deeply in it in order to reach consumers worldwide.

The FIFA Women's World Cup, which was introduced in 1991, has also, over time, won a global audience. FIFA reported that at least 764 million in-home viewers watched the women's tournament in Canada in 2015, which was a new record, making it the second most popular FIFA-sponsored event in the world after the men's tournament. Further, football's governing body stated that approximately eighty-six million people followed the matches online or on mobile devices and that key television markets, such as the United States, Japan, and Western Europe, enjoyed record numbers of viewers. For example, the final match of the tournament, won 5–2 by the United States over Japan, was the most viewed football match, men's or women's, in the history of US television.[35]

ADVERTISING

The advertising of products and services has long been a part of World Cup history. Over time, the methods used in advertising at football matches have become much more sophisticated and nearly ubiquitous. Old-fashioned wooden signboards behind goals at either end of the pitch have given way to rotating, electronic advertising devices. At home, television has offered even more methods to commercialize the game. Every aspect of the broadcast of a match can be sponsored by a corporation or organization. The halftime interval of major games not only offers in-game analysis but also provides opportunities for advertisements from major sponsors. Electronic ads are superimposed onto game images, so that a given brand is always before one's eyes while watching a match. To be sure, some of the crassest forms of branding and commercialization of football have taken place at the club level, at which every part of a stadium, every uniform, and every publication is seen as a chance to send an economic message and earn money. Nevertheless, the techniques and mechanisms developed for club football have filtered into the landscape of competitions between nations, including World Cup qualifying and finals matches. The game of football is a global commodity, and advertising revenue has clearly grown and added to its economic significance over the course of the twentieth and early twenty-first centuries.

Since Havelange, Dassler, and Nally revolutionized the economic model for football's global tournament in the 1970s and '80s, advertising has become an increasingly important and sophisticated part of the competition. In recent decades, the World Cup has clearly become big business, and many multinational companies understand the importance of maximizing the event for possible economic profit. The 1994 tournament in the United States, for example, presented corporations and advertising agencies with challenges and opportunities. As we have seen, football in the United States competes with a wide range of other sports—American football, basketball, baseball, and ice hockey, for example—for spectators, media coverage, and advertising dollars. Moreover, in the early 1990s there was no strong domestic league in the United States to generate interest in the World Cup. How then to best proceed with advertising campaigns to make football and its foremost international competition appealing to US fans? Advertising agencies adopted a number of interesting and effective techniques for the 1994 competition. One ad, for example, that first aired during halftime of the United States vs. Switzerland match, featured Deion Sanders, a prominent athlete of the day, who had become famous as an American football star but who had also dabbled in professional baseball. The ad promoted Powerade, which had been introduced for the 1992 Olympic Games in Barcelona by Coca-Cola, a long-standing corporate sponsor of international football. The ad played on the athletic ability of Sanders to suggest that he would next take up football (soccer) as a new sport. The implication of the ad was clear—Americans should do the same by taking up the world's game and drinking Powerade to help them in their pursuit of athletic glory. The ad also used Americans' relative unfamiliarity with football to its advantage. At one point in the ad, a referee whistles Sanders for a yellow-card violation, and the latter, without missing a beat, grabs the piece of paper from the former and signs his autograph and says, "Must be a fan." It is a clever piece of advertising improvisation.[36]

Another 1994 ad, however, adopted a direct approach to showcase the appeal of football. Snickers featured Tab Ramos, one of the US national team players, in a piece that claimed he ate candy bars to satisfy his hunger during grueling training sessions for the World Cup. In its presentation, the ad is similar to many other sporting advertisements. It features the athlete in action, highlights his physical preparation for and dedication to his sport, and suggests that the featured product, Snickers, is part of the reason he has come so far in athletic competitions. Whether a US national team player actually ate candy bars to satisfy his hunger is not the main point of the ad. By using Ramos, a major US company showed that it was willing to promote the home team in a global competition as an attempt to gain market share and brand awareness in an expanding audience: football fans. A final example of advertising executives trying to bridge the gap between American sports fans and football was the 1994 Adidas commercial that featured cuts of footballers while the song "Take Me out to the Ball Game," a baseball favorite, was played. The suggestion is clear: there is a new game in town that can grow to be as popular as America's original sporting pastime. Adidas, of course, has been heavily involved in promoting and sponsoring the World Cup for decades, and some of its executives, as we saw above, even set the model for how to do so.[37]

Adidas, a multinational sporting apparel giant, was at it again in 2006 in the run-up to the tournament in Germany. A well-known commercial of the day focused on the emotional nature of the game and its ability to connect people across cultures and historical epochs. The ad features two young Spanish-speaking boys—José and his friend—who decide to play a game of pickup football. Their pitch is nothing more than a dusty patch outside the modest apartments their families occupy. The two boys begin to pick players to fill out their respective sides. Soon many great players—Zidane, Kaká, David Beckham, and Oliver Kahn, to name just a few—show up to join the game. Things take an interesting historical turn when José chooses Franz Beckenbauer, who had been retired from football for many years by 2006, for his pickup side. Nevertheless, a youthful Beckenbauer jogs out to join the game and meets his surprised teammates. In response, and with the urging of Zidane, José's friend then selects Michel Platini, the legendary but retired French footballer.

In the game that ensues, world-class talent and ability is on display, but the two young boys are not intimidated, nor do they back down from the famous footballers in their midst. In fact, José remains at the center of the story. He flips the coin to determine ends of the pitch, tackles the ball away from the professionals, and sends off Kaká after he fails to convert a goal-scoring opportunity. At the end of the game, José's mother calls him home. He grabs his ball from a prostrate Kahn, who is arguing with several other players about whether the last kick, struck by Frank Lampard, had crossed the goal line or not. Suddenly, all of the star players are gone and José happily returns home with the ball tucked under his arm.

The commercial, called "José + 10," includes many interesting advertising hooks. The setting for the pickup game is simple, which emphasizes that football is a popular game played anywhere open ground can be found. The two boys are clearly involved in a fantasy match that allows them to call forward their favorite present and past players, but they are not overly impressed by the stars who show up. Although José is Spanish-speaking, he is clearly wearing a German national shirt in a nod to the 2006 competition site. In using images of Beckenbauer and Platini from their playing days, the commercial not only makes a historical connection to some of the greatest players of the 1970s and '80s but also introduces a certain timeless element. In one's imagination at least, football stars from the past do not age and are available to play with one in a pickup game. Finally, the simple dirt field reminds one of the origins and the basics of the game. Ball and pitch are all that one needs. Not everyone grows up with the game in such a gritty atmosphere, but many do. The suggestion of the ad is that no matter how famous one becomes, one should always remember the roots of the sport.[38]

In the same year, 2006, Nike released a series of football commercials under the logo "Joga Bonito," which is Portuguese for "play beautifully." The phrase is also close to *jogo bonito* or the "beautiful game," which had long been associated with Brazilian football. For these ads, Nike engaged Eric Cantona, the famous but controversial French player, to act as emcee and guide through the various spots. By 2006, Cantona was retired from the game but had gained some fame as a reformed bad boy superstar. Loaded with obvious talent, he had also engaged in several fights with teammates, opponents, and officials. As a player for Manchester United he had gone into the stands at Crystal Palace to kick a heckling fan. He was convicted of assault and served an eight-month ban from football. After this incident, his on- and off-the-field behavior improved, and he stayed involved with the game and took up a career as an actor.

Cantona is featured in most but not all of the "Joga Bonito" ads, whose basic message is to play skillful, entertaining football that will engage the world's fans. In one spot, he literally invades a German sporting studio to interrupt two dull broadcasters to announce that henceforth there will be no more liars and cheats in the game. The game will be played with skill, heart, and honor. The piece then cuts to several beautiful goal-scoring moments, including a scene featuring Ronaldinho, the Brazilian superstar, scoring and dancing. In another "Joga Bonito" ad, Wayne Rooney, the English star, is at a Manchester United training ground and grows frustrated with the play of his goalkeeper. He decides to head into goal himself, much to the exasperation of his manager, Sir Alex Ferguson. Rooney, however, plays the game like he's a kid again and bounces out of his goal to lead a head-on rush against the opposing team. He scores, but then is quickly scored upon as he dashes madly back to try to defend his goal. The point of the ad is straightforward: even the highest-paid professionals sometimes just need to ignore the norms of the game and play.

Many of the other commercials in the series feature members of the Brazilian national squad, who, more than anyone else, should embody the concept of the "beautiful game." In one ad, several members of the team—Ronaldinho, Ronaldo, Robinho, and Roberto Carlos—are in a locker room preparing for a match. They perform various dribbling tricks, pass the ball around the narrow space with great creativity, and simply enjoy the spirit of playing with one another. All the while, a samba beat is in the background. Cantona had introduced the piece by saying that if one wants to make beautiful music, then one has to play in an orchestra—in other words, as a team. The "Joga Bonito" commercials attempted to sell football (and Nike products) to a global audience, but they also represented a self-critical assessment of the game. In many of the segments, the simple joy of playful competition is emphasized, and the overly tactical, sometimes cynical side of the sport is critiqued. The message was simple: "For the good of the game and its fans, play beautiful soccer (again)."[39]

Advertising has been and will remain central to the economics of the World Cup. The mechanisms by which it is offered to spectators at stadia or at home have evolved greatly since 1930 and immensely since the 1960s with the use of television to broadcast games live. Technological change, a hallmark of the modern and contemporary eras, has transformed advertising techniques. Placards and boards inside stadia have given way to twenty-four-hour viewing cycles, in which advertising and branding have continued to play central parts. The coming of cable channels, the Internet, and cell phones has sped up the process whereby football as a global sport can be packaged, bought, sold, and consumed. Although national teams from around the world wear few commercial logos on their uniforms as compared to club players, the World Cup itself is completely saturated with advertising logos and heavily commercialized. Indeed, one of the long-standing complaints about football is that it, like so many modern sports, has become more of a commodity to be bought and sold than a game. Some of the best-known advertisements of the past twenty years have made this argument by suggesting that the game should remember its simple roots and play should be for the joy of competition, not for commercial gain. Adidas, Nike, and other global companies, which have made a fortune marketing sports of all kinds over the past several decades, are, ironically, bringing the message of football's traditional, non-commercialized roots to fans around the world.

PLAYERS' SALARIES AND BONUSES

Some players have clearly achieved economic benefits for participating in the World Cup. This benefit comes in different forms, but two primary ways in which players can profit financially from being a member of a national side are through bonuses and a boost to their club salaries. Team bonuses are paid out in a variety of schemes and vary from one national organization to another and from one World Cup to another. Players have also, from time to time, fought with their countries' football authorities over the size and timing of paying bonuses. Player pressure has sometimes been effective in raising the amount of money included in bonuses. National footballing organizations add economic incentives to performing well, advancing deep in, and perhaps even winning a tournament. For Brazil 2014, the national organizations of Germany, Brazil, England, and Spain were willing to provide bonuses of 300,000, 330,000, 433,000, and 720,000 euros, respectively, to each player on a title-winning side.[40]

FIFA has also developed a scheme for paying prize money to World Cup teams. For the 2010 tournament in South Africa, for example, a total of $420 million was paid out in prize money, some of it going for the first time to domestic clubs that held the contracts for participating players. In addition to a $1 million payment as a preparation fee, each team at the finals received a minimum of $8 million for the group stage. Prize money increased for each subsequent round of the tournament, with the eventual winner, Spain, receiving a payment of $30 million. The second-place team, the Netherlands, received $24 million. In essence, then, Andrés Iniesta's winning goal for Spain, in a 1–0 victory in the final, was worth $6 million to the Spanish football federation. In 2014, the champion, Germany, was given a $35 million payment as winner of the tournament. For 2018, the champion, France, took home a bonus of $38 million.[41] This prize money is paid to the national football associations, which usually use it, or a part of it, to reward their players' performances.

Moreover, some players' salaries have risen over the course of their careers after participating in a World Cup. The amount of increase in salary is dependent on many factors but is clearly linked to some straightforward sporting accomplishments, such as number of game appearances, perceived contributions to one's team's success, and scoring goals. Moreover, appearances in the final round games are much more important to a player's potential earnings than games of lesser importance, such as international friendlies. In today's game, top players have a number of competitions—domestic leagues and cups, international cup matches, and regional international matches, such as the European Championships—in which they can display their talent. Nevertheless, World Cup matches still serve as special opportunities to showcase one's ability. This is especially true for young or less well-known players from countries that do not have wealthy or well-funded domestic leagues. For such players, such as athletes from African nations, a deep run in the global tournaments can be a springboard to a lucrative playing career in Europe, especially in one of its major leagues. England, Spain, Italy, Germany, and France, for example, currently have numerous players from a large number of countries around the world. The working assumption on the part of these European teams and leagues is that if a player can play well at the highest level of competition against the top players in the world, then that player can be successful at the club level.

Samuel Eto'o of Cameroon, for example, is one of the best African strikers of all time and broke in with his national team as a teenager. He played in the 1998 tournament at the age of seventeen and also participated in the 2002 competition. He has enjoyed a long professional career, primarily in Europe, and has been engaged by major clubs, such as Real Madrid, FC Barcelona, Inter Milan, and Chelsea. His World Cup experience was part of what brought him to the attention of these clubs. His further club performances kept him very much in demand. In 2004, for example, Barcelona paid a transfer fee in excess of twenty million euros for Eto'o.[42] A year later, he was able to negotiate a substantial salary increase with the Catalan team, for which he would star for several years.

The opposite assumption, that highly played club players should be able to assert themselves in World Cup competition, has not always been borne out. For example, Lionel Messi of Argentina and FC Barcelona, who is widely regarded as one of the best players of his generation and of all time, has had relatively little success in international tournaments. He did help lead his national team to a second-place finish in the 2014 tournament, but the ultimate prize, a championship, has eluded him. Similarly, Cristiano Ronaldo of Portugal, who plays for Juventus Turin and who is also regarded as one of the best club footballers of his generation, has not enjoyed much success in

World Cup competitions. His Portuguese national side was able, however, to win the European Championship in 2016.[43]

Of course, the money earned by footballers, especially in the world's top leagues, depends on many factors, including long-term potential, availability, market demands, health, and projected economic return. Nevertheless, young players sometimes acquire the type of global exposure during a World Cup that allows them to command significant salaries at the club level. Established players can solidify their status during the global competitions as a way of proving their market value to their clubs. While it is impossible to sort out precisely all of the economic factors to come to an exact economic "dividend" for playing in a World Cup, it is clear that in many cases players profit financially by exhibiting their talents in the quadrennial tournaments. This is especially true of the period after the mid-1990s and the famous Bosman decision in 1995 that allowed for the free movement of European players within the European Union when their contracts with teams expired. Before that decision, clubs were forced to pay each other transfer fees, even for players who were no longer under contract. In addition, by 1999 deals were in place that lifted restrictions on the number of non-European players that could be employed by clubs and leagues in Europe. Those two measures had dampened the European and global market for footballers and tended to hold their salaries down. After 1995 and in the era of free transfer, players, especially elite ones and stars from World Cup competitions, have had more control over their financial status.[44] Non-elite players, especially those from outside of Europe, have not always fared as well in the more open post-Bosman market.[45] Even before 1995, however, some players were able to translate World Cup performances into better salaries or indirect gains, such as starring in advertisements.

Pelé, for example, the Brazilian star of the late 1950s and '60s, played most of his club career at Santos. He broke in with the club at age fifteen, started to play for the Brazilian national team at sixteen, and made his World Cup debut at seventeen in Sweden in 1958. He would go on to be a mainstay of the national team for the next twelve years. Late in his career, he signed with the New York Cosmos of the North American Soccer League (NASL). He played in the United States for two years and helped the Cosmos become an international sensation, if only for a short time. While in New York, Pelé was able to translate his fame and iconic status into real financial gain. He has remained both an ambassador for the game, appearing at many later tournaments, and a spokesman for many products and companies with global reach, such as Mastercard. While not earning a salary commensurate with his level of play in the late 1950s and '60s, Pelé gradually benefited economically from his footballing fame and his long-term association with the World Cup.

Johan Neeskens, the Dutch midfielder, eventually parlayed his international performances into commanding higher salaries. A star of the famous "Clockwork Orange" teams (so called because of the precision of their play and the color of their uniforms) that finished second in West Germany (1974) and in Argentina (1978), he was also an important cog in the highly successful Ajax club teams of the early 1970s. A highly skilled midfielder who was responsible for linking up the play of both his national and club teams, Neeskens signed with Barcelona in 1974, where he stayed for five seasons. He moved late in his career to the Cosmos, where he played from 1979 to 1984. Once again, the NASL provided an aging football star an opportunity to make a high salary at the end of his playing career. He signed with the New York team for an annual salary of approximately $300,000.[46]

The famed Mozambique-born Portugal-based striker Eusébio made a similar move to the NASL late in his career. After rising to fame at the 1966 World Cup in England, at which he scored nine goals and attracted the attention of the press, and playing for over a decade with the Portuguese national team, he made stops with several clubs in North America in the late 1970s. Whereas he had originally signed as a teenager with Benfica of Lisbon in 1960 for an annual salary of $1,700, in 1975 he joined Boston for a salary of approximately $1,000 a week. By then, he was only a shadow of the player who had led Portugal to a third-place finish in the 1966 tournament and who had helped to eliminate Brazil at the same competition. Numerous knee operations had reduced Eusébio's speed, power, and quickness, but he was still considered a strong draw in North America, even as the NASL began to have economic problems in the late 1970s. While never commanding the salary and attention of some stars, Eusébio did manage to earn substantial money at the end of a long and fabled international and club career. The move to the United States was also significant for him because the Portuguese authoritarian leader Antonio Salazar had declared him a "national treasure" and prevented any move abroad where he might have garnered a higher salary than in Portugal.[47] It was only late in his career that he was able to make the financially beneficial move to the NASL.

A player of a later generation, Ronaldo of Brazil, broke in with his national team in time for its triumph at the 1994 World Cup in the United States. Although he did not play in that competition, he was already highly regarded by his teammates. The defender Cafu said that at the age of seventeen Ronaldo was a "phenomenon," a title that would become one of his playing nicknames. By 1998, he was regarded as one of the best strikers in the world. He would play for many famous European clubs, including Barcelona, Inter Milan, Real Madrid, and AC Milan. In 1998, his national team finished a "disappointing" second to host France, but it was able to prevail and win the tournament in

2002 in South Korea and Japan. It is impossible to sort out to what degree World Cup success helped to determine Ronaldo's salary—after all, he was already a famous footballer before he played in the final round of the 1998 tournament—but clearly his performances at the international level helped solidify and sustain his club standing and earning power over many years. In 1996, Nike, the international sporting goods giant, signed him to an endorsement deal worth $180 million. He subsequently starred in a number of Nike television ads—for example, during the 1998 and 2002 tournaments, in both of which he competed.[48] For players of Ronaldo's status, club and international performances, financial fortune, and media and television exposure are inseparably intertwined. In his case, star power, on display in the World Cup and at the club level, brought with it clear and substantial financial rewards.

CONCLUSION

The global economic dimensions of the World Cup have grown dramatically over the course of the last hundred years. FIFA and its corporate sponsors have learned to use broadcast media, especially television, as partners in creating great wealth and revenue from the global tournaments. In the television age, corporate sponsors will pay millions of dollars to lend their names to football's foremost international competition. In return, they hope to garner sales and brand recognition from their affiliation with the global game. Many players, although certainly not all, have also benefited economically from the growth in popularity of the tournament. Over time and in an uneven process, some football players have been able to translate strong performances at the international level into better salaries and endorsement deals. The cost to them has come in the way of the increased number of matches that they must play on a near continuous basis.

The World Cup, then, has become a huge economic engine over the course of its existence.[49] The money it generates, however, has not always been evenly or equitably distributed. Clearly, FIFA itself has received its fair share of the economic spoils from the tournament. Some national football federations also have done well financially based on good outcomes and finishing among the top teams at the competition. Other national bodies, whose teams have not done quite as well at the matches, have earned far less money from their participation. Some players have benefited economically from playing in the World Cup. The tournament gives them exposure, which they can hopefully use to gain better contracts and advertising opportunities. Many other players, however, either because they played too early in the history of the tournament or because they or their teams did not fare well during the competition, have not been able to take away much, if any, direct financial benefit from the World Cup.

Most problematic of all, in terms of calculating short- and long-term financial outcomes, has been the tournament's impact upon local and national economies. For every claim about enhanced revenue from ticket sales, merchandise, or hotel bookings, there have been stronger counterclaims that staging the World Cup is a net economic drag upon the host country. Nevertheless, countries around the world believe that the prestige of playing host to the competition offsets any financial shortfall that might be associated with it. Moreover, the bidding nations always present plans for stadia construction, expanded infrastructure, and hotels that suggest they will not only turn a profit for FIFA, the national footballing federations, and the players, but also for the communities and people where the games will be played. They also count on the "happiness" effect of being hosts to a major sporting event.

Most sports economists are clear, however, that the financial benefit of such a competition on construction, jobs, wages, and sports tourism in given locations and countries is minimal or perhaps nonexistent. They use sophisticated models to address these questions about the short- and long-term economic impact of global sporting events upon a hosting nation. The World Cup has the ability to raise revenue through ticket sales, on-site merchandising, hotel bookings, and sport tourism, but most of this money is offset by the costs of staging the tournament. Nevertheless, bidding to be the site of a World Cup is often intense and hotly contested. Indeed, indirect economic variables, such as the possible financial benefits of national pride and periods of "feel-good" psychology and consumer confidence, also play a role in countries pursuing the privilege of staging the tournament. Moreover, the ability of football's preeminent global competition to generate increasing amounts of capital is likely to continue to grow. Broadcasting rights, advertising dollars, and sports merchandising will ensure that the world's game remains a financial juggernaut in the future. How all of the money generated by the World Cup is distributed to FIFA officials, national football associations, participating teams, local economies, and players, however, will also remain hotly contested.

Finally, as an economic phenomenon, the World Cup is clearly linked to world historical developments in the modern era. For example, the revolution in media technology—radio, television, and the Internet—has dramatically affected the global reach of the football tournament. Advancements in transportation—air travel, for example—have made it possible to stage the quadrennial competitions in South America, Europe, Asia, Africa, and North America. Changes in work and the growth in leisure time in the nineteenth, twentieth, and twenty-first centuries have created more fans to watch and follow World Cup matches. The more frequent movement of labor—in this case, players—has also been a hallmark of the modern period. In many important and fascinating ways, the economic development of the World Cup of football has paralleled recent world historical trends.

DOCUMENTS AND ARTIFACTS RELATED TO THE ECONOMICS OF THE WORLD CUP

A. Geoff Hurst's Bronzed Boot from the 1966 World Cup Final, National Football Museum, Manchester, UK. https://www.nationalfoot ballmuseum.com/collections_detail/geoff-hursts-bronzed-boot-from-the -1966-world-cup-final

  1. What does a bronze boot tell us about the commercialization of the World Cup in 1966?
  2. Who was Geoff Hurst? Research his playing career. What type of salary did he command in the 1960s?

B. Adidas Telstar Ball, 1970, in David Goldblatt and Jean Williams, *A History of the World Cup in 24 Objects*. De Montfort University, Leicester, UK. https://www.dmu.ac.uk/documents/world-cup-2014/world-cup -24-objects.pdf

  1. What did Adidas hope to accomplish by lending its name to the official game ball for the 1970 World Cup?
  2. What was the significance of the design of the ball?

C. FIFA, "FIFA World Cup 1974: Final Competition, Technical Study." https:// resources.fifa.com/image/upload/world-cup-1974-500965.pdf?cloudid =wnzpp4kcraivkmgremag

  1. From this report, what types of economic impacts did the 1974 World Cup have for the host country, West Germany; the national teams; and the players?
  2. What kinds of economic information did FIFA choose to include in this technical report? What type of information might you have expected that FIFA would have included in the report?

D. Hosting the 1986 Soccer World Cup. Hearing before the Subcommittee on Commerce, Transportation, and Tourism. Committee on Energy and Commerce, US House of Representatives, on H.J. Resolution 219, "A Joint Resolution Declaring the Support of the US Government for the Efforts of the US Soccer Federation to Bring the World Cup to the United

States in 1986." HathiTrust Digital Library. https://hdl.handle.net/2027 /uc1.31210024777243

1. What economic reasons did the US House of Representatives cite for supporting the US Soccer Federation's (USSF) bid to host the 1986 World Cup?
2. From the subcommittee's report, can you discern economic or other reasons why FIFA ultimately decided not to accept the bid?

E. Sam Knight, "How Football Leaks Is Exposing Corruption in European Soccer," *New Yorker*, May 27, 2019. https://www.newyorker.com/maga zine/2019/06/03/how-football-leaks-is-exposing-corruption-in-european -soccer

1. What arguments does the author use to support his claims about economic and political corruption in European soccer?
2. Research football officials' (FIFA and UEFA) claims about what they have done in the last several years to clean up economic corruption in world football.

SUGGESTIONS FOR FURTHER READING AND RESEARCH

Arbena, Joseph L., ed. *Sport and Society in Latin America: Diffusion, Dependency, and the Rise of Mass Culture.* Westport, CT: Greenwood, 1988.

Clignet, Rémi, and Maureen Stark. "Modernization and the Game of Soccer in Cameroon." *International Review of Sport Sociology* 9, no. 3 (1974): 81–98.

Fishwick, Nicholas. *English Football and Society: 1910–1950.* Manchester: Manchester University Press, 1989.

Fynn, Alex, and Lynton Guest. *Out of Time: Why Football Isn't Working.* London: Simon and Schuster, 1994.

———. *The Secret Life of Football.* London: Queen Anne, 1989.

Ginsborg, Paul. *Silvio Berlusconi: Television, Power, and Patrimony.* London: Verso, 2004.

Harding, John. *For the Good of the Game: The Official History of the Footballers' Association.* London: Robson, 1991.

Horne, John, and Wolfram Manzenreiter, eds. *Football Goes East: Business, Culture, and the People's Game in China, Japan, and South Korea.* London: Routledge, 2004.

Hutchinson, John. *The Football Industry: The Early Years of the Professional Game.* Edinburgh, UK: Richard Drew, 1982.

Jennings, Andrew. *Foul! The Secret World of FIFA: Bribes, Vote Rigging, and Ticket Scandals.* London: HarperSport, 2006.

Jones, Stephen. "The Economic Aspects of Association Football in England, 1918–1939." *British Journal of Sports History* 1, no. 3 (December 1984): 286–99.

Kuper, Simon, and Stefan Szymanski. *Soccernomics.* New York: Nation Books, 2009.

Mason, Tony. *Association Football and English Society: 1863–1915*. London: Harvester, 1980.

Szymanski, Stefan. *Money and Soccer: A Soccernomics Guide*. New York: Nation Books, 2015.

Thompson, E. P. "Time, Work, Discipline, and Industrial Capitalism." *Past and Present* 38 (December 1967).

Tischler, Steven. *Footballers and Businessmen: The Origins of Professional Soccer in England*. New York: Holmes and Meier, 1981.

Vamplew, Wray. *Pay Up and Play the Game: Professional Sport in Britain, 1875–1914*. Cambridge, UK: Cambridge University Press, 2004.

Walvin, James. *The People's Game: The History of Football Revisited*. Edinburgh, UK: Mainstream, 1994.

Yeo, Stephen, and Eileen Yeo, eds. *Popular Culture and Class Conflict, 1590–1914*. Brighton, UK: Harvester Press, 1981.

NOTES

1. Chris Gratton, Nigel Dobson, and Simon Shibli, "The Role of Major Sports Events in the Economic Regeneration of Cities: Lessons from Six World or European Championships," in *Sport in the City: The Role of Sport in Economic and Social Regeneration*, eds. Chris Gratton and Ian P. Henry (New York: Routledge, 2001), 35–45. The evidence offered in this article is not drawn from football matches per se, but does touch directly on the topic of sports generating income for local and national economies. The authors' conclusions about the economic impact of hosting major sporting events are, on the whole, optimistic, which is not the opinion of other sports economists, such as Stefan Szymanski. See Simon Kuper and Stefan Szymanski, *Soccernomics* (New York: Nation Books, 2009), 235–52. Kuper and Szymanski also cite influential studies done by other sports economists (Rob Baade, Victor Matheson, and Holger Preuss).

2. See Kuper and Szymanski, *Soccernomics*, 235–52, who survey most of the relevant studies and data on hosting World Cup and other international football tournaments.

3. On television and football, see John Sugden and Alan Tomlinson, *FIFA and the Contest for World Football: Who Rules the Peoples' Game?* (Cambridge, UK: Polity Press, 1998), 73–83.

4. FIFA.com.

5. Kuper and Szymanksi, *Soccernomics*, 238–44.

6. Quinton Fortune, "South Africa Spent 2.4 Billion Pounds to Host the 2010 World Cup: What Happened Next?" *The Guardian*, September 23, 2014, https://www.theguardian.com/football/2014/sep/23/south-africa-2010-world-cup-what-happened.

7. David Goldblatt, *The Ball Is Round: A Global History of Soccer* (New York: Riverhead Books, 2008), 521–26.

8. Eduardo Galeano, *Soccer in Sun and Shadow*, trans. Mark Fried (London: Verso, 1998), 147.

9. Goldblatt, *The Ball Is Round*, 524–25.

10. For a number of years, there has been a growth industry in publishing on FIFA's economic scandals, secrecy, and ongoing investigations. See, for example, Ken Bensinger, *Red Card: FIFA and the Fall of the Most Powerful Men in Sports* (London: Profile Books, 2018); Andrew Jennings, *Foul! The Secret World of FIFA: Bribes, Vote Rigging, and Ticket Scandals* (London: HarperSport, 2006); Andrew Jennings, *The Dirty Game: Uncovering the Scandal at FIFA* (London: Century, 2015); and David A. Yallop, *How They Stole the Game* (London: Poetic Publishers, 1999).

11. According to the FIFA marketing website, partners are offered, in addition to all of the standard sponsorship rights, "the possibility to tailor their sponsorship according to their marketing strategy and needs. For example, they can individually use the official logo and create composite logos. This not only allows them to differentiate themselves creatively from uninvolved third parties but also gives them an excellent marketing tool." FIFA Partners, FIFA.com.

12. Ibid.

13. FIFA.com. On the issue of transnational corporate sporting sponsorships, see George H. Sage, *Globalizing Sport: How Organizations, Corporations, Media, and Politics Are Changing Sports* (Boulder, CO: Paradigm, 2010), 164–67.

14. For some of the history of World Cup bidding, see Sugden and Tomlinson, *FIFA and the Contest for World Football*, 100–124.

15. On the economics of bidding for major sporting events, see P. R. Emery, "Bidding to Host a Major Sports Event: Strategic Investment or Complete Lottery," in *Sport in the City*, eds. Chris Gratton and Ian P. Henry (New York: Routledge, 2001), 90–108.

16. Leo H. Kahane and Stephen Shmanske, eds., *The Oxford Handbook of Sports Economics*, vol. 1: *The Economics of Sports* (Oxford: Oxford University Press, 2012), 453–56. This section of the handbook is titled "Benefits to Local and National Economies from Hosting the World Cup Finals" and is written by Rob Simmons and Christian Deutscher.

17. Gene Kim and Clancy Morgan, "Brazil's Empty $300 Million World Cup Stadium," *Insider*, June 27, 2018, https://www.insider.com/300-million-world-cup-stadium-is-nearly-abandoned-2018-6.

18. Robert Baade and Victor Matheson, "The Quest for the Cup: Assessing the Economic Impact of the World Cup," *Regional Studies* 38 (2004): 341–52.

19. Kuper and Syzmanski, *Soccernomics*, 247–51.

20. 2018 World Cup Qualification, FIFA.com.

21. Galeano, *Soccer in Sun and Shadow*, 197.

22. Stefan Szymanski, *Money and Soccer: A Soccernomics Guide* (New York: Nation Books, 2015), passim. The Champions League matches league-winning and other qualifying teams from one year in an extensive tournament the following year. Qualification is based on the strength of European domestic leagues. The competition lasts from the fall of one year into the late spring/early summer of the next and employs first a round-robin format before proceeding to knockout stages. Liverpool won the 2019 Champions League.

23. See chapter 5, on football as a sporting spectacle.

24. As the global popularity of football grew over the course of the twentieth century, star players became celebrities in their own right and increasingly mixed with famous actors, musicians, and other performers. Some football players, therefore, became part of the cult of celebrity, which has also been a hallmark of modern society and culture. See Daniel Alan Herwitz, *The Star as Icon: Celebrity in the Age of Mass Consumption* (New York: Columbia University Press, 2008).

25. On the history of the World Cup draw, see FIFA, "History of the World Cup Final Draw," InfoPlus, FIFA.com, https://www.fifa.com/mm/document/fifafacts/mcwc/ip-201_10e_fwcdraw-history_8842.pdf.

26. "Did the 1966 World Cup Mark the Birth of Modern Football?," bbc.co.uk; Fabio Chisari, "When Football Went Global: Televising the 1966 World Cup," *Historical Social Research* 31, no. 1 (2006): 42–54.

27. Felix Richter, "Billions of Dollars for Billions of Viewers," statista.com, June 21, 2018.

28. Seb Joseph, "The Media Trends Defining the World Cup, in 5 Charts," digiday.com, June 19, 2018.

29. Galeano, *Soccer in Sun and Shadow*, 168.

30. As noted elsewhere, FIFA, the global governing body, is attempting to clean its political and economic house. Sepp Blatter is currently suspended from all FIFA functions.

31. Adam Brandon, "World Cup Reorganisation: Freshening Up or Diluting Down?" worldfootballindex.com, April 1, 2017.

32. FIFA.com.

33. FIFA.com.

34. FIFA.com, Media Release, December 16, 2015; 2018 FIFA World Cup Russia, FIFA.com.

35. FIFA.com.

36. Shareen Pathak, "Rewind: The Day Soccer came to U.S. Advertising," adage.com, July 10, 2014.

37. Ibid.

38. YouTube, "Adidas José + 10 Impossible Team Commercial," youtube.com, April 14, 2017, https://images.app.goo.gl/t4Sf8hRULFgEwyBx6.

39. *Irish News*, "Joga Bonito: Remembering When Nike Brought 'The Beautiful Game' to Our Screens," irishnews.com, February 9, 2017.

40. *Fields of Green*, "World Cup Players Compete for Country, and Bonus Money," thefieldsofgreen.com, June 10, 2014.

41. FIFA.com.

42. "Samuel Eto'o," transfermarkt.com.

43. Messi and Ronaldo have both been involved in messy tax fraud claims in Spain. See, for example, *BBC News*, "Lionel Messi Tax Fraud Prison Sentence Reduced to Fine," bbc.com, July 7, 2017; and Kathleen Elkins, "Soccer Star Cristiano Ronaldo Fined over $20 Million for Tax Fraud," cnbc.com, January 22, 2019. Messi was required to pay approximately $288,000 as part of his tax settlement. In addition to fines for tax fraud, Ronaldo faced charges of rape—which he strongly denied—in the United States, as of early 2019. See Tariq Panja and Kevin Draper, "Cristiano Ronaldo's DNA

Sought by Las Vegas Police in Rape Investigation," *New York Times*, January 10, 2019, https://www.nytimes.com/2019/01/10/sports/cristiano-ronaldo-lawsuit.html.

44. Martin Littlewood, Chris Mullen, and David Richardson, "Football Labour Migration: An Examination of the Player Recruitment Strategies of the 'Big Five' European Football Leagues 2004–5 to 2008–9," *Soccer and Society* 12, no. 6 (2011): 788–805.

45. Joseph Maguire, *Global Sport: Identities, Societies, Civilizations* (Malden, MA: Blackwell, 1999), 100–101.

46. Frank Litsky, "Long Ordeal Nears an End for Neeskens," *New York Times*, July 3, 1981.

47. Goldblatt, *The Ball Is Round*, 426.

48. Adam Reed, "Brazil Soccer Star Ronaldo Becomes the Majority Owner of a Top Spanish Club," cnbc.com, September 4, 2018.

49. This chapter on the economics of the World Cup of football has not even attempted to calculate the amount of money exchanging hands because of betting on the tournament. To do so would involve guessing about the aggregate economic effects of legal and illegal, formal and informal activities, which is beyond the scope of the present study. For some brief discussion of World Cup betting, see "Betting History of the World Cup," oddsshark.com, which is itself a betting site and is already taking wagers on the 2022 World Cup in Qatar. For a scholarly discussion of betting in American sports, see Douglas T. Putnam, "Beating the Spread," in *Controversies of the Sports World* (Westport, CT: Greenwood Press, 1999), 131–48.

Chapter 4

The World Cup and Gender, Race, and Ethnicity

Race, ethnicity, and gender are three important analytical categories for world and sports historians. They have helped scholars and students to understand the ways individuals and societies order themselves and function socially and culturally. Much has been written about these categories theoretically and how they should be applied across chronological epochs. As we have seen, in the modern era football became codified with set rules, and competitions, such as the World Cup, were standardized. During this time, race, ethnicity, and gender clearly influenced or shaped how people related and reacted to the dramatic and even explosive growth in football. In this chapter, these analytical categories will be used to provide a lens through which one can see how football has often mirrored and occasionally driven social and cultural developments at the national and even global level. The first half of this chapter explores the evolution and global significance of women in football over the last century. It focuses on the growth of international competitions and the FIFA World Cup for women, but it also explores the way gender assumptions and even stereotypes have affected the game.[1]

The second half of the chapter looks at the racial and ethnic composition of three teams in detail—Brazil from the 1930s to the 1950s, France from the late 1950s to the 1990s, and Germany in the 2014 tournament—to gauge the way race and ethnicity have woven their way into debates about national football cultures. Further, the second section shows how discussion of these matters has been crucial to shaping national perspectives but has also caused pushback on the part of critics unwilling to embrace diverse teams as "representative" of their country. Finally, this chapter looks at how the World Cup has gradually and often haltingly opened up to include more teams from Africa and Asia, making the football tournament over time a more global and diverse sporting event. Analyzing the World Cup of football using the categories of gender, race, and ethnicity shows that there are no easy or uniform answers to the question of national or personal identity in the modern era. Indeed, sporting culture is just as likely to show the limitations as the progress of social and cultural integration in contemporary societies.

WOMEN, GENDER, AND FOOTBALL

On April 10, 2016, the Women's National Team of Colombia played a "friendly" match against the US Women's National Team (USWNT) in Chester, Pennsylvania. The game was significant for a number of reasons. A friendly match in world football is usually an opportunity for national teams to try out players and tactics in a relatively relaxed environment because the outcome does not affect qualifying for competitions such as the World Cup or the Olympics. The US team was fresh off of its 2015 victory in Canada, which was followed by a triumphant tour on home soil. Star players, such as Carli Lloyd, Hope Solo, Alex Morgan, and Megan Rapinoe, were repeatedly interviewed by the media and feted by fans. The team made the customary trip of championship teams to the White House, where President Barack Obama praised its achievements.

Nevertheless, the friendly match against Colombia was overshadowed by the recent news that five American players had filed a wage discrimination complaint against the United States Soccer Federation (USSF). Their argument was that women players should earn fair and equitable amounts of money compared to their American male counterparts and work, train, and play in conditions similar to the US men's national team. At the 2015 Women's World Cup in Canada, for example, some of the games were played on artificial surfaces, something that would never be allowed for a men's major football tournament. The women clearly had a point. By 2016, the popularity of the US women players was equal to or greater than that of the men. In addition, large numbers of viewers had tuned in to watch women's matches featuring the United States in Canada in 2015. One of the primary reasons often cited for the disparity in monetary compensation between male and female athletes in all sports is that the men simply draw larger crowds, command more advertising, and create more revenue. More money generated equals more money to disperse among the athletes. The USWNT, however, could legitimately claim that at least in 2015 it had been more than capable of raising the same kind of revenue as the men's team.

Moreover, no one could believe in 2016 that the US women were less successful on the pitch than the men. In addition to the most recent World Cup, the women could point to a long history of victories at the international level, especially in Olympic competitions (2008, 2012), but also at earlier World Cup tournaments (1991, 1999).[2] The US men, who have made significant strides in world football over the past several decades, would still not be among the favorites at a World Cup or international competition in 2016. That role would fall to the Germans, French, Argentines, Spanish, Dutch, or Brazilians, among other global football powers.

In April 2017, the USSF reached a new Collective Bargaining Agreement (CBA) with the women's national team. The agreement went some distance toward meeting the women's demands for better pay and better working conditions, including items such as increasing per diem payments while on national team tours. Further, the USSF seemed to pledge more institutional support for the new women's professional league, the National Women's Soccer League (NWSL) in the United States. The agreement did not result in an equal pay for equal work settlement that would have allowed women's national team players to earn as much as their male counterparts for appearing in matches. As the negotiations showed, the pay structures between the men and women players were quite different and could not be easily reconciled. Nevertheless, the new collective bargaining agreement was on balance a significant step forward for women's football in the United States. Moreover, the active involvement of high-level women US players had driven the negotiation process. They were instrumental in allowing for an agreement to be reached.[3] The new CBA addressed, however, only some of the women's grievances. In March 2019, the US Women's National Team's pursuit of equal or equitable treatment in pay, playing conditions, travel, and medical treatment continued when twenty-eight of its leading players sued the US Soccer Federation for gender discrimination. The outcome of this legal action is still open.[4]

Clearly, the actions and attitudes of women national football players were becoming increasingly significant and newsworthy. For example, when the friendly matches of 2016 gave way to the competition at the Rio Olympics in 2016, global tensions would be revealed. In Brazil, the US women bowed out, surprisingly, in the quarterfinal round to Sweden and won no medals. Hope Solo, the longtime US goalkeeper, called the Swedish players "cowards" for supposedly being unwilling to press their attack and being overly defensive in the match. Her comments went viral and created much ill will, leading ultimately to her suspension from the USWNT in late summer 2016.[5] For better or worse, the US women had become global players, whose performances and comments were followed by a world audience.

The Colombian women who played that friendly match in Pennsylvania were also dealing with their own set of problems and issues in the spring of 2016. Colombia had also done well in Canada in 2015, finishing the competition with a strong showing. Several of its players, including Lady Andrade, were recognized for their skill and flare in their matches against Mexico, France, England, and the United States. The fortunes of the team seemed to be on the rise. However, the Colombian national football foundation had failed to pay the players the salaries and bonuses supposedly agreed upon for a good showing at the competition. Thus, in protest, Andrade and others sat out of the match against the United States. The "friendly" was dominated by commentary about the off-the-field issues facing both teams. The US women felt strong enough in their recent fame to sue their own national governing body. Some of the Colombian women felt so aggrieved by their financial situation that they chose not to play. In a microcosm, the match in Chester, Pennsylvania, showed how far the women's game had come in recent decades and how far it still had to go.

WOMEN AND FOOTBALL BEFORE THE FIFA WORLD CUP

On one level, it is surprising that it took so long to organize an official women's FIFA-sponsored World Cup. After all, women joined in all types of folk sports as participants or spectators, including those that involved a ball and resembled early versions of what we today call football. This is true whether one is looking at early North American, Asian, African, or European cultures. Women's engagement in these games differed from that of men, but they were not denied participation as such. When the game of football was organized in the nineteenth century, however, and rules were codified to govern its play, men attempted to exclude women almost completely from the game that emerged in England's public schools and early amateur and professional leagues. Women were not allowed in the public schools. Strong male beliefs about the supposed physical weakness of women were also widely held. The nineteenth-century version of football seemed to be the preserve of men, and women were shunted to its margins. The history of women's participation in football culture in this era is not as bleak, however, as it is often portrayed. Claims of male privilege and divided spheres of influence and participation in the Victorian era (late nineteenth and early twentieth centuries), one male and public and one female and private, are almost always overstated and overdrawn. Further historical research will surely do more to restore women, both as participants and spectators, to the early history of football.

Nevertheless, many amateur and professional leagues around the world and national footballing associations made it difficult, if not impossible, for several decades for women to play organized football matches. There were few opportunities to stage international competitions until well after the Second World War. There were exceptions to this rule, such as when the Scottish Football Association in 1892 helped sponsor a women's match, or when some teams such as Dick, Kerr's Ladies were formed during the First World War and played charity and other matches around the north of England. Various national football associations, however, failed to provide official sponsorship or recognition of these early attempts to organize women's football. In fact, most national associations hampered the development of women's football considerably in the interwar era and beyond by banning them from using stadiums registered to the national associations. Without much, if any, financial support or infrastructure, women's football was largely marginalized well into the post–Second World War era. To be sure, women's matches were still played—teams like Dick, Kerr's Ladies, for example, continued to tour until 1965—but it was clear that they would be conducted without official sponsorship and aid from the male-controlled football associations throughout the world.[6] Many of the national associations only lifted their bans on women's football in the 1970s (West Germany, 1970; England, 1971; and Brazil, 1979).

In addition, in the nineteenth and for much of the twentieth century, gendered notions about what was appropriate physical activity and exercise for women contributed to a cultural climate in which women had to break through any number of stereotypes about the lack of female stamina, energy, skill, and strength. These stereotypes were propagated by national athletic bodies, medical associations, and the popular press. Women's progress in sports sometimes seemed frustratingly slow. Women did manage, however, to counter many of these stereotypes and achieve significant athletic breakthroughs throughout the twentieth century. They did so sooner in individual sports like tennis and golf (one thinks of the careers of women athletes such as Suzanne Lenglen and Babe Didrikson, for example) than in the male-controlled world of football, which took more time to concede much ground to women as players.[7] Even without support from national or club organizations, women continued to play football, and eventually global competitions were held in the early 1970s and '80s. These tournaments, which sometimes drew very large crowds, were not recognized by FIFA. Teams from Denmark (1970, 1971), Italy (1982, 1986), and England (1985, 1988) won these competitions. They remind us that women's football could survive and even thrive without the help of FIFA and men's national associations.[8]

Global feminism of the 1960s and '70s, which argued for more opportunities for women in society, further supported the growth of women's football. Sports experienced periods of gradual opening up and significant structural changes, such as the introduction of Title IX in the United States. Title IX was a section of the 1972 Education Amendments and stated that if educational institutions received federal financial assistance, they could not discriminate on the basis of sex. Although the legislation has been interpreted to mean different things, has sometimes been challenged in the courts, and is currently part of the debate about gender identity (transgender rights, for example) in the United States, its importance for the advancement of women's sports cannot be underestimated. The debate about gender equity in US college and university sports continues, but there have clearly been many more opportunities for women to participate in athletics since the 1970s.[9] Title IX has not just opened up sports such as football for American women; players from other countries have come to the United States to play on university-sponsored teams as well. Christine Sinclair, a Canadian striker, starred collegiately at the University of Portland in Oregon, for example. In addition, Title IX has been seen globally as a watershed in trying to achieve gender equity in sports. The idea behind it is similar in spirit to the establishment and maintenance of women's professional football leagues in countries such as Sweden, Japan, Germany, and France. The post-1960s and '70s era has seen, therefore, many more institutions and organizations offering sporting opportunities for women around the globe than existed in the first half of the twentieth century.[10]

One might consider, for example, the career of Sarah Zadrazil of Austria as representative of a certain path open to contemporary women's football players. From St. Gilgen, in the province of Salzburg, she proved early on that she was a high-caliber player and distinguished herself in Austrian youth leagues; she then made her debut in the Austrian Bundesliga at the age of fourteen for USK Hof bei Salzburg. Her performances caught the attention of the coaching staff at East Tennessee State University (ETSU), who recruited her to play college football in the United States from 2012 to 2016. Although ETSU is not one of the powerhouses of women's college sports in the United States, it did provide Zadrazil with valuable playing experience and an education. After graduating from ETSU in 2016, she returned to Europe and was recruited to play professionally in Germany with FFC Tribune Potsdam. As early as 2010, she won a spot on the Austrian national team, which has been on the rise in recent years. She was a key cog on the side that reached the semifinals of the Women's European Championship in 2017.[11]

Thus, Zadrazil took full advantage of the opportunities—youth leagues, college teams (in her case in the United States), professional clubs, and national sides—open to highly skilled and motivated women football players in the early twenty-first century. Of course, most women players will not be selected to represent their countries or be good enough to join a professional league, but many of them have and are playing in youth leagues and school systems around the world. In many countries, the number of women players is on the rise, and the game is establishing itself more and more as part of national and professional sporting cultures.

Table 4.1.   **Women's Soccer Leagues around the World (not all fully professional)**

Country	League	Number of Teams	Years of Operation
Australia	W-League	9	2008–
	Women's National Soccer League	6	1996–2004
Denmark	Elitedivisionen	8	1973–
England	FA Women's Super League 1	12	2011–
France	Division 1 Féminine	12	1992–
Germany	Frauen-Bundesliga	12	1989/1990
Japan	Nadeshiko League Division 1	10	1989–
Mexico	Liga MX-Femenil	19	2017
Norway	Toppserien	12	1987–
Spain	Primera División de la Liga de Fútbol Feminino	16	1988–
Sweden	Damallsvenskan	12	1988–
USA	National Women's Soccer League	9	2013–
	Women's Professional Soccer	6/7	2009–2012
	Women's United Soccer Association	8	2001–2003

Sources: dbu.dk (Denmark); dfb.de (Germany); Tom Dunmore, *Historical Dictionary of Soccer* (Lanham, MD: Rowman & Littlefield, 2015), 261; fawsl.com (England); fff.fr (France); fotbal.no (Norway); Timothy F. Grainey, *Beyond Bend It Like Beckham: The Global Phenomenon of Women's Soccer* (Lincoln: University of Nebraska Press, 2012), 258–63, 265; laliga.es (Spain); ligafemenil.mx (Mexico); nwslsoccer .com (USA); ozfootball.net (Australia); SvenskFotball.se (Sweden); Jean Williams, "Football and Feminism," in *The Cambridge Companion to Football*, ed. Rob Steen, Jed Novick, and Huw Richards (Cambridge: Cambridge University Press, 2013), 188–94; w-league.com.au (Australia); Worldfootball.net.

WOMEN'S WORLD CUP: 1991–PRESENT

Unlike many other women's football matches in the period between the end of the nineteenth century and the 1970s and '80s, the 1991 World Cup would have the official sponsorship of the male-dominated FIFA and the various national football associations of the participating countries. To be sure, financial and moral support for the women's tournament differed from country to country, and not nearly as many nations participated, at least initially, in the women's tournament as they did in the men's competition in the 1990s. Nevertheless, a sea change in global sport had occurred in the post–Second World War era that was sped up by the feminist movement within athletics in the 1970s and '80s, which helped create a FIFA-sanctioned Women's World Cup to be played in 1991. International rules for play on the field were well established, of course, by this point in time. As with the men's game, the fascination with statistics and record keeping was a big part of cup competition right from the very beginning. Finally, the women's tournament, which did not initially draw a lot of international media attention and advertising dollars, would soon find its audience.

In the brief history of the official FIFA Women's World Cup since 1991, there have been only four victor nations: Germany, Japan, Norway, and the

United States. The United States won the first Cup played in China by defeating Norway, 2–1, in the final. Attendance for all of the games played was 510,000, and only twelve nations participated in the first women's tournament. In 1995, the competition was held in Sweden, where the Norwegian national women's side was able to win the world title by defeating Germany, 2–0. Again, only twelve teams competed in the cup. Attendance for all of the matches was 112,213. Despite the low in-person attendance, the 1995 final was watched on television reportedly by one in four Norwegians.[12] The 1999 World Cup in the United States in many ways represented a breakthrough for women's football. The competition was expanded to sixteen teams, which showed the continuing global reach of the women's game. Second, attendance for the matches—1,194,215—was considerably higher than in 1991 and 1995. The final match played between China and the United States ended dramatically with a penalty shootout won by the latter. It was witnessed by a reported crowd of over ninety thousand in the Rose Bowl in Pasadena, California.[13] This game became emblematic of the growing popularity of women's football. A picture of a jubilant Brandi Chastain, who had scored the winning penalty, appeared on the cover of *Sports Illustrated*, one of the flag-bearers of sports media in North America.[14]

The 2003 tournament was again scheduled for China, but global concern about the SARS (Severe Acute Respiratory Syndrome) disease caused FIFA to move the competition on short notice back to the United States. The host nation, however, could not defend its title, and Germany, which had fielded numerous strong teams for the competition but had not yet been able to capture the ultimate prize, won the cup for the first time. Attendance for the matches, played among sixteen teams, was 656,789. As compensation for not hosting the cup in 2003, China was given the honor in 2007, without any selection process on the part of FIFA. The Germans were able to defend their title by defeating Brazil, 2–0. Sixteen teams competed in the matches in China in 2007, and the overall attendance for the games was 1,156,988. In 2011, the women's tournament was played for the first time in Germany. The hosts, two-time defending champions, were unable to make the final, which Japan won in dramatic fashion on penalty kicks over the United States. It was the first victory by an Asian nation in the women's tournament.[15]

The 2015 Women's World Cup was held in Canada. The tournament was noteworthy for several reasons. First, the number of participating nations rose to twenty-four, which meant that there was a greater presence of teams from Africa, Asia, and Central America than in earlier competitions. For example, Ivory Coast, Cameroon, Thailand, Ecuador, and Costa Rica fielded women's tournament finalists for the first time in their history. The expanded format for the 2015 women's tournament meant that two European nations, Switzerland and Spain, would also make their premier on football's biggest world stage.

Even though they were not able to advance very far in the tournament, the presence of these teams added additional global attention to the cup. The additional teams also created the possibility for the further growth of women's football around the world. How much money and organizational support might be provided for teams from these countries between the World Cup competitions would remain a key question going forward.

The competition in Canada also threw into sharp relief the question of gender equity in global sport. Many of the women players noted that they would have to play their matches on artificial surfaces, which tend to cause more injuries than natural grass. The women and their fans and supporters rightfully claimed that the men's competition would never be played under such conditions. On the other hand, the 2015 women's tournament was a sporting success in terms of the quality of competition, media and advertising, and as a showcase for female athletes from around the world. Although the United States would win the final in dominant fashion over Japan on the strength of Carli Lloyd's first-half hat trick (three goals), much of the rest of the competition, especially its knock-out phases, was marked by tight games and evenly matched teams. The cup in Canada showed the depth of talented women's players from around the world, be they Nigerian, Japanese, German, Swedish, English, Brazilian, or Canadian.[16]

The women's game seemed to have taken another leap forward with the 2015 cup. Attendance for the matches in Canada was strong (1,353,506), and there was significant global media coverage of the games. For example, extensive television coverage of the tournament in the United States carried over into a triumphant televised celebration after the competition was over. The US women were feted wherever they went in the late summer of 2015 and became sporting celebrities. They were not alone; several of the players from other teams—Marta of Brazil and Lotta Schelin of Sweden, for example—also became better known to a global audience.[17]

The 2019 Women's World Cup was played in France and continued to show the global growth of the tournament. The United States won the competition by beating the Netherlands, 2–0, in the final. France had hosted the men's World Cup in 1998 and the European Championship in 2016, so the infrastructure was in place to support the women's matches. In addition to the United States and the Netherlands, several teams, including England, France, Italy, Sweden, Spain, Canada, and Nigeria, played attractive and determined football throughout June and early July 2019. France's team has been on the rise as a global force in the last two decades and benefited from playing at home. It could not, however, advance past the US team's combination of 2015 veterans and rising young players.

Megan Rapinoe won both the Golden Ball (best player) and Golden Boot (leading scorer) at the 2019 competition. Moreover, she was a very public voice in representing the women's game and its international progress, as well as in addressing issues of gender, social, and economic inequality. She several other US players were embroiled for part of the tournament in a dispute with US president Donald Trump over the issue of a possible visit to the White House, which became a flashpoint in the polarized political environment in the United States. Inevitably, Rapinoe's gender identity—she and a number of other high-profile US women's World Cup players are lesbians—was drawn into the social media commentary on the competition, its outcome, style of play, and the politics of sports in general. By the end of the tournament, chants of "equal pay" could be heard at the championship game in Lyon. The 2019 Women's World Cup represented the degree to which sports and global, political, and economic issues have become intertwined in the first decades of the twenty-first century. It also showed the continued strength of the women's game as a global commodity. FIFA estimated that approximately one billion viewers took in some part of the tournament, and attendance topped one million fans for the fifty-two games held in nine venues throughout France.[18]

The modern women's World Cup in the post-1991 period has also produced its share of record-breaking stars and notable performances. In addition to those mentioned above—Brandi Chastain's penalty in 1999 and Carli Lloyd's hat-trick performance in 2015—there have been the longevity records of players, such as Homare Sawa of Japan and Formiga of Brazil, who have competed in six and seven championships, respectively. Sawa has long been considered an ambassador of women's football, and Formiga has shown remarkable endurance. Five other players—Kristine Lilly of the United States, Bente Nordby of Norway, Birgit Prinz of Germany, Karina LeBlanc of Canada, and Christie Rampone of the United States—have played in five women's World Cups. Lilly holds the women's record for most match appearances, at thirty. And Rampone and Formiga played the game at the highest competitive level into their forties. Prinz is one of the all-time leading scorers in the women's tournament. She scored fourteen goals over the course of four competitions and was the leading scorer (seven) at the 2003 tournament in Germany. Several other players have scored goals in four competitions, including Sun Wen of China, Mia Hamm of the United States, Bettina Wiegmann of Germany (all stars of the 1990s), and Abby Wambach of the United States, a top performer in the 2000s. Marta of Brazil holds the record for most goals—seventeen—scored in the final rounds of the women's World Cup.[19]

The women's World Cup also has many honors. The Golden Ball is awarded to the competition's best overall player; the Golden Boot to the top goal scorer; and the Golden Glove to the best goalkeeper. There are also awards for making the all-star team and fair play. Star players, their records, awards, and performances have established for the women's tournament the same type of international yardsticks as those of their male counterparts, who receive similar awards for excellent play at their competitions. Even though the FIFA-sponsored women's tournament is of much more recent vintage than the male version, it has established its own history based on the accomplishments of its best players and teams. As with all modern sports, the ability to reach back and compare athletic achievements over time is crucial to the way games are played and understood by competitors, fans, casual observers, and scholars. Women's football has *always* had a past—even when it was formally marginalized for much of the twentieth century—but that past can be more easily documented and analyzed in the era (post-1991) of the official FIFA Women's World Cup.

Attendance at live matches of the women's World Cup has fluctuated some over the course of the past twenty-five years, but if one excludes the 1995 cup in Sweden, where attendance was low, the match average for the other six cups is between a low of 19,615 for the 1991 cup in China, and a high of 37,319 for the 1999 tournament in the United States. The China–United States final in 1999 remains one of the most watched games in women's football history. The tournament in Canada averaged approximately twenty-six thousand attendees per match, and this figure takes into account the expansion in the number of participating teams (twenty-four) and therefore a correspondingly larger number of games (fifty-two). Clearly, these numbers indicate a healthy interest in watching the women play live. They also provide some indication of the possible economic benefits to hosting a women's tournament, especially in countries like Germany, China, Canada, France, and the United States, where the infrastructure—stadia, transportation, hotels, training grounds—is largely already in place to hold massive international competitions. In such cases, unlike, say, in Brazil in 2014 for the men's tournament, there is less need to allocate large amounts of public funds to build facilities and manage them for a major global sporting event. France, for example, was in a good economic position to host the Women's World Cup in 2019.

Table 4.2. Women's World Cup

Year	Place	Winner	Teams	Matches	Attendance	Average Attendance
1991	China	USA	12	26	510,000	19,615
1995	Sweden	Norway	12	26	112,213	4,316
1999	USA	USA	16	32	1,194,215	37,319
2003	USA	Germany	16	32	656,789	20,525
2007	China	Germany	16	32	1,156,955	36,155
2011	Germany	Japan	16	32	845,751	26,430
2015	Canada	USA	24	52	1,353,506	26,029
2019	France	USA	24	52	1,131,312	21,756

Source: FIFA.com.

Global viewership for the women's World Cup over the years has grown significantly as well. In 2015, FIFA reported that an estimated 764 million viewers watched some part of the competition in Canada. In total, there were globally 7,781 hours of the matches broadcast, which was a 31 percent increase over 2011. Not only were more people watching the women's competition in 2015 than earlier, but they also had the possibility of taking in a wider variety of matches and pairings. Given the technological changes since 1991, it is not surprising to learn that an estimated eighty-six million people viewed the games of the 2015 World Cup online or on some type of mobile device. A tendency toward wider platforms for viewing sporting events will be part of women's football in the future. Overall, the 2015 competition broke broadcasting and marketing records in France, Japan, and the United States. The final match between Japan and the United States was the most watched match in US history, beating out all of the US men's World Cup and qualifying matches.[20]

The women's World Cup, much like the men's tournament, has also had its share of spectacular performances—spectacular both in the sense of superior athletic achievement, the type of performance that impresses both the avid football fan and the casual observer, and in the sense of a performance that can be part of an overall historical narrative about sport, athletics, women, nation, and identity. Several individual women and teams point out the dual meaning of this idea of spectacular performance in football. For example, Marta, the single-named virtuosa from Brazil, has often been named the best female player in the world. She embodies many of the same footballing qualities that have made her male countrymen so popular in world and professional football for many decades. She is talented on the ball, inventive, willing to run at opposing players, has a flare for the game, and can be quite dramatic on the field. Marta has, however, never been able to bring a World Cup or Olympic title to her home nation of Brazil. She and her teammates lost in a semifinal penalty shootout against Sweden in the 2016 Rio games. They followed up that defeat with a loss in the third-place game against Canada and finished without a medal at their "home" games. Nevertheless, Marta is widely recognized as a supremely talented football player and creative genius, even as she has sometimes drawn controversy to herself through on-field histrionics.[21]

The German women's national team has most often been seen as a successful collective that performs consistently well in global competitions. Much like the German men's team, the country's women seem to always be among the favorites in global competitions and win their fair share of Olympic (2016) and world titles (2003 and 2007), but without the single star player who has the name recognition of a Marta. To be sure, excellent German women players, such as Prinz, Anja Mittag, and Dzsenifer Maroszán, have given many dramatic footballing performances. Most fans of the game, however, would be hard-pressed to name these players, remember their top performances, or refer to them as spectacular players. The German team's style and achievements seem to fit a global narrative about its country's identity that borders on stereotype: efficient, hard-working, but not dramatic. As with all national stereotypes, there is much that is unfair and unfounded in this assessment, but it shows how international football, and especially World Cup competitions, can help create and reinforce notions of national identity, even if those notions sometimes seem superficial and imposed from popular culture. On the other hand, as will be explored below, international football can also be a mechanism for probing, expanding, and even exploding stereotypes.[22]

Japan's play in the women's World Cup and the Olympics has also been seen through well-established global narratives. The Japanese women's team is often thought of as extremely well organized and capable of sophisticated passing and play. At their best, as in the women's tournament of 2011, the Japanese players embody a technical virtuosity that makes them one of the best performing teams in the world. Japanese women football players try to create intricate passing patterns on the field and then suddenly burst forward or put a shot on goal from a well-designed move. Moreover, the Japanese women are often lauded for their ability on the ball and the fairness of their play. Some of the best football technicians of the last twenty years—Sawa, Yuki Nagasato, and Aya Miyama, to name but a few—have come from Japan, and the country has produced many spectacular individual players. Nevertheless, fans and commentators often comment on the discipline in the Japanese women's football team and thereby play on national stereotypes about efficiency and collective will.

Japan's performances in two recent women's tournaments represent the highs and lows of global football and show once again how international events can be drawn into a global sporting event. In 2011, the Japanese women won the competition in dramatic fashion, defeating the US team in a final match decided by a penalty shootout. The Japanese women were technically sound, well organized, and showed a willingness to fight on the pitch. The game was given an added degree of drama because it took place not long after the catastrophe at Fukushima, where an earthquake and resulting tsunami had led to a major nuclear accident. At the end of the 2011 competition, the Japanese women, in a poignant gesture, held up a sign thanking the world for international support following the multiple disasters at home. That sporting event's outcome seemed to dovetail nicely with international sentiment. According to much popular opinion, the Japanese deserved to win.[23] As Abby Wambach, the ultracompetitive star US forward, put it: "I reason that their country needs the win more than ours does."[24] Four years later, however, in the 2015 final, the Japanese women were overwhelmed by a superior US team, 5–2. The match was essentially decided in the first half, when the American team scored four goals.

The American women's national team and its performances often seem to fit several national and global narratives. Along with the Germans, the Americans have consistently put out strong international sides in women's football. Over the past thirty years, the US side has achieved impressive victories and performances and had long winning streaks in friendlies and international competitions alike. The US team is almost certainly aided by the large number of female players in the country, the well-organized school system that supports a wide range of women's sports, and its domestic professional leagues. The American women's team is often seen as physically strong, hypercompetitive, and sometimes even arrogant. An example of the last would be Hope Solo's comments after the United States loss to the Swedes in the 2016 Rio Olympics.

However, the US women's team has undoubtedly generated some of the most dramatic and memorable performances in recent global football. Fans of the American team can almost recite a litany of top moments in the global game. There is Chastain's cup-winning penalty on home soil during the 1999 women's World Cup. The emotion of the victory seemed to be caught in her gesture of ripping off her jersey and celebrating in full view of a global audience. In the 2011 tournament in Germany, Abby Wambach scored a header off a cross from Megan Rapinoe in the 122nd minute of a competition against Marta's Brazil. The goal seemed to reemphasize the competitive nature of the American women's team. The team would, however, go on to lose the final match to Japan. In 2015, Lloyd scored three goals in the first half of the final game against Japan. She punctuated that performance with an audacious third goal from midfield that beat the outstretched arms of a tumbling Ayumi Kaihori, Japan's goalkeeper. Her performance was electric and filled with sheer athletic drama. It was the kind of moment that becomes part of the overall memory of world football. Players, fans, the media, and scholars can and will refer to it much as they do the performances of famous male players, such as Pelé in the 1950s and '60s, Johan Cruyff in the 1970s, or Diego Maradona in the 1980s. Such performances become part of the history of the game. They provide common points of reference that can be analyzed by fans, commentators, and students of football.[25]

The history of the French women's national team in recent decades reveals another type of international narrative. In the 1990s, the French had precious little success in global football—they missed the first three official women's World Cups altogether—and the country did not seem interested in fielding a highly competitive women's team. Whether it was the World Cup, the Olympics, or European Championships, the French women were hardly competitive and never a threat to the stronger footballing nations of the United States, Germany, and Scandinavia. Beginning around 2000, however, the French team greatly gained in stature; it is now usually considered among the favorites in any international tournament and is often said to play some of the best and most free-flowing football in the women's game. Several factors have helped foster the French women's team's rise in recent years. First, infrastructure has been put in place so that women have the facilities and support to train at the highest professional levels. Top French teams, such as Lyon and Paris Saint-Germain, have also created women's club teams to help support the players financially between international competitions. In fact, in Canada 2015 seventeen of the twenty-three players on the French roster were then engaged by the two French super clubs. The numbers were similar a year later at the Rio Olympics; fourteen of the eighteen players came from the two clubs. In addition, the French women's team might have gained from the performance of the ethnically diverse French men's team in 1998.[26] Success can breed success and help to break down gender and racial barriers. Other far-reaching social changes, such as the support of greater cultural and sporting activities for women in France, have also played a role in fashioning a more competitive and successful national football team.

The French women's team also looks much like its male counterpart. It draws players from different ethnic and social groups in France. Some of its players are descendants of parents who came from countries or territories that once had been formal parts of the French empire or are still associated with the Francophone world. A prime example is Louisa Nécib, who has sometimes been dubbed "Ziza" by the French and world football press. The name is essentially the female equivalent of Zizou, which is the nickname of French male legend Zinedine Zidane. Like Zidane, Nécib is of Algerian background and was born and raised in Marseille, in the south of France. Like Zidane, she was, until her retirement in 2016, widely considered one of the most skillful French players and one of the driving forces of the national team. Nécib was not quite able to match Zidane's success on the field.[27] Despite dramatic improvement in recent years, the French women's team has not yet captured a world, Olympic, or European title. Nevertheless, it remains one of the most popular teams to watch because of its style, flare, and gifted players.

Of course, the emergence and development of the FIFA Women's World Cup and skillful and impressive national teams over the past thirty years has not meant that resistance to women participating in global sports has disappeared. Even as the tournament has grown and embedded itself in the sporting landscape, it has sometimes proven difficult to find financial sponsors

Chapter 4

for women's professional football leagues. In the United States, for example, several professional leagues have come and gone in the last few decades. In Europe, the situation is somewhat better, especially if women's professional teams are sponsored by the same big clubs that run male teams. For example, Arsenal, Chelsea, Liverpool, and Manchester United in England, Barcelona in Spain, and Lyon in France currently operate women's teams. Professional clubs and leagues are extremely important, of course, to sustaining women's football in the years between the quadrennial World Cup tournaments.[28] Critics of women's professional leagues, especially in the United States, have often argued that they do not generate enough revenue to sustain themselves. The history of Major League Soccer (MLS), the men's professional league in North America, however, seems to show that the right type of business plan, a mixture of homegrown and imported players, and firm economic commitment from owners, sponsors, and fans can build and sustain professional football leagues. The same type of careful financial formula could and should work for the women's game as well.

Several nations, in addition to fielding strong international teams, have helped grow the women's game by sponsoring important domestic leagues. Japan, Germany, Sweden, and Norway have emerged, for example, as countries heavily invested in developing women's football. Recently, Mexico introduced a professional league with significant financial backing and fan support. These domestic leagues help address one of the vexing problems for women football players globally: how to find the monetary and material support to help them develop and stay in the game between global competitions. Since the early 1990s, several domestic leagues in the United States have provided playing opportunities not only for US players but for players from around the world, including star players such as Marta from Brazil and Nadine Angerer from Germany. Similarly, domestic leagues in Sweden, Germany, and France have given opportunities to American women players to ply their trade. For example, Ali Krieger of the United States played professional football for many years in Germany with FFC Frankfurt. In the past few decades, several American players, including Kristine Lilly, Michelle Akers, Hope Solo, and Christen Press, have found a professional home in Sweden with clubs such as Göteborg and Tyresö. An interesting global exchange of top women players developed over the course of the 1990s, 2000s, and 2010s. Financial concerns and gains, just like in the men's game, have driven this exchange, but often the most crucial factor for women players has been economic survival.

As with all women's sports in the modern era, world football has also had to deal with the issues of sexual identity and politics. For example, top athletic achievements and spectacular performances have not spared the women's game from sexist rhetoric. Josef (Sepp) Blatter, who was, as noted previously, the head of FIFA for many years, remarked in 2004 that women players should "play in more feminine clothes like they do in volleyball," and suggested that they could "wear tighter shorts."[29] Although he was roundly criticized at the time by several women footballers and managers, his comments, coming from the head of world football's governing body, drew global attention to how far attitudes toward women and sport still had to go in some circles. Although said in jest, David Letterman's comments about the 1999 US women's football team—he called them "Babe City" and invited them onto his late-night show—still revealed an openly sexualized attitude toward women players. By 2015, the rhetoric had changed. President Obama called the winning women's team "badasses" at a White House reception and used the occasion to champion gender equality in sports and same-sex marriage by calling attention to Abby Wambach's post-victory celebration in Canada with her female partner, Sarah Huffman, a former professional and US national team player. Wambach, along with Megan Rapinoe, was one of the most prominent and outspoken lesbian football players at the 2015 cup.

On the other hand, several women's football players have also used ingrained sexual attitudes to their advantage to become marketing celebrities. For example, Alex Morgan is one of the most recognizable faces on recent US women's national teams. She has also enjoyed endorsement deals with Nike, Coca-Cola, AT&T, and Panasonic, among other corporate sponsors. Most of the ads she does have featured not only her football skills but her physical attractiveness as well. Morgan is not the only woman football player who has been able to translate her talent and celebrity into commercial endorsements; players such as Nécib from France, Schelin of Sweden, and Marta of Brazil have also earned money off the field through sponsorships. Most of these ads highlight the players' football skills as well as their physical attributes. Of course, male footballers, such as Cristiano Ronaldo of Portugal and David Beckham of England, have also used their physical attractiveness to land advertising opportunities. Complicated cultural notions about gender, sexuality, and physical attractiveness are frequently on display in the presentation and selling of modern athletes, be they women or men.

RACE AND ETHNIC IDENTITY

Germany won the 2014 men's World Cup in Brazil, defeating Argentina in the final and Brazil in the semifinal match. The latter, a 7–1 loss, was a crushing blow to the host team. The players on the German team that won in 2014 came from diverse ethnic and racial backgrounds. In attack, the

Germany, World Cup Winners, 2014 (*Action Plus Sports Images/Alamy Stock Photo*)

squad featured an aging but still effective Miroslav Klose, whose family is originally from Poland. Midfielder Mesut Özil is of Turkish background; his grandparents came to Germany as part of the "guest workers" movement in the 1960s and '70s. Another midfielder, Sami Khedira, is of Tunisian heritage. In the central defense for Germany stood Jérôme Boateng, whose half-brother, Kevin-Prince Boateng, played for Ghana. Klose, Özil, Khedira, and Boateng teamed up with players like Bastian Schweinsteiger, Manuel Neuer, and Thomas Müller to create a formidable unit, which in German was known simply as *die Mannschaft*, or national squad. Many other teams at the 2014 cup—France, Belgium, the United States—featured a kaleidoscope of ethnicities and races, which would seem to make global football a yardstick for contemporary social and cultural integration. Many of the teams at the 2018 competition in Russia were also racially and ethnically diverse.[30]

The multicultural integration found on many contemporary football teams, however, obviously does not show that the modern world has moved into some kind of "post-racial" utopia. On the contrary, their composition throws up as many questions about ethnic and racial identity as it answers. For example, even though Boateng had helped his national side to a title in 2014, a right-wing politician in Germany mentioned him by name as an "undesirable neighbor." The politician later apologized for his remarks.[31] Many of the players who represent racial and ethnic diversity on national teams are of course native-born citizens of the countries they represent.

Özil, for example, was born in Gelsenkirchen in the former West Germany in 1988, just one year before the fall of the Berlin Wall. He came up in the youth system of his local club, Schalke 04, before joining Werder Bremen, Real Madrid, and eventually Arsenal of London. Following a poor showing in Russia in 2018 and controversy connected to his being photographed with the Turkish president, Recip Tayyip Erdoğan, he retired from international football in 2018.[32] Born in Germany, Özil's Turkish heritage has nevertheless complicated his playing career.

Boateng was born in Berlin to a German mother and Ghanaian father and currently plays for Bayern Munich. Christian Benteke of Belgium was born in 1990 in Kinshasa, which was then Zaire and is in the modern-day Democratic Republic of the Congo. He moved to Liege, Belgium, in 1993 with his parents to escape the corrupt regime of Mobutu Sese Seko and grew up and played youth football there. His family's sojourn is a direct reflection of the long colonial involvement of Belgium in the Congo region. As Laurent Dubois has so expertly shown for the case of France and especially for its championship team of 1998, the history of football can tell us much indeed about imperialism, post-imperialism, and global patterns of movement.[33] A further examination of national football teams from the most recent World Cups would reveal many stories like those of Özil, Khedira, Boateng, and Benteke.

Racial and ethnic diversity, let alone cultural tolerance and acceptance, and world football have had a very difficult relationship in the twentieth and twenty-first centuries. A survey of the powerful German teams of the 1960s and '70s, for example, would not turn up players of Turkish, Tunisian, or Ghanaian background. The migration of peoples from these countries to Germany only began in earnest in these decades and beyond. One would not suspect that the sons and grandsons of "guest workers" and other migrants to Germany would be old enough to have made their mark until recent decades. Of course, Germany's restrictive citizenship laws, which had been in effect since 1913 and did not change for good until 2000, made it difficult for minorities to integrate themselves into society. These laws and the cultural assumptions behind them made it hard for people of non-German ethnic backgrounds to enjoy the full legal benefits of being "German" until quite recently.[34]

The situation was only marginally better in a country like Brazil, whose national side featured players of different ethnic and racial backgrounds in the 1950s. Even the casual fan of world football knows the name Pelé; many football experts regard him as perhaps the best player in the history of the game. Of African heritage, he became famous as a young member of the 1958 Brazilian team and stayed with the national side all the way until its famous 4–1 victory in 1970 against Italy. Brazil was able to win three—1958 in Sweden, 1962 in Chile, and 1970 in Mexico—of the four cups contested in those years. While Pelé has become the icon of those teams, he clearly had an

Brazil, World Cup Winners, 1958

Brazil, World Cup Team, 1970 (*PA Images/Alamy Stock Photo*)

exceedingly strong supporting group. For the 1962 final he was injured and unable to help the team repeat as world champions. Several players on that team represented a wide spectrum of racial and ethnic backgrounds. The same was largely true of the 1958, 1966, and 1970 Brazilian squads. Some of the legends of Brazilian football graced those various teams: Vavá, Didi, Mário Zagallo, Garrincha, Rivellino, Nilton Santos, Gérson, Tostão, Jairzinho, and Carlos Alberto. Together, they represented a broad swath of the ethnic and racial spectrum of 1950s and '60s Brazil.

Together, they also created a pool of well-trained, hardworking, and focused football players. A journalist reported that Gérson was certain of Brazil's victory in the 1970 competition: "Brazil will only lose the Cup if they break the leg of Pelé, the arm of Tostão, the knees of Gérson, the head of Rivellino or if they kill our team."[35] In addition to talent, that team was filled with confidence.

In the earliest years of the World Cup, the 1930s, the football association of Brazil was, however, not as welcoming to players of African background. In fact, it was the winning side of Uruguay that featured the original black superstar of the World Cup, José Andrade. His nickname was "the Black Marvel" or "the Black Pearl," a name that was later bestowed on Pelé from Brazil.

Andrade's best days as a player were probably in the 1920s when he helped Uruguay to back-to-back Olympic titles in Paris in 1924 and Amsterdam in 1928, but he was still effective enough to be named to the 1930 all-star team at the World Cup. He was a fast and skillful player. While

Uruguay, World Cup Team, 1930

Brazil, World Cup Team, 1930 (*Getty Images*)

Andrade was playing for Uruguay, other South American teams, such as Brazil, were still debating whether to include players of African heritage in their national rosters. The irony is that Andrade's father, insofar as can be established, probably had been a slave in Brazil in the late nineteenth century and had fled to Uruguay,[36] which had a tradition of engaging black players in its national squad. In the 1916 South American championship, for example, Uruguay beat Chile 4–0, with two "Africans"—Isabelino Gradín and Juan Delgado—in the lineup. Chile protested the result because of their inclusion. As Eduardo Galeano has commented: "Back then [1916], Uruguay was the only country in the world with black players on its national team."[37]

There were already a number of excellent Brazilian football players of African heritage throughout the country in the first decades of the twentieth century. Some of the Rio and São Paulo teams, especially those with closer connections to working-class, lower-class, or mercantile sections of Brazilian society, included and featured players of African or mixed racial background. The prolific Arthur Friedenreich, for example, was born to a German father and an Afro-Brazilian mother. He is said to have scored over 1,300 goals in competitive matches before he stopped playing in 1935 at the age of forty-three. Fausto dos Santos, another Brazilian player of African descent, was a dynamic midfielder in the 1930s who played to good effect in 1930. Domingos da Guia was a strong fullback from this era. Leônidas da Silva, an immensely talented player, was nicknamed "the Black Diamond." Leônidas would play in the 1938 Brazilian squad that went to the tournament in France. That team was more inclusive than the 1930 and 1934 teams had been; it featured players of African, European, and mixed ancestry. Still, throughout the 1920s and '30s, race and racism weighed heavily on the Brazilian game and national team. To play in the Seleção—the name given to the national squad—was rare for black players. At both the club and national level, players like Leônidas suffered an enormous amount of racial abuse. Friedenreich and Domingos did as much as they could to cover their "blackness" and tried to pass as white or of mixed ancestry in Brazilian football. The former's light skin and straightened hair made this easier, and he was accepted by white elites and black fans alike. Domingos, too, tried to pass himself off as a mulatto by covering his hair with a cap or straightening his hair. For Leônidas, whose skin color was much darker, passing as anything but a "black" player was virtually impossible. The 1938 Brazilian team represented an important moment in greater acceptance of ethnic and racial diversity in its national team's composition, but a further breakthrough in matters of race and football did not come until the 1950s and '60s and the many triumphs of the Pelé-led teams.[38]

Uruguay might have featured a black superstar, Andrade, in the 1924 and 1928 Olympic teams and in its 1930 World Cup–winning squad, but that did not necessarily mean that Uruguayan society was any freer from racism than Brazil at the time. Uruguay is a small country that had to draw on all social levels in order to field winning football teams. Moreover, the number of people in Uruguay of African background could not compare with the number of Afro-Brazilians, who were descendants of the slave culture that had been such a large part of South America's largest country for centuries. Including, accepting, embracing, and celebrating black star players in Brazil was socially and culturally problematic. Moreover, Brazilian elites, drawn largely from European backgrounds, could still try to convince themselves that the country was large enough and strong enough to be successful in world football without reaching into the working and laboring classes to promote and feature too many black and mixed-ancestry players. The lack of success at the international level would prove this assumption wrong and make more room for Brazilian players from a wider ethnic and racial spectrum beginning in the late 1930s and in earnest in the 1950s.[39]

Brazilian football's history with race and ethnicity exemplifies how challenging social and cultural issues have been dealt with, or not, in modern sport. Of course, many other nations have had to deal on one level or another with similar challenges of racial and ethnic diversity in a globalizing world. Another nation whose encounter with race and ethnicity in its footballing culture has been especially profound is France. In the post–Second World War era, France, like many of the former European empires, had to face up to decolonization and changing relationships with its former subject states.

This process could and did turn violent in some situations, as in the French attempts to hold on to Indochina (Vietnam, Cambodia, and Laos) and Algeria. Both of these conflicts turned into protracted and bloody wars. In addition, France, even as a victor nation from the Second World War, had to come to grips with its diminished political and economic global position after 1945. Moreover, French society itself was changing as migrants from the former colonial possessions in Africa and Asia came to the metropole in increasing numbers in the second half of the twentieth century. Football, it seemed, could provide a possible vehicle to deal with some of these national, social, and ethnic tensions.[40]

France's experience with social and cultural integration through football has been, however, decidedly mixed in the last several decades. At the 1958 competition, for example, France fielded a highly entertaining team that also highlighted the ethnic diversity of the country. The side's leading scorer was Just Fontaine, who had been born in Morocco to a Spanish mother. Another of its star players was Raymond Kopa, who was of Polish background. His family had come to France as part of a labor migration to supply mineworkers. He also did his best, often under trying circumstances, to integrate himself into his adopted homeland. As Pierre Lanfranchi and Alfred Wahl put it, he often claimed to "[defend] the French colours to the limits of his power."[41] There was also Roger Piantoni, who was of Italian heritage. In Sweden, France lost to the eventual champion Brazil and its young star Pelé in a semifinal match. This tournament was to launch the fortunes of the Brazilian national team in the 1960s and '70s and be credited with helping to heal ethnic and racial divides in that country. On the other hand, France's national team was about to slide into one of its international low points. It would fail to make four of the next World Cups and most of the European Championships. The French domestic game would suffer as well, with several teams failing or merging with one another to survive. Attendance at matches in France declined severely, and football did not seem to be part of the national culture or the debate on race and ethnicity throughout most of the 1960s and '70s.

The fortunes of the French national football team improved dramatically in the 1980s and '90s, however. The squad reached the semifinals of the 1982 and 1986 World Cup tournaments in Spain and Mexico, respectively. It won the 1984 European Championship played at home. Led by its outstanding midfield of Michel Platini, Jean Tigana, Alain Giresse, and Luis Fernández, dubbed the "magic square" for their excellent combination play, France returned to international prominence in global football, a position it had not enjoyed since the late 1950s.

Of course, fans and the media could not overlook the obvious role race and ethnicity played in the success of the French national squad. Tigana was born

France, World Cup Team, 1986 (*Joel Robine/Getty Images*)

in Bamako in what was then called the French Sudan but today is known as Mali. Fernández had been born in Spain and naturalized as a French citizen as late as 1981. Even the great Platini, who had been born and raised in France, was of Italian ancestry on both sides of his family. He would go on to cut an international career as a player, manager, and later as a FIFA executive. It was in this last role that he would get caught up in the scandals and accusations that came to a head in 2015.[42]

The question of ethnic and racial integration and the French national team continued to be a theme into the 1990s. Building on the renaissance in footballing culture ushered in by the 1980s generation, a new group of French stars emerged who eventually would win the World Cup in 1998. That team beat Brazil in the final, 3–1, in the Stade de France before eighty thousand fans. The team would follow up that victory by winning the European Championship two years later in the Netherlands by defeating Italy. Another golden age of French football seemed to have been established, and it was accomplished with a team that represented the full breadth of the racial, ethnic, and post-imperial spectrum of French society. For example, among the twenty-three players named to the 1998 national squad were athletes who came, or whose families came, from Armenia, Algeria, Guadeloupe, New Caledonia, Argentina, Ghana, Senegal, Italy, French Guiana, Martinique, and metropolitan France. Seemingly, the team was a testament to a successful social integration of French society. The fact that it did so

France, World Cup Team, 1998 (*Allstar Picture Library/Alamy Stock Photo*)

well on the football pitch could show the benefits of living in and even embracing a multi-racial, multi-ethnic society.[43]

Sports such as football can be a part of ongoing social change, such as overcoming social stereotypes and modeling racial and ethnic inclusion. It is naïve, however, to believe that what one witnesses on the football pitch—a multi-racial team—ever comes easy or represents a permanent state of social change. Developments in sports may also mirror deep social cleavages within a given country, or even globally. The French national team's recent history shows how problematic race and ethnicity remain in contemporary society. Even in the 1990s, when the team was winning the world title, there were voices within France that claimed it did not represent the true nature of the country. It was clear for some that the team was too international, too cosmopolitan, too "black." These voices only grew stronger in the 2000s, when the team's performances on the playing field began to change. For example, France crashed out of the 2010 tournament in South Africa in spectacular fashion, leading to much unrest in the team and between it and French football officials. Recently, France's footballing fortunes improved again when, fielding largely the same type of multi-racial, multi-ethnic squad that has been a hallmark for French teams since the 1980s, it finished second at the European Championship in 2016 and won the 2018 World Cup in Russia.

French society continues to be roiled by ethnic and racial tensions. Far-right populist politicians continue to keep up the drumbeat against immigrants and

France, World Cup Champions, 2018 (*Kremlin.ru*)

foreign-born citizens. France has also had to endure a series of terrorist attacks inspired by or carried out by the Islamic State (ISIS). One terrorist bomb even went off outside of the Stade de France while a friendly match between France and Germany was being played inside.[44] All of these developments tear at the very fabric of French society and show that whatever racial and ethnic progress has been brought about by footballing culture and success on the pitch in the last several decades, much work remains to be done.

In the near century since the creation of the World Cup of football, however, nothing has added to its ethnic and racial diversity as much as its gradual opening up to include more teams from Africa and Asia in the competition. The early tournaments, those taking place before the Second World War, were affairs that featured teams solely from the Americas and Europe. They were staged alternately in Uruguay (1930), Italy (1934), and France (1938). Nor was there any process to allow teams from Asia and Africa to qualify for the World Cup in the 1950s. Gradually, in the 1960s and '70s, squads from North Korea, Israel, Morocco, Australia, Zaire (Democratic Republic of the Congo), Tunisia, and Iran took part in football's premier international competition. In the 1980s and early '90s, however, only four teams from Asia and Africa were allowed to qualify for the World Cup finals. Nevertheless, Morocco in 1986 was able to top its group ahead of England, Poland, and Portugal. It was the first African team to do so. A turning point came in 1998. At the same competition that saw a multi-ethnic and multi-racial French team triumph, the tournament took a major step toward more global representation. In France, five teams from Africa (Cameroon, Morocco, Nigeria, South Africa, and Tunisia) alongside four teams from Asia (Iran, Japan, Saudi Arabia, and South Korea) played.

Many teams from sub-Saharan Africa—Nigeria, Ghana, and the Ivory Coast, for example—have begun to assert themselves in recent competitions and become fixtures in international matches. They have played attractive football at World Cups. In 1994, Nigeria, for example, won its group impressively. Ghana reached the final tournament in 2000 (Round of 16), 2010 (Quarterfinals), and 2014 (Group Stage). The Ivory Coast, which made the World Cup finals in 2006, 2010, and 2014, has produced several star players, such as Didier Drogba, Yaya Touré, and Emmanuel Eboué. The movement toward greater inclusion of African teams culminated in the awarding of the 2010 World Cup to South Africa. Spain won the competition, but it marked the first time football's foremost international event had been held outside of the Americas or Europe.[45] Ethnic and racial considerations were also clearly part of the decisions to send the tournament to Russia in 2018 and to Qatar in 2022. The competition in Russia marked the first time football's preeminent event was held in a Slavic country in Eastern Europe. FIFA's decision to hold the tournament in Qatar is, of course, controversial. As was discussed above, Qatar has no professional league of its own; its entire football infrastructure has to be built, and slave labor or its equivalent is being used in the construction. For Sepp Blatter, president of FIFA at the time of Qatar's selection, and his inner circle, however, the stated goal in 2022 was to bring the World Cup to a Middle Eastern nation in order to solidify football's claim to being a truly global game. After holding the cup in South Korea and Japan in 2002 and South Africa in 2010, Russia and Qatar represented new geographic and ethnic frontiers for FIFA. It remains to be seen how the competition will be conducted in Qatar, a country under political pressure in the region and globally. Discussions about race and ethnicity will continue, however, to be a dominant theme at the 2022 World Cup.

CONCLUSION

Considerations about race, ethnicity, and gender have clearly played important parts in the evolution of modern football. The game has changed remarkably since the first men's FIFA World Cup in 1930, which featured only a handful of teams from South America, the United States, and Europe. At that time, there was no thought given to a similar competition for women—their game had been pushed to the margins of sporting life—and most nations only uncomfortably dealt with the issue of including players of non-European background in their teams. When they did so, it was often only with reluctance, and the players still experienced a great deal of prejudice and isolation.

Racial, ethnic, and gender inclusion in world football improved only marginally in the period between the late 1930s and the immediate aftermath of the Second World War. In the 1960s and '70s, movements and agitation for greater racial, ethnic, and gender equality in many countries across the globe took root and gradually changed the cultural landscape of several societies, which opened up slightly, or even moderately, to allow more women, more people from a wider array of racial and ethnic backgrounds, and more countries from Africa and Asia to play the world's game at global tournaments. The obvious impact of these social changes was not fully felt until the 1990s when a women's FIFA-sponsored World Cup became a global footballing fixture, and ethnic and racial diversity became more common on many national teams. There were earlier and important signs, however, of these social and cultural shifts in the 1960s—one thinks of the racial and ethnic composition of the great Brazilian teams of that era—and in the 1970s with the establishment of legislation such as Title IX in the United States, the rise of global feminism, and the staging of successful women's tournaments without FIFA's support. These developments, and much more, helped create more space in football for a wider spectrum of people, including women, to play the world's game at the highest level. Football's twentieth-century history, therefore, helps us to see and understand much about how race, ethnicity, and gender considerations have shaped our recent past.

Nevertheless, it would be a serious mistake to conclude that the history of football and the World Cup has been one that clearly maps out racial, ethnic, and gender progress and that some sort of racial and gender "equality" has been achieved. The developments discussed in this chapter—the creation of a FIFA World Cup competition for women or the emergence of players from former colonial empires in various national teams—continue to cause controversy in some circles. The critics of the women's game are still numerous, and racial and ethnic tolerance in football is still often a fragile and elusive thing as many fans of club teams could attest. Some national sides are resistant to fielding teams that are ethnically or racially diverse. The ubiquitous signs one sees in stadiums of "No to Racism" just prove that it is all too alive and well in many countries and locations around the world. Thus, football, and its history with race, ethnicity, and gender developments, remains as problematic as social change in the modern era itself. Reasons for optimism about integrated and tolerant societies, reflecting supposed racial, ethnic, and gender "progress" should be tempered by the harsh realities of slurs and projectiles sometimes flung in too many stadiums. The vitriol and hatred are also often expressed in contemporary social media and on the Internet, where commentators and fans alike can post, in seeming anonymity, any number of hateful racial, ethnic, or gender-based statements. As anyone who has gone online to try to find serious discussion of football knows, rational discussion often degrades rapidly into name-calling and bullying that features a wide variety of epithets.

As with the politics and economics of the game, footballing culture is a lens to understand racial, ethnic, and gender changes and how they have been promoted and contested in the modern world. Clearly, much has changed in the game since the introduction of the first men's World Cup in 1930. More players and teams from around the globe are now included in the competition. Many national teams are formed by drawing athletes from all racial and ethnic sectors of a given society. Nevertheless, resistance to and contempt for these moves can also be found in world football. Thus, one is left with a very mixed view of how racial and ethnic change has fit uneasily into the evolution of the World Cup in the modern era. At a bare minimum, one must concede that issues of racial and ethnic identity, however they are constructed and fought over, have been central to the history of football throughout the twentieth and twenty-first centuries. Central debates about a nation's core values and identity, therefore, have been displaced and displayed on the pitch. This will undoubtedly remain the state of affairs for the foreseeable future.

Similarly, great changes in women's football have taken place in recent decades. The introduction of a FIFA Women's World Cup in 1991 and the creation and expansion of women's professional leagues in many countries have provided new opportunities for high-level competition, fame, and occasionally, even fortune, for today's top women players. But the fate of the women's game in many parts of the world, especially in Africa, Asia, and parts of South America, is still uncertain. In many places, financial and institutional support for women's football is unstable. The situation is better in North America and Europe, where national sides and leagues enjoy stronger economic backing. Even in these places, however, women football players have often had to struggle for recognition and money. In the United States, for example, several professional leagues have come and gone since the 1990s. In countries such as Spain and Italy, where the game of football is clearly the national sport, women players have fought hard for institutional backing, monetary support, and public recognition and have only very recently made gains in each of these areas. The situation is better in most of Scandinavia, Germany, France, and England. In these countries, professional leagues have helped sustain women players between international contests such as the World Cup, the Olympics, or the European Championships.

Gender considerations thus leave the student of modern football and world history with a host of questions. How far has the game of women's football come since the 1990s? Is the progress made in some countries a road map for what can be achieved globally or at least in certain regions of the world? Do shifts in a sport—football—indicate or dovetail with changes going on in society? Will women's football suffer from a pushback against notions of gender equality in the years ahead? These are difficult, open-ended, and ongoing questions. An understanding of how gender norms and attitudes have penetrated modern societies in the past is the starting point for any serious discussion of these issues today and in the future. Football's World Cup competitions, both for men and women, have been and will remain an important and complicated vehicle for studying racial, ethnic, and gender identity in the modern era.

DOCUMENTS AND ARTIFACTS RELATED TO GENDER, RACE, ETHNICITY, AND THE WORLD CUP

A. FIFA, Asia's First World Cup Team, 1938 (Dutch East Indies), 1938 FIFA World Cup France. https://www.fifa.com/worldcup/videos/fascinating-story-of-asia-s-first-world-cup-team-2438675

1. Research the colonial role played by the Netherlands in the twentieth century. Why was a small European nation in control of what would become present-day Indonesia?
2. How well has Indonesia, as an independent nation, done in World Cup qualifying? What is the state of football in the country?

B. Dick, Kerr's Ladies postcard, 1920s, National Football Museum, Manchester, UK. https://www.nationalfootballmuseum.com/collections_detail/dick-kerrs-ladies-postcard-1920s

1. How do the players on the Dick, Kerr's Ladies team present themselves on this postcard? What visual image do you think they are trying to create or project?
2. Who, do you imagine, would send and receive postcards with images of women footballers in the interwar period?

C. "Flashback: Group B: 1995 FIFA Women's World Cup," National Football Museum, Manchester, UK. https://www.nationalfootballmuseum.com/exhibitions/flashback-group-b-1995-womens-world-cup

1. From this source, what was the state of women's football at the time of the 1995 World Cup?
2. Research which women's teams participated in the 1995 finals.

D. FIFA, Ando Kozue, Japanese Women's National Team, Jersey. https://
fr.fifa.com/photos/galleries/kozue-ando-jpn-1552274#the-jersey-kozue
-ando-japan-seen-1476410

    1. Research the career of Ando Kozue and the Japanese national team for
which she played.

    2. What image of Kozue is projected in the photos from this gallery? Is
FIFA creating or controlling this image?

E. Andrew Das, "U.S. Women's Soccer Team Sues U.S. Soccer for Gender
Discrimination." *New York Times*, May 8, 2019, sec. Sports. https://www
.nytimes.com/2019/03/08/sports/womens-soccer-team-lawsuit-gender
-discrimination.html.

    1. What arguments do the US Women's team members cite as grounds for
their legal action? Are you persuaded by these arguments?

    2. From this article, can you imagine what arguments the USSF (United
States Soccer Federation) will use to counter the claims of gender
discrimination?

SUGGESTIONS FOR FURTHER READING AND RESEARCH

Alegi, Peter. *African Soccerscapes: How a Continent Changed the World's Game.*
Athens: Ohio University Press, 2010.

Alegi, Peter, and Chris Bolsmann. *Africa's World Cup: Critical Reflections on Play,
Patriotism, Spectatorship, and Space.* Ann Arbor: University of Michigan Press,
2013.

Cahn, Susan K. *Coming on Strong: Gender and Sexuality in Twentieth-Century
Women's Sport.* Cambridge, MA: Harvard University Press, 1994.

Corner Kick: The Official Newsletter of the 1999 FIFA Women's World Cup. Los
Angeles: FIFA Women's World Cup Organizing Committee, 1999.

Cronin, Mike, and David Mayall. *Sporting Nationalisms: Identity, Ethnicity, Immigration, and Assimilation.* London: Frank Cass, 1998.

Dauncey, Hugh, and Geoff Hare. *France and the 1998 World Cup: The National
Impact of a World Sporting Event.* London: Frank Cass, 1999.

Dubois, Laurent. *Soccer Empire: The World Cup and the Future of France.* Berkeley:
University of California Press, 2010.

Elsey, Brenda, and Joshua H. Nadel. *Futbolera: A History of Women and Sports in
Latin America.* Austin: University of Texas Press, 2019.

Galeano, Eduardo. *Soccer in Sun and Shadow.* Translated by Mark Fried. London:
Verso, 1998.

Grainey, Timothy F. *Beyond Bend It Like Beckham. The Global Phenomenon of
Women's Soccer.* Lincoln: University of Nebraska Press, 2012.

Gumbrecht, Hans Ulrich. *In Praise of Athletic Beauty*. Cambridge, MA: Belknap Press of Harvard University Press, 2006.

Hill, Dave. *Out of His Skin: The John Barnes Phenomenon*. London: Faber and Faber, 1989.

Jacobs, Barbara. *The Dick, Kerr's Ladies*. London: Robinson, 2004.

Jenkins, Garry. *The Beautiful Team: In Search of Pelé and the 1970 Brazilians*. London: Simon and Schuster, 1999.

Longman, Jere. *The Girls of Summer: The U.S. Women's Soccer Team and How It Changed the World*. New York: Perennial, 2001.

Mangan, J. A. *Europe, Sport, World: Shaping Global Societies*. London: Frank Cass, 2001.

———. *Making European Masculinities: Sport, Europe, Gender*. London: Frank Cass, 2000.

Miller, Marla. *All-American Girls: The U.S. Women's National Soccer Team*. New York: Pocket Books, 1999.

Wambach, Abby. *Forward: A Memoir*. New York: Dey Street, 2016.

Williams, Jean. *A Beautiful Game: International Perspectives on Women's Football*. Oxford: Berg, 2007.

———. "Rise Like a Phoenix: The History of Women's Football and the Women's World Cup, 1869–2015." Sport and Translation (blog). Joint blog series on the Women's World Cup with AHRC funded Women, Work, and Value in Europe 1945–2015. University of Bristol, June 2, 2015. http://sportandtranslation.blogspot .com/2015/06/rise-like-phoenix-history-of-womens.html.

Williams, Jean, and Rob Hess. "Women, Football, and History: International Perspectives." *The International Journal of the History of Sport* 32, no. 18: 2115–22.

NOTES

1. For a good introduction to some of the most important issues of gender analysis and football, especially in Latin America, see Brenda Elsey and Joshua H. Nadel, *Futbolera: A History of Women and Sports in Latin America* (Austin: University of Texas Press, 2019).

2. FIFA.com.

3. Ryan Rosenblatt, "7 Questions Now That the USWNT Players and U.S. Soccer Have Agreed to a New CBA," foxsports.com, April 5, 2017. The new CBA, which is in effect until 2021, does not address all of the issues raised by the original wage discrimination complaint, which was, as of January 2019, still before the Equal Employment Opportunity Commission (EEOC).

4. Andrew Das, "U.S. Women's Soccer Team Sues U.S. Soccer for Gender Discrimination," *New York Times*, March 8, 2019. https://www.nytimes.com/2019/03/08 /sports/womens-soccer-team-lawsuit-gender-discrimination.html.

5. *Guardian*, "USA's Hope Solo Given Six-Month Ban for Calling Sweden 'A Bunch of Cowards,'" theguardian.com, August 24, 2016.

6. For more on the Dick, Kerr's women's teams, see Barbara Jacobs, *The Dick, Kerr's Ladies* (London: Robinson, 2004).

7. Susan K. Cahn, *Coming on Strong: Gender and Sexuality in Twentieth-Century Women's Sports* (Cambridge, MA: Harvard University Press, 1994), 7–83.

8. Jennifer Doyle, "Recovering from Soccer's Divorce," Fox Sports, July 7, 2011.

9. Much of the controversy over Title IX from the time of its adoption to the present has centered on the issues of interpretation and implementation. In general, Title IX has come to rely on a three-pronged test for nondiscrimination: Are activities, including athletic participation, in proportion to the sex/gender enrollment of a college or university? Have academic institutions made past efforts to expand activities and opportunities for underrepresented sexes/genders on campus? And are the interests, including athletic interests, of underrepresented sexes/genders currently being addressed? The Office of Civil Rights (OCR), which oversees enforcement of Title IX, issued legal clarifications in 2005 and 2010. The OCR is supposed to look at the interests of all students at academic institutions.

10. Kahn, *Coming on Strong*, 246–79.

11. women.soccerway.com. See also, Clara McCormack and Kristen Walseth, "Combining Elite Women's Soccer and Education: Norway and the NCAA," *Soccer and Society* 14, no. 6 (2013): 887–97.

12. Attendance for the 1995 Women's World Cup might have been held down by the small capacity of venues used in Sweden. Three of the five stadia used for the competition had a capacity of ten thousand fans or less. On the report of one in four Norwegian fans watching the 1995 final, see Jeré Longman, "Women's World Cup: Norway's Rivalry with the United States Is Intense," *New York Times*, nytimes.com, June 13, 1999.

13. Jennifer Doyle reminds us that records show that one hundred thousand fans filled the Azteca Stadium in Mexico City for a women's final match in the 1971 Copa Mundial, which was not sanctioned by FIFA. Denmark won that game over the host, Mexico, 3–0. Jennifer Doyle, "Recovering from Soccer's Divorce," Fox Sports, July 7, 2011.

14. *Sports Illustrated*, cover photo, July 19, 1999.

15. FIFA Women's World Cup, 2011, FIFA.com.

16. FIFA Women's World Cup, 2015, FIFA.com.

17. FIFA Women's World Cup, 2015, FIFA.com.

18. On the 2019 tournament in general, see FIFA Women's World Cup, 2019, FIFA.com. On some of the political controversites surrounding the competition, see Cody Benjamin, "Women's World Cup 2019: USWNT's Megan Rapinoe Says She Is 'Uniquely and Very Deeply American,'" CBS Sports, cbssports.com, July 3, 2019. For statistics on global viewership of the 2019 competition, see Ben Strauss, "Women's World Cup Final Delivers Viewers for Fox, Despite Early Start Time," *Washington Post*, washingtonpost.com, July 8, 2019.

19. FIFA.com.

20. Statista.com.

21. For more on Marta, see chapter 5.

22. Gertrud Pfister, "Sportswomen in the German Popular Press: A Study Carried Out in the Context of the 2011 Women's Football World Cup," *Soccer and Society* 16, nos. 5–6 (2015): 639–56.

23. Jeré Longman, "A Resilient Team Soothes a Nation," *New York Times*, nytimes.com, July 17, 2011; Justin McCurry, "Women's World Cup Victory Brings Joy to Japan," *The Guardian*, theguardian.com, July 18, 2011.

24. Abby Wambach, *Forward: A Memoir* (New York: Dey Street, 2016), 110.

25. See chapter 5.

26. FIFA.com.

27. FIFA, "Classy Cadamuro Bids Football Farewell," FIFA.com, August 14, 2016. Cadamuro is Nécib's married name; she married an Algerian international player, Liassine Cadamuro.

28. Timothy F. Grainey, *Beyond Bend it Like Beckham: The Global Phenomenon of Women's Soccer* (Lincoln: University of Nebraska Press, 2012), 256–65.

29. Marcus Christenson and Palul Kelso, "Soccer Chief's Plan to Boost Women's Game? Hotpants," *The Guardian*, www.theguardian.com, January 15, 2004.

30. 2014 FIFA World Cup, Brazil and 2018 FIFA World Cup, Russia, FIFA.com.

31. Philip Oltermann, "German Right-Wing Party Apologises for Jérôme Boateng Comments," *The Guardian*, theguardian.com, May 29, 2016. The politician involved was Alexander Gauland of the Alternative for Germany (AfD) party.

32. Christian Radnedge, "Özil Retires from International Football Feeling 'Unwanted,'" Reuters, reuters.com, July 22, 2018.

33. Laurent Dubois, *Soccer Empire: The World Cup and the Future of France* (Berkeley: University of California Press, 2010).

34. "Law on Nationality," Federal Foreign Office, Germany.

35. As quoted in Garry Jenkins, *The Beautiful Team: In Search of Pelé and the 1970 Brazilians* (London: Simon and Schuster, 1999), 32.

36. Hans Ulrich Gumbrecht, *In Praise of Athletic Beauty* (Cambridge, MA: Belknap Press of Harvard University Press, 2006), 249–51.

37. Eduardo Galeano, *Soccer in Sun and Shadow*, trans. Mark Fried (New York: Verso, 1998), 38–39.

38. Andreas Campomar, *Golazo! The Beautiful Game from the Aztecs to the World Cup: The Complete History of How Soccer Shaped Latin America* (New York: Riverhead Books, 2014), 76–80, 158–62, 175–76, and 240–47.

39. Ana Paula da Silva, "Pelé, Racial Discourse and the 1958 World Cup," *Soccer and Society* 15, no. 1 (2014): 36–47.

40. Dubois, *Soccer Empire*, passim.

41. Pierre Lanfranchi and Alfred Wahl, "The Immigrant as Hero: Koa, Mekloufi, and French Football," in *European Heroes: Myth, Identity, Sport*, ed. Richard Holt, J. A. Mangan, and Pierre Lanfranchi (London: Frank Cass, 1996), 117.

42. Richard Halifax, "Platini Vows to Return to Football after Swiss Justice Move," independent.ie, January 16, 2019. No criminal case was opened against Platini; he was, however, named in the proceedings against Sepp Blatter.

43. Dubois, *Soccer Empire*, 124–32.

44. Liz Alderman, "Suicide Bombers Tried to Enter Stadium," *New York Times*, nytimes.com, November 14, 2015.

45. The journal *Soccer and Society* devoted all of issues 1–2 of volume 11 (2010) to articles on and analysis of the 2010 World Cup in South Africa.

Chapter 5

Football as Spectacle

One of the most intriguing developments in the modern game of football is the way it has become a commodity. Football as a sporting spectacle has been packaged and sold in many ways over the course of the last 150 years. The play of the game, its rhythm and flow, is part of its global appeal. The players' skill, physical prowess, and stamina are often on display. Moreover, the artistry of football has made it engaging to a wide audience, to fans witnessing it in stadia and on fields of play everywhere, and to those listening to or watching it on radio, television, or, today, the Internet. Star players are talked about and written about as heroes, antiheroes, and supporting cast. The game has an immediate visceral and physical appeal, which can and has been sold and consumed. Football is therefore also one of the foremost products of sporting culture in the modern world.[1] An analysis of football in the World Cup competitions can also reveal much about modern consumerism, celebrity status, and the effects of worldwide communication techniques beyond just their economic impact. To understand the evolution of sport through looking at the spectacle of football is to gain a deeper appreciation for modern globalizing tendencies not yet discussed in *The World Cup as World History*.

As a sporting spectacle, the World Cup of football has been consumed in many different ways over the course of its history. Currently, football fans have a multitude of opportunities to follow the tournament as it is played out over several weeks in a host country. The games are broadcast live throughout the world and then often shown later in their entirety or in highlight fashion. Studio panels dissect the games to analyze teams' strategies and tactics. The players' performances are scrutinized in great detail. In today's technology-driven world, statistics on time of possession, passes completed, and distances run are as common as shots, shots on goal, and corner kicks were to a previous generation. In addition, the evolution of the Internet has given football fans a myriad of other platforms and formats to follow, discuss, argue about, and bet on games. The consumption industries that drive the modern world are very much a part of the global game of football and perhaps nowhere is that more obvious than during the World Cup.

ARENAS AND CROWDS

One of the oldest ways to be a part of the spectacle of World Cup football is as a fan witnessing a game in person. Part of the global appeal of the game is the atmosphere generated by crowds gathered in stadia during the month-long schedule of matches. Part of the fans' experience of tournament games is what goes on inside the stadia in which the games are played. Sports historians have written extensively on some of the most famous football sites from around the globe—the Maracanã in Rio de Janeiro, the Centenario in Montevideo, Wembley Stadium in London, or the San Siro in Milan, for example. They often employ language such as "cathedral," invoking religious imagery to convey the feeling and fervor contained within the stadia. Other scholars have discussed the anthropological effects of being in a crowd and the series of emotions—anticipation, exhilaration, aggression, anger, joy, and release—that can accompany watching a football match, especially a high-level World Cup game, in person. Regardless of how one interprets the phenomenon of attending a game, in religious, secular, or psychological terms, the grandiose scale and physical beauty that some of its stadia have acquired have undoubtedly enhanced the game of football. For fans drawn to the spectacle of football, some of these stadia have acquired a near mythical quality.[2]

Uruguay in 1930 used the very first competition to construct a massive new modernist stadium, the Centenario, as the centerpiece for the competition. Even though it was not fully ready when the cup began, it eventually became the symbolic centerpiece of the first tournament, a landmark in sporting architecture, and one of the most famous stadia of the day. As we saw in a previous chapter, it took its name from the one-hundred-year anniversary of Uruguayan independence, an occasion that had helped persuade FIFA to stage the competition in the South American country in the first place. The stadium was also a sign of the economic stability and prosperity of Uruguay in the decade after the First World War. The building of the Centenario symbolized the political, economic, and sporting aspirations and standing of an entire country. It helped, of course, that Uruguay won the inaugural competition in its brand new and architecturally beautiful stadium.[3]

Centenario Stadium (*INTERFOTO/Alamy Stock Photo*)

Twenty years later, in 1950, the World Cup was played in Brazil, and another stadium would become famous as a site for football's spectacle. Located in Rio de Janeiro, the Maracanã was at the time the largest stadium in the world. For the final match of the competition between Brazil and Uruguay, a record crowd of nearly 200,000 filled the stadium. Unfortunately for the hosts, they lost the final to their South American rivals, a defeat so devastating that some sporting observers have stated that it created a national malaise in Brazil until 1958, when Brazil finally won its first World Cup.[4] The Maracanã also holds the world record for the largest crowd to see a club competition in Brazil. In 1963, over 177,000 fans filled its rungs to watch Flamengo and Fluminense, two of the most famous Brazilian club teams, play a match.[5]

Such huge numbers of fans gathered in one place was only possible because of the then common design of most major football stadia. Before security concerns took over and officials, teams, and leagues reconfigured their sites such that every fan has to have a seat, many people stood to watch and witness a match. Often, this was done by standing on terraces that could accommodate huge numbers of individuals and created a dynamic atmosphere within the stadium. Fans on the terraces could literally feel the rhythm of the

Maracanã Stadium (*dpa picture alliance/Alamy Stock Photo*)

game as people around them pushed forward in anticipation of a goal or to voice their opinion about a play on the pitch. Old-time fans sometimes claim that the in-person experience of watching a game has forever changed with the advent of all-seater stadia, which have eliminated the terraces. The new or rebuilt stadia, however, have also meant greater safety for fans watching matches, because injuries and occasionally tragedies could unfold on the old terraces when the fans pushed forward onto people in the surrounding crowd.[6] The Maracanã itself was later reconfigured so that it would hold approximately one hundred thousand fans. It fell on hard times as the domestic Brazilian leagues declined in importance because the country's best players went to Europe. The local teams were also often grossly mismanaged.[7] However, the stadium was restored in time for the 2014 tournament, when it was used as the site for the final between Germany and Argentina.

Several other stadia have acquired near mythical status for their role in staging World Cup matches. The Azteca Stadium in Mexico City, mentioned previously, has hosted two tournament finals, one in 1970 and another in 1986. It is famous for its size—it holds well over one hundred thousand fans—its altitude (7,280 feet above sea level), and the proximity of the fans to the playing field. The combination of these three factors makes the Azteca one of the most intimidating sites in the world in which to play a football match. The Azteca Stadium's conditions also make for a special type of footballing spectacle. The San Siro in Milan, yet another famous stadium, has been redesigned and

Azteca Stadium (*Wikimedia Commons, Karl Oppolzer*)

San Siro Stadium (*Flickr/prijordao*)

Old Wembley Stadium (*London Aerial Photo Library/Alamy Stock Photo*)

rebuilt several times to increase its capacity. For the 1990 competition in Italy, it accommodated seventy-five thousand fans. It is also home to two of Italy's most famous clubs: AC Milan and FC Internazionale.

Wembley Stadium in London has long been considered one of the "cathedrals" of the game. In its heyday, Old Wembley, built in 1922–1923, was large enough for 127,000 fans and was host to the 1966 World Cup final between England and West Germany. It was torn down in 2002–2003 and replaced in 2007 by a new Wembley Stadium that remains a crucial part of the footballing landscape in England and a primary location for the consumption of the sport as spectacle.[8]

Built for the 1998 World Cup, the Stade de France in suburban Paris features an elliptical design and an ultra-modern sporting environment for the football fan. Its tinted glass roof covers the playing field and the stands and provides an extraordinary viewing experience. Like many other notable sporting structures of the late twentieth and early twenty-first centuries, the Stade de France has many amenities intended to enhance the fans' enjoyment of the game and increase their consumption. It has several dozen bars, numerous stores, three restaurants, and a movie theater. Unfortunately, a terrorist attack occurred there on November 13, 2015, during an international match between France and Germany. Fortunately, the terrorists were unable to enter the stadium, in which French president François Hollande was watching the match. They detonated their devices outside the facility. The terrorist attack was another cruel reminder that extremists could attempt to hijack sports and use them as a platform for political purposes.[9]

Table 5.1. World Cup Stadia, Capacity (approximate at the time they held the World Cup)

Year	Place	Stadium	Capacity
1930	Uruguay	Centenario (Montevideo)	100,000
1934	Italy	Stadio Nazionale (Rome)	55,000
	Italy	San Siro (Milan)	40,000
1938	France	Stade Olympique (Paris)	60,000
1938	France	Stade Vélodrome (Marseille)	48,000
1950	Brazil	Maracanã (Rio)	200,000
1954	Switzerland	Wankdorf (Bern)	64,000
1958	Sweden	Råsunda (Stockholm)	52,000
1962	Chile	Nacional (Santiago)	77,000
1966	England	Wembley (London)	99,000
1970	Mexico	Azteca (Mexico City)	107,000
1974	W. Germany	Olympiastadion (Munich)	77,000
1978	Argentina	Monumental (Buenos Aires)	75,000
1982	Spain	Bernabéu (Madrid)	90,000
	Spain	Camp Nou (Barcelona)	120,000
1986	Mexico	Azteca (Mexico City)	115,000
1990	Italy	Olimpico (Rome)	74,000
	Italy	San Siro (Milan)	75,000
1994	USA	Rose Bowl (Pasadena)	94,000
1998	France	Stade de France (Paris)	81,000
2002	S. Korea	Daegu (Daegu)	67,000
2002	Japan	International (Yokohama)	70,000
2006	Germany	Olympiastadion (Berlin)	72,000
2010	South Africa	Soccer City (Johannesburg)	85,000
2014	Brazil	Maracanã (Rio)	75,000
2018	Russia	Luzhniki (Moscow)	78,000
2022	Qatar	Iconic (Lusail)	80,000 (projected)

Note: Estimating the capacity of football stadia is complicated. In some instances, such as Chile 1962, the official listed capacity of the Nacional Stadium was approximately 67,000 fans. Nevertheless, the semifinal match between host Chile and defending champion Brazil drew almost 77,000 fans to the stadium. Moreover, several World Cup stadia, such as Wembley Stadium in London, the San Siro in Milan, the Camp Nou in Barcelona, the Maracanã in Rio de Janeiro, and the Azteca in Mexico City, have been reconstructed and reconfigured several times during the twentieth and twenty-first centuries.

Source: FIFA.com; stadiumDB.com; stadiumguide.com; footballhistory.org; acmilan.com; Tom Dunmore, *Historical Dictionary of Soccer* (Lanham, MD: Rowman & Littlefield, 2015), 90–120; Simon Inglis, *The Football Grounds of Europe* (London: Willow Books, 1990), 11, 51, 99, 108, 196, 212, 236, 240.

Within these and many other stadia, one can witness an obvious element of football as spectacle: the involvement of crowds at games and tournaments. From its inception in the late nineteenth century, modern football quickly became a popular sport and drew large numbers of fans to various contests. By the time the first World Cup was staged in 1930, numerous football matches had been played in front of very large audiences. For example, Hakoah Vienna, an important Jewish club team of the interwar era, toured the United States and played a match in front of forty-six thousand fans at the old Polo Grounds stadium in New York in 1926.[10] Plenty of club and national team matches could boast similar figures for attendance in the 1920s and '30s. Once the World Cup was introduced in 1930 and continued to grow thereafter, it drew large numbers of fans to live matches.[11] Indeed, one part of the popularity of the tournament has been the fans' tour to a host country to follow one's national team. Sports tourism has therefore become big business in the era of the World Cup, even as it has become easier and easier to follow the matches on television and the Internet.

The individual fan and the crowd are a fundamental and important part of the spectacle of the World Cup of football. It is difficult to analyze with any precision the attitudes of individual fans to matches, but many scholars have worked on the subject of crowd reaction and fans.[12] This has been especially the case when fans have grown unruly and even violent. There has been, for example, much discussion and many academic attempts to analyze the "hooligan" effect in world football. Hooligans, defined as fans looking for physical or violent encounters with fans from the opposing side, have been quite noticeable in many national footballing cultures, perhaps especially in the English game in the 1980s, but also in many other countries and competitions.[13] As recently as the summer of 2016, one saw violence involving Russian and English fans outside stadia at the European Championship in France. Club teams in numerous countries, such as Italy, Argentina, Brazil, and Serbia, have had to deal with violent fans both inside and outside of playing venues. The World Cup has also had its fair share of raucous fans, but most of its competitions have come off without the displays of severe violence and confrontation that have plagued some club matches. For example, at the 1985 European Cup Final between Juventus of Italy and Liverpool of England, thirty-nine people, most of them Italians, were tragically killed at the Heysel Stadium in Brussels, Belgium. They were rushed by opposing supporters and crushed to death when a wall collapsed. Another six hundred fans were injured in the terrifying incident, which also helped lead to changes in stadia construction and management for high-profile matches and major tournaments.[14]

One of the most interesting studies of the psychology of the hooligan or violent fan is Bill Buford's *Among the Thugs*. Buford, an American journalist, tried to understand the tendency toward violence among football supporters by going among them in the 1980s and early '90s, including attending a match during the 1990 World Cup tournament in Italy.[15] He found no single motivation that alone could account for violent behavior. Many different factors seemed to flow together to create the circumstances for fans to "go off," as he put it. The hooligans were affected by both the anonymity of being in a crowd and the perceived need to act out and prove themselves to known compatriots. Real or imagined political, economic, or cultural grievances, such as the financial downturn experienced in Britain in the 1970s and '80s, might have motivated them. Most frightening of all in Buford's account is the possibility that human beings simply have a psychological capacity for violence. He suggested that when social norms and control are breached, as they might be at a football match, then the will of the crowd, if predisposed toward aggression and looking for an enemy, might find its outlet by participating in violence. For Buford, psychological factors are part of the explanation for hooligan activity and violence.

Of course, violent reactions associated with football matches are just one possible crowd reaction. Whereas most games build a certain level of tension and anticipation in the football fan, they do not usually spill over into aggressive or brutal behavior. Indeed, the majority of games are played without any incidents caused by hooligans. Crowd involvement at a football match, including singing and chanting, can add to the overall enjoyment of witnessing the sporting spectacle in person. There is, therefore, a broad spectrum of experiences one encounters in stadia worldwide and as a part of a football crowd witnessing a sporting spectacle.

WORLD CUP STARS AS SPORTING ICONS

Another method for understanding football as a sporting spectacle is to examine the way star players, male and female, have been represented and "sold" to various audiences over the years. Some of them, such as Pelé, Diego Maradona, and Franz Beckenbauer, have acquired cult-like status for their on-field accomplishments. They have become world football's icons. That is, certain World Cup stars seem to have established the mold for other players to follow. They have become positive and sometimes negative models against which the sport of football measures itself and its ability to attract and keep fans. Football players are held up as part of the spectacle of the game and as primary vehicles for consuming it—ticket sales, endorsements, television packages, advertising, and merchandising all ultimately depend on their play and performance. They therefore are also heavily scrutinized and sometimes sharply criticized for real and perceived sporting or personal failures. Thus, the construction of sporting icons is a delicate and ongoing balancing act. Today's hero can also be tomorrow's fallen and problematic star. Through an examination of star players, their World Cup successes and failures, and the ways they have been advertised and represented to the public, one gains another window onto football as a sporting spectacle and its meaning in a globalized world.

One player who clearly has added to the appeal and spectacle of World Cup football is Edson Arantes do Nascimento, better known throughout the football world simply as Pelé. In chapter 4, discussion of Pelé and his exploits focused on the labored progress in racial relations within Brazilian football and society brought on by the great success of the teams he helped lead in the late 1950s and 1960s. One cannot, however, underestimate the contributions he made to the game as a star athlete at a time when the game was growing in global popularity on television and through advertising. Pelé was not football's first superstar, but he may be the most important player in its history as spectacle. In addition to playing in parts of four World Cups (1958, 1962, 1966, and 1970)—he was unfortunately injured and unable to compete in most of the matches of the 1962 and 1966 cups—he scored hundreds of goals for club and country, many of them in dramatic fashion, over a playing career that spanned twenty-one years. Garry Jenkins writes that "Pelé once compared scoring a goal to an orgasm. At those moments can scoring a goal seem better than sex, I wondered? 'It depends on the goal, but yes it can.'"[16]

After leading Brazil to triumph in 1970, Pelé became part of a wave of famous players who came to the United States to help the then fledgling North American Soccer League (NASL) establish itself. The NASL was extremely popular in the late 1970s. Crowds numbered in the tens of thousands at matches in many US cities. Pelé was part of the skyrocketing fame of the New York Cosmos, the best-known and most successful of all the NASL franchises. Even after the league declined and then collapsed, he remained a popular individual in the United States and throughout the football-playing world. Indeed, his most important contribution to the popularity, branding, consumption, and spectacle of football may be his role as unofficial ambassador for the game. His name has become synonymous in some circles for football played at its best, the beautiful game.[17]

The reasons for Pelé's position in the history of the game are complex. Certainly, he came along at the right time. The revolution in global communications—television, in particular—made it possible for athletes such as

Pelé, 1960

Pelé to become household names and global commodities.[18] But first there had to be a product. One could, of course, sell success. As a three-time World Cup champion, one could package Pelé as a winner. Moreover, he had scored or helped create some of the greatest goals in the history of the competition, including the celebrated last goal of the 1970 tournament against Italy. That particular effort is often cited by football enthusiasts and officials as the greatest single team goal ever scored.[19] Of course, such claims are merely grist for the mill of conversation, discussion, and argument about football's past. Everyone has an opinion about the greatest goal, save, assist, pass, dribble, etc. of all time. In the age of YouTube and the Internet, fans, sportscasters, and scholars are more willing than ever to share their lists of favorites.

Pelé's appeal, however, goes beyond team or individual highlights and accomplishments. He was undoubtedly one of the most complete football players ever. He was strong, fast, smart, and had a tremendous "feel" for the game. Fans watching him would notice the grace with which he moved and the beauty of his play. There was a recognizable aesthetic quality to Pelé's performances, of the kind that some scholars, such as C. L. R. James, have analyzed for participants in other sports.[20] To watch Pelé was to learn to appreciate and perhaps even love the artistry possible in athletic competitions. The spectacle he offered, therefore, went beyond merely goals and assists, wins and losses. He was the beautiful athlete in motion, whose level of play could be seen, understood, and appreciated by both the casual fan and the lifelong aficionado of football. Pelé's qualities as a player made him not only a global superstar of his era but a model against which later players would be compared. His game came as close to art as any athlete in any sport has achieved.[21]

Football analysts, scholars, and serious and casual fans alike usually agree that Diego Maradona was another of the game's greatest players, and an iconic player. From Argentina, he burst onto the football scene at a young age and impressed people deeply with his skills, especially his ability to dribble the ball past opponents at will and with pace. Maradona was one of those players, like Ronaldinho of Brazil or Lionel Messi, a fellow Argentinian of a later generation, who seemed to have command of the ball at his feet. Maradona became famous for his performance in the 1986 World Cup in Mexico, especially for his play against England. In that game, he managed to show his virtuosity and his gamesmanship. He scored one of the greatest goals in the history of football by slaloming among several defenders before slotting the ball into the goal beyond the flailing figure of the English goalkeeper, Peter Shilton. It was a spectacular individual effort and cemented Maradona's reputation as one of the most skilled players in football history. Invariably, it will be shown in the run-up to every new global competition and is often voted "the goal of the century."[22]

Maradona also scored one of the most controversial goals in the history of the World Cup in the same game against England. In a tight contest, a few minutes before his famous run through the English defense, Maradona used his hand, a clear violation of the rules, to "head" the ball over Shilton and into the goal. Despite the vehement protests of the English team, the goal stood and helped carry Argentina to victory in the match, 2–1. Argentina would continue on to capture the championship trophy in 1986, besting West Germany, 3–2, in the final. Maradona added to the controversy of the England match by saying that his second goal had been scored partially by the "Hand of God," an expression that has entered into World Cup history. A tacit admission of his misdeed, the comment was interpreted differently by various audiences. It could mean that his game was aided by cunning (in Argentina, for example), or that he realized the deep implications of what he had done and explained it with an ironic expression (to neutral observers), or that he had cheated but would not accept responsibility for his act (in England). Regardless of how one understood Maradona's comments, the "hand of God" goal, controversial as it was, would become part of the visual and iconic history of the World Cup. It is played again and again in the lead-up to each new tournament.

By the end of the 1986 World Cup, Maradona was a football phenomenon. As a player whose image and exploits could be branded and sold, he was much in demand. He had a very successful, although sometimes

Maradona, "Hand of God Goal," 1986 World Cup vs. England (*Bob Thomas/Getty Images*)

controversial, career at the club level, primarily with Napoli in Serie A, the top division in Italy. In Naples, he would become a favorite and feted son of the city. His career, however, also demonstrates another aspect of the global game: how difficult it is to maintain a certain sporting image once it has been created and one has achieved cult-like status. Maradona would eventually fall hard from his playing peak of the mid-1980s. He was unable to help Argentina defend its title in 1990 as it lost in the final to a German side in a competition held in Italy, where he had been playing for many years and had become famous. By the time of the World Cup in the United States in 1994, Maradona was more or less a shadow of his former self, a player who could no longer produce the kind of athletic performance that was so much a part of the consumer nature of the world's game. When he let out a primordial scream into a television camera after scoring a goal in a game against Greece, it might have seemed like the football superstar was announcing himself once again on the global stage. It turned out, however, to be a last gasp effort to retain his position in the game. Almost immediately thereafter, he failed a drug test and was banned from any further matches in 1994.[23]

The celebrity culture of football, so much on display in Mexico in 1986, in Italy in 1990, and in the United States in 1994, had done much to create Diego Maradona as a sporting superstar. It advanced his cult as one of the greatest players of the game and made him financially well-off and a marketing phenomenon. It would also turn against him and show the fragility of trying to maintain global status in an interconnected world. The press published stories about his decline into drug dependency and significant weight gain. His personal struggles were displayed for all to see. Few would recognize the wunderkind of the world's game who had burst onto the football scene in the puffy man who roamed the sideline as Argentina's coach at the 2010 tournament in South Africa. His talent on the field and his fame as a national player did not prevent him from being let go as manager after that competition, amidst much political wrangling in the Argentine Football Association (AFA). His place in football's history, as a gifted player on the pitch and a problematic individual off of it, has become part of the history of the sport and how it has been understood over the last few decades.[24]

Maradona was and is a football archetype: the gifted but also tragically flawed player. He came from the social and economic margins of Argentinian society and gained international fame and fortune. The game that made him and the culture around it also took their toll. Over time, he seemingly could not stand up to the pressure of being a football superstar. On the pitch, he was also often a marked man who was fouled hard and continuously, which did not help him to maintain his playing prowess. Drug use, weight gain, political controversy—he traveled to Cuba for treatment and while there made several positive comments about Fidel Castro, the communist leader of that island nation, for example—were all part of the Maradona profile. As he grew older, he was less able to impose himself on the pitch. Until the end of his career, however, he remained defiant and outspoken. He once said that "it was not the drugs that stopped me playing. . . . There are a lot of powerful men in football. They've tried to kill me, destroy me, but they cannot. They want to destroy me as I am one of the few players who says things that these people do not like."[25] Regardless of his relationship with football's "powerful men" and his polarizing place in the history of the game, he had become by then a folk hero in many circles, both in his native Argentina and in his adopted city of Naples. Nevertheless, he was seemingly haunted by the success he achieved. He complicated his standing and stature in the game through hard living and bad habits.

Maradona is the most famous archetype of the gifted but flawed figure in world football, but he is certainly not alone in that category and stands in a long tradition of tremendously talented but also troubled players. For example, José Leandro Andrade, star of the great Uruguayan teams of the 1920s, battled alcohol and illness most of his adult life and died penniless in Montevideo in 1956. Heleno de Freitas, a Brazilian great of the 1930s and '40s, died, most likely, from the effects of late-stage syphilis. George Best, the Northern Irishman who became famous at Manchester United as a countercultural icon in the 1960s and '70s, also drank himself into an early grave. Many football players have decisively influenced the game but have not necessarily managed the fame that came with that accomplishment. Maradona, a global icon because of his play at the World Cup, stands at the head of that list.

Bobby Moore of England, who captained the World Cup–winning side of 1966, represents a decidedly different type of player and image from Pelé or Maradona. He did not possess the grace of a Pelé or the pace and dribbling skills of a young Maradona. Nevertheless, Moore has gone down in the history of football as an icon and archetype of the game: the player who "reads" the game from the back of the formation and organizes his team well. He is universally regarded as one of the best defenders to have competed in a World Cup. Pelé himself made that claim after seeing Moore perform in 1966. The latter was noted for his ability to recognize the strategy and tactics of the opposing teams. He discerned during the course of play how attacks might unfold and moved to foil them through correct positioning and well-timed tackles. He might very well then win the ball back for his side and begin the counterattack from his defensive position. He was the strategist on the field, the general who marshals his forces.

In addition to his play with the English national squad, Moore captained West Ham United in London for many years. During his football career,

Bobby Moore, 1963 (*Dutch National Archives*)

he also became a sympathetic character; he was successfully treated for cancer during his playing days, before later succumbing to the disease and dying at the young age of fifty-one.[26] Other players, most notably Franz Beckenbauer of West Germany, who became known as the "Kaiser" on the field, also fall into the category of the dominant defender on the pitch, who organizes play from the back of the team's formation. He played the role of

Franz Beckenbauer (right) in duel with Johan Cruyff, 1974 (*Dutch National Archives*)

libero—that is, he roamed alternately behind and in front of his defensive line. He could be found, however, in a wide range of defensive, midfield, and even attacking positions.[27]

Players such as Moore and Beckenbauer and the images they create from World Cup play can also help one to understand and possibly break down racial and ethnic stereotypes. In the game of world football, as in many sports, there has often been a temptation or at least an inclination to see white players as more intelligent, more gifted at organization, and more cerebral, and black athletes as more physical and more "naturally" talented but lacking the understanding and oversight to interpret the games they play. These pernicious stereotypes can be difficult to overcome, and they show themselves in a wide range of situations. Crude forms of these racial and ethnic stereotypes can be seen in events such as the 1936 Berlin Olympics, when Adolf Hitler's hateful racial ideology was confronted by the powerful and winning performances of African American athletes such as Jesse Owens. Of course, the Nazis made much of the sporting accomplishments of their so-called Aryan athletes in 1936.[28] Similarly, Jackie Robinson's reintegration of baseball in 1947—a few African Americans had played the sport professionally in the late nineteenth century—was necessary to overcome that sport's racist history. He proved that people from any background could play and compete in what was considered a cerebral sport. One sees echoes of these types of cultural stereotypes in debates about African American quarterbacks in American football. One sees clearer evidence of these racial stereotypes in the choices made about managers and coaches in a wide spectrum of professional sports.[29]

In football's history, there is the possibility of contextualizing these racial stereotypes and perhaps overcoming them. Bobby Moore might not have been the greatest athlete ever to play football, but he certainly did not get to the right place on the pitch through intelligence alone. And Franz Beckenbauer might have given off a sense of aloofness and dominance in his style of play, but he, too, was a gifted athlete who could impose himself physically upon a game. Moreover, the legacy of Moore and Beckenbauer has been carried on by players such as the great central defender Marcel Desailly of France, who helped control and organize his defense throughout the World Cup of 1998. Desailly hails from Ghana and was part of the racially inclusive side that represented France in that competition. Thiago Silva, the Brazilian defender of mixed ethnic background and frequent captain of his team, is largely regarded as one of the best players of his generation at that position. His organizational skills were so clearly missed in the semifinal match—he was suspended because of an accumulation of yellow cards—against a dominant Germany in the 2014 competition. The well-organized, cerebral, calm defender who marshals the game from the back is a role that has been occupied, therefore, by players of black, white, and mixed ethnic ancestry throughout the history of the World Cup. Recognizing this state of affairs can help one to break down the social and cultural stereotypes about "naturally gifted" versus "cerebral" athletes. The exploits and achievements of football players from across the racial spectrum defy easy categorization.

One of the most intriguing of iconic football players is Johan Cruyff of the Netherlands. He was a bridge figure in the history of the sport—between Pelé and Maradona—who came of age with the club team Ajax of Amsterdam and the Dutch national team, as television was continuing to grow the global audience for football. At the same time, a countercultural movement was afoot in most of Western Europe and the United States. Playing in the late 1960s and throughout most of the 1970s, Cruyff was part of a generation of football players who modeled the changes of the era on and off the pitch. He and many others grew their hair long and dressed in the fashion of the day. In interviews, he could be blunt and straightforward. Although the huge sums of money that would transform football had not yet flowed into the game, Cruyff also knew how to market his name, image, and brand. He would question the role of received authority in society and was part of a general movement toward more personal freedom, especially as the younger generation in the Netherlands and Europe demanded it.[30]

On the field, Cruyff was, however, both a brilliant individualist and the consummate team player. At both the club and national level, he showed

Johan Cruyff (*Dutch National Archives*)

plenty of flair in his game and could dribble and maneuver around defenders with an array of moves and techniques. But it was as the central character in the evolution of what was then called Total Football that Cruyff became famous first for Ajax and then for the Netherlands in the 1974 World Cup in West Germany. Total Football has been discussed and defined differently by various football authorities and sports historians.[31] Simply put, it was a system of play that relied less on players occupying a constant position on the pitch and put more emphasis on the free-flowing nature of the game. Players might interchange positions during an offensive maneuver or as part of a quick conversion into a defensive posture. Total Football required players to be flexible and quick in their thinking. It also demanded that they attack as one, as a unit, with even the goalkeeper playing an offensive role. In addition, the whole team, reading the play of the opponent, also had to shift and defend as a whole. It meant that the team often pressed high up the field, pressured the other team, and tried to regain control of the ball as quickly as possible. Above all else, Total Football relied on the quick evaluation of available space on the football pitch. The Netherlands, with Cruyff and other standout players, used the entire width of the field and exploited runs and passes into space to open up their opponents. As the Dutch artist Jeroen Henneman once commented: "Football was always unconsciously about space. The good players were always the ones who instinctively found positions to receive the ball in space."[32]

Total Football was only successful with players trained in its intricacies, and it grew out of the club system of the Netherlands. At Ajax, coach Rinus Michels became the primary proponent of the free-flowing style of play. Nevertheless, it took a generation of skillful players such as Cruyff, Johan Neeskens, Johnny Rep, and Rob Rensenbrink to make it work. It also could not immediately be adopted by other teams, although its legacy lives on in the post-1970s game in many guises. For example, FC Barcelona, with its intricate short-passing schemes and interchange of midfielders and forwards, owes much to the Total Football concept. Not surprisingly, when Cruyff finished his playing career, which included a stint in the United States with Los Angeles and Washington of the North American Soccer League, he coached at Barcelona from 1988 to 1996.[33] He died there in 2016 at age sixty-eight, from lung cancer.

Cruyff, the counterculture icon, became the architect of and one of the central players in the Dutch team's Total Football, which was nicknamed "Clockwork Orange," after the color of the national team's jersey and the famous Stanley Kubrick film of the era. It was, however, not the first time in world football that a brilliant individualist would fit into a great team concept. Commentators and fans always discuss and debate which players represent best which archetypes and traditions of the game and who first invented or introduced a style of football. The great Hungarian star Ferenc Puskás, who played his club football for Real Madrid (1958–1966) in its most dominant era, once said that the elements of Total Football were already present in the 1950s.[34] In his opinion, some of the same principles used by the Dutch in the World Cup tournaments of 1974 and 1978 and Ajax Amsterdam in the early 1970s were championed by the Hungarian sides that were so highly competitive in international football in the first half of the 1950s. Indeed, Hungary was the favored side to win the 1954 competition. The West German team pulled off what came to be called the "Miracle in Bern," after its victory in the championship match in the Swiss city that hosted the final.[35]

The Hungarian style of play in the 1950s, the trainers who taught it, and the organization that sponsored it came, in turn, primarily out of the generation of the 1930s, when Central European football, primarily that of Budapest, Prague, and Vienna, was at its height. At that time, some of the best national and club-level matches were played in three of the successor states—Czechoslovakia, Hungary, and Austria—of the old Habsburg Empire. If one kept digging further into the history of innovative concepts in football, therefore, one might alight upon the Austrian "wonder team" (*Wunderteam*) of the early 1930s as a group that introduced new strategies of play. At the center of that team stood a player, Matthias Sindelar, not unlike Cruyff. Slender, skillful, confident, and able to impose himself on the game by sending others into space, he was the driving force that made that Austrian side go and might have brought it to a World Cup victory in 1934, if not for the poor political situation surrounding it at the time. Sindelar, who did not make the transition into the "all-German" team of 1938, which was created after the annexation of Austria into Nazi Germany, died before the beginning of the Second World War in mysterious circumstances. His death might have been an accident, suicide, or murder, as he was not a fan of the new authoritarian regime that took hold in his native country.[36] In any case, one might characterize him as a practitioner of Total Football before the term existed. As Roman Horak and Wolfgang Maderthaner have commented: "Sindelar embodied . . . a style characterized by sophisticated technique, intelligent movement off the ball, accurate passing on the ground."[37] They could have been describing the playing style of Cruyff and many of the Dutch stars of the 1970s.

Players like Sindelar and Puskás remind us of an important point that has been made by David Goldblatt, one of the foremost historians of the game of football. As he notes, our historical sense of the archetypes of global football, of the cultural icons that have made the game, of those players who have created the spectacle of the sport, is often heavily conditioned by the use of available media. Many great football stars before the 1960s and '70s did not have the advantage of playing before local or international television audiences. Insofar as our ideas about football as a spectacle are greatly shaped by our viewing, watching, and consuming the sport through vehicles such as television, this means that we may very well raise up and create cult-like status around players like Pelé, who played long enough to benefit from the transition to television, or Maradona, who played his entire career in the television era, but we have much less of a visual impression of stars of earlier eras, such as Sindelar, and hence their cultural impact upon the game and society has been much more limited.[38] Goldblatt is certainly right about how we have literally viewed football. Without many visual representations of players such as Sindelar (and hundreds of others), we rely upon what was reported about their exploits and impact in newspapers or perhaps on radio. That information comes down to us in a host of languages that make it difficult if not impossible for us to read about them and their exploits. These pre-television-era players from countries throughout the world never really had the opportunity to achieve the status of global superstars and international cultural icons. Although it is pure speculation, it is interesting to imagine what players like Sindelar, and many others, might have come to represent if they had played their entire careers in front of television cameras. Their images, styles of play, and cultural status would then have been packaged and sold as part of the global spectacle of football. Perhaps as sports historians and fans learn more about football players from the pre- or mostly pre-television era, such

Table 5.2. Sampling of Significant Footballers Who Played in the Pre- or Mostly Pre-Television Era

Name	Country	World Cups
Paulino Alcántara	Philippines/Spain	No World Cups
José Andrade	Uruguay	1930
Bellini	Brazil	1958, 1962, 1966
Larbi Ben Barek	Morocco/France	No World Cups
Didi	Brazil	1954, 1958, 1962
Just Fontaine	France	1958
Garrincha	Brazil	1958, 1962, 1966
Alcides Ghiggia	Uruguay	1950
Salif Keïta	Mali	No World Cups
Sándor Kocsis	Hungary	1954
Leônidas da Silva	Brazil	1934, 1938
Giuseppe Meazza	Italy	1934, 1938
Luis Monti	Argentina/Italy	1930, 1934
Ferenc Puskás	Hungary/Spain	1954, 1962
Helmut Rahn	West Germany	1954, 1958
Nílton Santos	Brazil	1950, 1954, 1958, 1962
Juan Schiaffino	Uruguay	1950, 1954
Matthias Sindelar	Austria	1934
Alfredo di Stéfano	Argentina/Spain	No World Cups
Fritz Walter	West Germany	1954, 1958
Mário Zagallo	Brazil	1958, 1962

Sources: Paul Darby, *Africa, Football, and FIFA: Politics, Colonialism, and Resistance* (Portland, OR: Frank Cass, 2002), 14; Tom Dunmore, *Historical Dictionary of Soccer* (Lanham, MD: Rowman & Littlefield, 2015), 24, 25, 66, 67, 122, 131, 135, 159, 160, 164, 176, 180, 205–6, 221, 223, 227–28, 259, 267; Brian Glanville, *The Story of the World Cup* (London: Faber and Faber, 2014), 17–19, 22, 28, 31, 39, 42, 63, 65–68, 72–75, 77–83, 91–97, 99, 102, 103–7, 112, 113, 117, 122, 128, 129, 138, 140, 144, 203; David Goldblatt, *The Ball Is Round: A Global History of Soccer* (New York: Riverhead Books, 2008), 492, 506, 571; Clemente A. Lisi, *A History of the World Cup, 1930–2018* (Lanham, MD: Rowman & Littlefield, 2019), 24–26, 29, 31–32, 37–40, 41, 42, 55–60, 61, 62, 65–66, 69–71, 72, 74, 76, 80–82, 84, 87–90, 91, 99, 100–104, 117, 125.

as those listed in table 5.2, and more images of those players are found—in newspaper photographs, early newsreels, or film—their stories can and will be woven into the cultural iconography of global football.

Outfield players, those who attack the goal, control the midfield, or defend the pitch from offensive moves, are not the only ones to define football. Central to the game and its image is also the goalkeeper. In the contemporary game, there are a large number of truly formidable and impressive goalies. Gigi Buffon of Italy has become famous for his long service between the posts for country and club. The American Tim Howard was a well-regarded goalkeeper for his nation. And Manuel Neuer is merely the last in a long line—Oliver Kahn, Andreas Köpke, and Toni Schumacher—of outstanding

German goalies. Today's goalkeepers are often tall and quite athletic. At times, they make the goal seem very small indeed. Gordon Banks of England drew rave reviews for almost literally "standing on his head" to make a number of great saves during the 1966 tournament. But Banks is usually thought of as the second-best goalie in the history of the game. The man who invented the modern model for today's goalkeeper is Lev Yashin of the Soviet Union, who has taken on legendary status in the history of football. He is the best example of the iconic modern goalie.

Yashin played in the late 1950s and throughout the 1960s, when television was just beginning to transform the way fans could watch and consume club and national matches. He became famous for his international performances, especially his work in goal at the 1956 Summer Olympics, the 1960 European Championship, and the World Cups of 1958, 1962, and 1966. In Sweden in 1958, for example, he played a tremendous game against Brazil, even though his side lost. Yashin was credited with keeping the score in check, as the Soviets went down to a 2–0 defeat. Because of his play and his propensity to dress in black, he became known as the "Black Panther" or "Black Spider." The former alluded to his tremendous reflexes; the latter to the impression that he had eight arms and legs with which to deflect and defend shots.[39]

Lev Yashin, 1969 (*SPUTNIK/Alamy Stock Photo*)

Yashin played for the Soviet Union when it was using sports of all kinds as a defense of and advertisement for its communist political and economic system. In the 1950s and '60s, the Soviets became competitive in the Olympic Games, for example. Yashin seemingly never balked at the sporting culture that created and supported him. He played his entire club career at Dynamo Moscow, which was the team of the Soviet police forces, including the KGB, or state secret police. When he was done as a player, he stayed on at Dynamo for another twenty years in one capacity or another. Despite his dedication to the club, Yashin left his mark on the game as an individual innovator. He created the role and image of the modern goalkeeper because he was so willing to depart from the then accepted practices of his position. For example, he came out of goal fearlessly to collect crosses and corner kicks. He left his goal line and penalty area to cut down the angles of attacking players and to disrupt their play. He used his fists to punch away difficult balls that he thought he could not collect cleanly. In all these ways, he was a football innovator who either invented new techniques for goalkeeping or expanded greatly on older ways of playing. Above all else, it was the aggressive and dominating nature of his game that stood out to contemporaries and later observers. He set the standard for the imperious goalkeeper, defying all comers. He was once quoted as saying that "the joy of seeing Yuri Gagarin—the famous Soviet cosmonaut—flying into space is only superseded by the joy of a good penalty save."[40] Yashin was a competitor.

Moreover, Yashin has literally been made into a sporting icon. In addition to receiving the Order of Lenin, the USSR's highest honor, in 1967, his image has been used on stamps and coins, and his likeness has graced several statues, including one at the Dynamo Stadium in Moscow and one in Rio de Janeiro, Brazil. In 1963 he won the Ballon d'Or, the trophy given to football's best player in a given year. He is the only goalkeeper to have ever been so honored. In 1994, FIFA created the Lev Yashin award for the best goalkeeper at the World Cup tournament. His testimonial match at the Lenin Stadium in Moscow was attended by one hundred thousand fans. Players such as Pelé, Eusebio of Portugal, and Beckenbauer showed up to add luster to the match and to help burnish his image as the best goalkeeper of his generation. Indeed, most expert polls conducted by FIFA, other organizations, or fan groups have named Yashin as the greatest goalkeeper of the twentieth century. When he died in 1990 of stomach cancer, he was given a state funeral and received more honors and accolades. He could not have known that the Soviet Union, which he had represented as goalkeeper, would implode politically and fall apart only one year later. Yashin's spectacular play for his nation and club had by then long passed into the collective imagination and historical narrative of the game. He had become part of the cultural iconography so crucial to football's global appeal in the modern period.[41]

WOMEN ICONS OF FOOTBALL

As women's football has grown in popularity in recent decades and their own version of a FIFA-sponsored football World Cup has been established, they, too, have in some instances become cultural icons and sporting archetypes. For example, Abby Wambach of the United States has been one of the most dominant players of the last generation. She retired from international play shortly after the successful US run to win the tournament in 2015, a competition in which she did not star but was still a very forceful presence. She left the international game with an impressive record. In addition to the world title from 2015, she was a crucial part of two Olympic-winning teams from 2004 and 2012. She was injured for the 2008 games. Olympic women's football, unlike the men's version, tends to involve the very best players and teams from around the world and, for that reason, serves as a type of "second" global championship.

Wambach scored an impressive 184 goals for her country, more than any other man or woman in international competition.[42] Her style of play, too, won admirers and created detractors. She was a big, physical presence at the top of any US formation and scored many of her best goals with her head. Wambach was fearless in the air and around the penalty box and sometimes seemed to overwhelm players with her size and strength. On set pieces—corner and free kicks—everyone knew that she was always a target. Her ability to play with her back to goal and create chances for herself and teammates set her apart from just about every other player in women's global football. Yet, those exact same qualities did not enamor Wambach with everyone in the women's game. Her dominance sometimes seemed to come too easily. Her physical advantages were perhaps too great. Those detractors tended to underestimate the courage, determination, skill, and effort she brought to the game.[43]

Wambach also presented a different type of cultural icon. Openly gay, she had a very public relationship with Sarah Huffman, to whom she was married from 2013 to 2016. After winning the 2015 Women's World Cup in Canada, she went over to Huffman, who was sitting in the crowd, and "whispered, 'I did it, we did it. Kiss me.'"[44] When the victorious US women's team visited, as was customary, the White House on October 27, 2015, President Barack Obama commented that she had not only set an example to young women aspiring to be football stars but to men and women everywhere. The president

Abby Wambach, 2015 (*Wikimedia Commons, Noah Salzman*)

said that she was "a world champion at last, draped in the Stars and Stripes, showing us all how far we've come—on and off the field—by sharing a celebratory kiss with her wife."[45] Unfortunately, the relationship ended in divorce not long after Wambach was arrested for driving under the influence of alcohol. She chose to go public about several addiction problems. In interviews, she was candid about how she had struggled with the rigors and pressure of playing football at its highest level and had begun using prescription painkillers and then became dependent upon them. Further, she said that she had turned to alcohol as well, in order to cope with depression. Eventually, she was caught in a cycle of addiction. Football fans, especially the legions of young women who have admired her, have had to digest all of the news about Wambach that has become known. Her forthrightness and honesty were the primary focus as she went through a very public ordeal. But the same powers that help create cultural icons in the world of football—newspaper reports, television coverage, internet sites, and social media—can sometimes also turn against a player as prominent as Wambach and begin to question her status as a cultural icon and possible role model for the game of football. Recently, however, Wambach made a successful public return and began offering commentary on football and the US women's national team in the run-up to the 2019 World Cup in France. Her legacy within the history of women's football seems secure.

A very different type of women's football archetype is Marta Vieira da Silva, known, according to the Brazilian custom, simply as Marta. Standing a diminutive five foot three, she is largely regarded as the most skillful female player in the world of the last generation. Often referred to as the female Pelé, Marta is known for her dribbling skills, pace, and quick and incisive understanding of the game. She started playing with the Brazilian national team and for several professional clubs at the age of seventeen and has been a fixture internationally since the 2003 Women's World Cup. She has played a central and attacking role for various Brazilian sides through a variety of international matches, including the 2007, 2011, 2015, and 2019 World Cups and various Olympic competitions. She has also played professionally in Sweden, Brazil, and the United States.

Marta's position in international women's football has been secured through a number of dynamic performances. She has competed in five World Cups (United States 2003, China 2007, Germany 2011, Canada 2015, and France 2019) and four Olympic Games (Athens 2004, Beijing 2008, London 2012, and Rio de Janeiro 2016). Among her most famous exploits is the 2007 semifinal match against the United States at the World Cup in China. In a game that the Brazilians dominated and won, 4–0, Marta was the central player and scored in the seventy-ninth minute what is largely regarded as one of the best goals by a woman. Using a variety of skills and moves, she outmaneuvered two American defenders before putting the ball past Brianna Scurry, the well-regarded American goalkeeper. It was the type of goal that has become legend in women's football history. It has also become part of the spectacle of the game, a goal that demonstrated the ability of one of the

Marta, 2014 (*Jean-Philippe Ksiazek/Getty*)

game's foremost players at the top of her game. Marta's reputation as a supreme talent has only grown since that time, and her services at the club level have been sought out by some of the best women's teams in the world.

Unfortunately, her spectacular career has also pointed out some of the limitations of the women's game even in the early twenty-first century. Although she has often been joined by a number of talented teammates, such as Formiga, Pretinha, and Cristiane, on Brazilian national teams, Marta has not been able to win any World Cup or Olympic titles during her remarkable career. She has risen to the status of cultural icon in the women's game globally but has not received the type of support from her home football association that is enjoyed by Wambach and her US teammates. The national team has not always been funded at a level that would allow it to train and compete at the highest level of women's international football. For example, the team has not always played enough "friendly" matches with other top-notch women's sides to keep its competitive momentum or to bring its talented individuals together to cohere as a unit. Thus, Brazil's women's team, with Marta as its iconic player, produces sometimes excellent and sometimes sub-standard results at the international level.[46]

The cultural and sporting legacy of a player like Marta is at least partially conditioned by gender stereotypes. In countries such as Brazil, Argentina, Italy, and Spain, football is still often regarded primarily as a male domain. Thus, the national teams from these and other lands sometimes struggle to find funding, sponsorship, and even acclaim at home, even as some of their star players, such as Marta, do much to expand the popularity and to add to the spectacle and marketability of women's football globally. On the other hand, there have clearly been breakthrough moments in the history of women's football, even in places where the game is still seen as a bastion of masculinity. In the 2007 Pan-American Games held in Rio de Janeiro, for example, Marta and her Brazilian teammates, having had the appropriate preparation for the competition, went undefeated. They put on an offensive display that thrilled fans of the women's game. During the competition, Marta scored twelve goals and was compared in the same breath with great male Brazilian players of the past, such as Pelé, Zico, and Romario. Perhaps most important of all, Brazil won the tournament in the Maracanã Stadium, the cathedral of Brazilian football, before 67,788 fans, proving that there was a popular base of support and interest in the women's game in the country. Nevertheless, finding the right combination of funding and infrastructure for women footballers, local clubs, and the national team has remained elusive in Brazil, even as the iconic position of a player like Marta has only been solidified in recent years. After losing in the 2019 Women's World Cup, she delivered an inspirational message to the next generation of female football players: "There's not going to be a Marta forever. Women's football depends upon you [young girls] to survive. So think about it. Value it more. Cry in the beginning so you can smile in the end."[47]

Many other women players have achieved breakthrough status in the years since 1991, when the FIFA Women's World Cup of football became an international fixture. Carli Lloyd of the United States has become known as a clutch player for her ability to score big-time goals in crucial matches, such as at the 2008 and 2012 Olympic Games and the 2015 tournament in Canada. In the final of that last competition against Japan, she scored a historic hat trick, including a goal from midfield. Mia Hamm, another American player, was a highly gifted forward—she scored 158 international goals—on the successful US teams of the 1990s and early 2000s and became well known internationally. Homare Sawa of Japan was one of the most influential players in the women's game. She was especially noted for her positioning and use of passing to open up space on the pitch. She played for over two decades (1993–2015) for her country's national team. Moreover, all of the women's players discussed in the chapter on gender and the development of the game—Alex Morgan, Louisa Nécib, and Lotta Schelin, for example—have gained international recognition, advanced the women's game considerably, and played the role of cultural icons either within their respective countries or at the international level. As with the men's game, a whole new generation of women players from many different countries—Nigeria, Cameroon, Ivory Coast, Denmark, Germany, Spain, Italy, Sweden, the Netherlands, Norway,

France, China, Japan, Argentina, Brazil, Chile, Colombia, Canada, England, Australia, and the United States, to name but a few examples—are influencing the development of the game, the way it is viewed as a sporting spectacle, and its aesthetic and artistic place in sporting culture. Hopefully support for women's teams throughout the world will continue to grow to allow their current and future players to contribute even more significantly to the game of football. The women's World Cup, the primary place where all of these developments are on display, is far younger than the men's version, but it has the same capacity to generate compelling sporting and historical narratives and cultural icons of the game.

CONCLUSION

In many respects it is easier to measure the political and economic impact of the sustained growth and global place of football's World Cup than it is to analyze its effect as a spectacle and cultural force. Nevertheless, it is important for both the sports and world historian to acknowledge and attempt to get at the aesthetic, artistic, and iconic aspects of the world's most popular sport. For many fans and casual observers alike, the most fundamental aspect of the game is watching it and appreciating the images, both temporary and permanent, that it creates. Much of our experience of the game comes through elemental senses—sight and sound—and therefore our most fixed notions of great players and games come to us from the era of television, in which those elements can be fixed, shared, and consumed by a truly global audience on a recurring basis. In the age of YouTube and the Internet, the most casual fan and the most serious scholar can look up footage of a young Pelé at the 1958 tournament in Sweden, or Maradona making his slalom run against England in Mexico in 1986, or Abby Wambach scoring a header in the 122nd minute against Brazil in the 2011 women's tournament in Germany. The images are there for anyone to view and analyze. Over time, perhaps more film and photographs of great players from the first half of the twentieth century and earlier World Cups will emerge and add images of those players to the iconic moments that have helped define the spectacle and history of the game of football.

Football has given us several recognizable and iconic players with whom fans can identify and whom scholars can analyze. There has been the brilliant all-around and supremely gifted athlete, Pelé; the ultra-talented and controversial master technician, Maradona; the cerebral iconoclast, who bends and wills himself into the flow of a great team, Cruyff; the cool-headed general who manages and marshals his side's defense and helps mount offensive moves from the back of the pitch, Moore; the physical, fearless, gender-challenging central attacker, Wambach; and the magically gifted, instinctive player who is not fully appreciated by her home fans, Marta. Yashin is the stalwart individual, who through strength, positioning, and sheer reflex stands alone to stop oncoming and on-rushing attacks.

All of these sporting characterizations can, of course, border on stereotypes and even caricature and would then be less valuable for scholarly analysis. But these players' World Cup performances, as shown in televised images, have helped create a common iconography of the game that has provided it with a global historical narrative. These players' status as sporting and cultural icons has created common points of reference for fans, officials, organizers, and commentators throughout the history of the World Cup, especially in the last fifty years of its existence as television broadcasting has become so central to the way sports are presented. It is not a coincidence, for example, that Pelé, because of his brilliance on the pitch and his position off of it, has become an unofficial ambassador of the game and makes an appearance of one type or another at virtually every World Cup and major football tournament. His image, his iconic status, immediately connects the current spectacle, the current iteration of a global tournament, with its history in a deep and personal sense. The best current example of an iconic player who links the past and present of the game is Lionel Messi of Argentina, who has the dribbling skills of Maradona and the grace of Pelé.

Lionel Messi, 2017 (*soccer.ru*)

The analysis of any sport cannot, therefore, be separated from the fundamental fact that it is a spectacle that has been represented in a broad range of images. This is especially true of football's World Cup, because it has reached a worldwide audience that allows a global conversation to take place about the meanings of the game, its players, and their cultural images. This quality of the sport—the fact that the spectacle being played out cannot be separated from the reactions of fans and viewers—has contributed greatly to the experience of consuming football as well. The history of the competition is intertwined with witnessing or experiencing the sights and sounds of the game. This is true whether or not the competition lives up to the spectacular expectations sometimes placed upon it. There have been many dismal World Cup moments. However, the anticipation that something dramatic might happen and become fixed as an image in the history of the game has drawn fans to live matches around the world. It has caused national committees and organizers to construct vast new stadia to host games. These places, these playing sites, have in turn also become part of the spectacle of the game. For some fans of the game there is an almost religious aspect to making a trip, a pilgrimage, to one of football's global cathedrals, such as the Maracanã in Rio de Janeiro, Wembley Stadium in London, or the San Siro in Milan, all of which have hosted World Cup games and many other notable matches. These sites, as places where some of the meaning of the game, its history, has been established, must be included in the narrative of world football.

Attending a World Cup match in person, to be in a crowd, is also part of experiencing football as a sporting spectacle. While one might need the tools of the social psychologist or cultural anthropologist to understand fully the effect of a sporting crowd to produce a range of emotions in an individual— elation, disappointment, anxiety, and anger, to name but a few of the more obvious mental states—it is clear that the crowd effect is part of the experience. Massive numbers of people gathered together heightens the tension of the game and adds to the sights and sounds of the spectacle. One can feel very much among one's peers or one's national group *or* as an outsider in hostile territory. The crowd amplifies and solidifies the sense of identity of the fans in the stadium. It is seemingly easy, at least for the duration of the game, to know who one is and to know who the "other" is. One wears common colors, carries banners announcing one's identity, shouts well-rehearsed slogans, sings well-known songs, and stands together at key moments or for the duration of the game. The opposition is dressed in the wrong colors, holds perhaps provocative signs, sings its own songs, and is loud and demonstrative at the wrong moments in the game. All fans are consuming the matches as sporting spectacles, but they do not consume them in the same way. Of course, in the history of world football this crowd effect has sometimes had negative consequences and spilled over into open confrontations and even violence, as emotions were called forth and the us-versus-them dynamic grew to a breaking point. These moments, or encounters of footballing confrontation, have been more prominent and obvious at the club level, where long histories and rivalries have provided the background and context for open antagonism. But they are not unknown to the World Cup and have been a part of its footballing landscape since its inaugural matches in 1930. Thankfully, more often than not the effect of the crowd, while ramping up fans' emotions and greatly influencing the way they experience matches, has been held relatively in check during most World Cup matches. Violence has indeed occurred, but it has not been the hallmark of the tournaments, and many have come off without severe confrontations.[48]

The crowd effect in football does have good aspects to it as well. The displays and demonstrations of national identity can be celebratory and good-natured and therefore appealing to fans from other nations. Some fans who do not have a team in the competition will adopt and follow a side depending on its display on the field or the sympathy it might generate. It used to be said that Brazil was every fan's second team—after one's own national side—because it supposedly played the best version of the so-called beautiful game, and its fans always seemed to be enjoying the spectacle. Indeed, the image of the Brazilian fans traveling to the global tournaments was of samba music and constant dancing. In recent years, that image has faded somewhat as the Brazilian team has not fared that well at World Cup tournaments, and other national teams have played football with equal flare. In general, there are at least as many fans who react positively to the effect of the crowd as those who engage in aggressive and even violent behavior. Even more remarkable are the moments when fans gain appreciation for the opposing teams in a World Cup match. At times, the display put on or the spectacle created by a given team simply captures the imagination of most if not all of the fans in a crowd or stadium.

World football's ability to create spectacular moments to draw in fans, commentators, and scholars alike helps us to understand football's global standing and its historical narrative. Players and matches, images and moments, can all be captured and presented to massive audiences, whether they are in-person crowds, television viewers, or Internet devotees. A common global visual and mental vocabulary is thereby generated that helps weave together an understanding of the game's place in social and cultural terms. This vocabulary, built up over several decades, allows one to discuss across generations and national borders the meaning of football in a world historical context. Cultural icons can be viewed by fans from numerous settings and time periods as points of historical reference, as part of a connective tissue that gives the game its worldwide appeal. These iconographic images and moments cover a wide spectrum of possibilities, from the spectacular athletic performance to the fallen hero. Generations of fans can interpret and reinterpret them. They help make football and the World Cup part of a global historical narrative.

The spectacle of World Cup football is therefore connected to several key world historical developments in the modern era. Through fans attending games in person at stadia and watching them on television or other media, football has created a community of global viewers with common reference points to famous players, teams, matches, and tournaments. The revolution in information technology has been instrumental in this community-building process because it has made sharing the images of star players and dramatic performances much easier in recent decades. Indeed, as we saw above, many players from earlier generations have not entered into the global historical narrative of world football because they competed and left their mark on the game before the advent of television and the Internet. They are, unfortunately, not as well known to the global football community. The creation of iconic football players in the modern period is also similar to the cult of celebrity that has developed in the entertainment and political worlds in the modern period. Athletic showcases, such as the World Cup, create the opportunity for some players to be recognized globally and become sporting icons. Thus, football has been woven into the cultural fabric of modern society.

DOCUMENTS AND ARTIFACTS RELATED TO THE SPECTACLE OF THE WORLD CUP

A. Centenario Stadium. https://www.stadiumguide.com/centenario

1. Use this site to understand more about the design and architecture of the Centenario Stadium in Montevideo, Uruguay.
2. Use the site to navigate to information about other world stadia used in World Cup competitions.

B. FIFA, Statistics. Statistics on every World Cup held since 1930, including attendance figures. https://www.fifa.com/worldcup/statistics

1. Use this FIFA site to find attendance of World Cup matches throughout the history of the tournament. How has attendance grown from the 1930s to the present?
2. From this site, how do you think that FIFA attempts to present and capture the spectacle of world football and its iconic players in images and text? In your opinion, how successful is this presentation?

C. President Richard Nixon meeting with Pelé, National Archives, 194508. https://www.docsteach.org/documents/document/president-nixon-meet ing-with-edson-pele-arantes-do-nacimento-retired-professional-brazilian -soccer-player-and-director-of-the-international-soccer-program-spon sored-by-pepsico-pele-autographs-a-soccer

1. What was the global reputation of Pelé at the time of this photo? To what degree do you think that he had already attained iconic status?
2. What political advantage do you think Richard Nixon hoped to gain by meeting with one of global football's stars?

D. *Diego Maradona*, a documentary film by Asif Kapadia, 2019. http://www .altitudefilment.com/film/sales/32/maradona

1. What is the presentation of Diego Maradona in this film?
2. How does this film attempt to deal with both sides of Maradona's football career? His superstar status? His image as a fallen idol?

E. Abby Wambach, "From Where I Stand," July 20, 2016. http://www.un women.org/en/news/stories/2016/7/from-where-i-stand-abby-wambach

1. What image of herself is Abby Wambach presenting in this statement?
2. What issues about the state of women's football in 2016 does Wambach raise?

SUGGESTIONS FOR FURTHER READING AND RESEARCH

Andersson, Torbjörn. "Swedish Football Hooliganism, 1900–1939." *Soccer and Society* 2, no. 1 (2001): 1–18.

Archetti, Eduardo. "Argentinian Football: A Ritual of Violence?" *The International Journal of the History of Sport* 9, no. 2 (1992): 209–35.

Arlt, Roberto. "Soccer and Popular Joy." In *The Argentina Reader*, edited by Gabriela Nouzellis and Graciela Montaldo. Durham, NC: Duke University Press, 2002.

Armstrong, Gary, and Richard Giulianotti, eds. *Football Cultures and Identities*. London: Macmillan, 1999.

Bale, John, and J. A. Maguire, eds. *The Global Sports Arena*. London: Frank Cass, 1994.

Bondy, Filip. *The World Cup: The Players, Coaches, History, and Excitement*. New York: Mallard Press, 1991.

Brown, Adam, ed. *Fanatics! Power, Identity, and Fandom in Football*. London: Routledge, 1998.

Burns, Jimmy. *The Hand of God: The Life of Diego Maradona*. London: Bloomsbury, 1998.

Castron, Ruy. *Garrincha: The Triumph and Tragedy of Football's Forgotten Footballing Hero*. London: Yellow Jersey Press, 2004.

Cheeseman, Doug, and Peter Robinson. *This Is Soccer: Images of World Cup USA 94*. London: Gollancz, 1994.

Clarkson, Wensley. *Ronaldo! Twenty-One Years of Genius and 90 Minutes That Shook the World*. London: Blake Publishing, 1998.

Edelman, Robert. *Serious Fun: A History of Spectator Sports in the USSR*. Cambridge: Cambridge University Press, 1993.

Finn, Gerry, and Richard Giulianotti, eds. *Football Culture: Local Contests, Global Visions*. London: Frank Cass, 2000.

Frankl, Walter. "Erinnerungen an Hakoah Wien, 1909–1939." *Bulletin des Leo Baeck Instituts* 64 (1983): 55–84.

Giulianotti, Richard, Norman Bonney, and Mike Hepworth, eds. *Football, Violence, and Social Identity*. London: Routledge, 1994.

Holt, Richard, J. A. Mangan, and Pierre Lanfranchi. *European Heroes: Myth, Identity, Sport*. London: Frank Cass, 1996.

Horak, Roman, and Wolfgang Maderthaner. "A Culture of Urban Cosmopolitanism: Uridil and Sindelar as Viennese Coffee-House Heroes." In *European Heroes: Myth, Identity, Sport*, edited by Richard Holt et al. London: Frank Cass, 1996.

Inglis, Simon. *The Football Grounds of Europe*. London: Willow Books, 1990.

Jenkins, Garry. *The Beautiful Team: In Search of Pelé and the 1970 Brazilians*. London: Simon and Schuster, 1999.

Johnes, Martin. "'Heads in the Sand': Football, Politics, and Crowd Disasters in Twentieth-Century Britain." *Soccer and Society* 5, no. 2 (2004): 134–51.

Lineker, Gary, and Stan Hey. *Gary Lineker's Golden Boots: The World Cup's Greatest Strikers, 1930 to 1998*. London: Hodder and Stoughton, 1998.

Luschen, Gunther, ed. *Cross-Cultural Analysis of Sports and Games*. Champaign, IL: Stipes Publishing, 1970.

Mangan, J. A. *Athleticism in the Victorian and Edwardian Public School: The Emergence and Consolidation of an Educational Ideology*. London: Falmer Press, 1986.

———. *Freeing the Female Body: Inspirational Icons*. London: Frank Cass, 2001.

Miller, David. *Cup Magic*. London: Sidgwick and Jackson, 1981.

Murphy, Patrick, John Williams, and Eric Dunning. *Football on Trial: Spectator Violence and Development in the Football World*. London: Routledge, 1990.

Palmer, Jon. *Superstars of the World Cup*. Clifton, UK: Parragon, 1998.

Pelé. *The Pelé Albums: Selections from Public and Private Collections Celebrating the Soccer Career of Pelé*. Sydney: Weldon, 1990.

Podalsky, Laura. *Specular City: Transforming Culture, Consumption, and Space in Buenos Aires, 1955–1973*. Philadelphia: Temple University Press, 2004.

Risoli, Mario. *When Pelé Broke Our Hearts: Wales and the 1958 World Cup*. Cardiff, UK: Ashley Drake, 1998.

Spaaij, Ramon, and Carles Vinas. "Passion, Politics, and Violence: A Socio-Historical Analysis of Spanish Ultras." *Soccer and Society* 6, no. 1 (2005): 79–96.

Sugden, John, and Alan Tomlinson. *Hosts and Champions: Soccer Cultures, National Identities, and the USA World Cup*. Aldershot, UK: Arena, 1994.

Taylor, Rogan, and Klara Jamrich. *Puskás on Puskás: The Life and Times of a Footballing Legend*. London: Robson Books, 1997.

Winner, David. *Brilliant Orange: The Neurotic Genius of Dutch Football*. London: Bloomsbury, 2000.

NOTES

1. Football's World Cup is also a "megaevent," a phenomenon of the modern era that has been studied at length recently. Other obvious megaevents would include the Olympic Games and world expositions or fairs. See Maurice Roche, *Megaevents and Modernity: Olympics and Expos in the Growth of Global Culture* (London: Taylor and Francis, 2002).

2. Simon Inglis, *The Football Grounds of Europe* (London: Willow Books, 1990). On Asian and African stadia and their role as cathedrals of the game, see Tamir Bar-On, *The World through Soccer: The Cultural Impact of a Global Sport* (Lanham, MD: Rowman & Littlefield, 2014). Chapter 5 is on football as a pagan religion.

3. Bill Murray, *The World's Game: A History of Soccer* (Urbana: University of Illinois Press, 1998), 62–64.

4. Andreas Campomar, *Golazo! The Beautiful Game from the Aztecs to the World Cup: The Complete History of How Soccer Shaped Latin America* (New York: Riverhead Books, 2014), 211–23.

5. William Schomberg, "No Regrets for Zico over New, Smaller Maracanã," Reuters, reuters.com, June 16, 2014.

6. The tragedy at Hillsborough Stadium in Sheffield on April 15, 1989, had many causes, including poor crowd control by the police, creating penned-in areas of the terraces, and constructing steel fencing at the edge of the pitch to prevent fan invasions. The Hillsborough terraces at the north end of the stadium were already full when more fans were suddenly allowed into the grounds as the match between Liverpool and Nottingham Forest was about to begin. Fans were accustomed to believing that more space could be found on the terraces where they could stand. At Hillsborough, this was tragically not the case, and ninety-six people were killed and 766 were injured. The event was one important spark toward the use of all-seater stadia.

7. Franklin Foer, *How Soccer Explains the World: An Unlikely Theory of Globalization* (New York: Harper Perennial, 2010), 115–40.

8. stadiumdb.com.

9. Rohan Banerjee and Adam Shergold, "Suicide Attacks near Stade de France," dailymail.com, November 13, 2015.

10. William D. Bowman, "Hakoah Vienna and the International Nature of Interwar Austrian Sports," *Central European History* 44 (December 2011): 642–68.

11. See chapter 3, table 3.1 for World Cup attendance figures.

12. See, for example, Steve Redhead, *Post-Fandom and the Millennial Blues* (London: Routledge, 1997); Daniel L. Wann et al., *Sport Fans: The Psychology and Social Impact of Spectators* (New York: Routledge, 2001); and Adam C. Earnheardt, Paul M. Haridakis, and Barbara S. Hugenberg, eds., *Sports Fans, Identity, and Socialization* (Lanham, MD: Lexington Books, 2012).

13. On the phenomenon of hooliganism, hard-core fans, and their activities, see Gary Armstrong, *Football Hooligans: Knowing the Score* (Oxford: Berg, 1998).

14. David Goldblatt, *The Ball Is Round: A Global History of Soccer* (New York: Riverhead Books, 2008), 543–45.

15. Bill Buford, *Among the Thugs* (New York: Vintage, 1993), passim.

16. Gary Jenkins, *The Beautiful Team: In Search of Pelé and the 1970 Brazilians* (London: Simon and Schuster, 1999), 125. Over the course of a long playing and public career, Pelé has also experienced problems. In 1970, the Brazilian military dictatorship investigated him for his political views. He had a very open argument with Brazilian football officials and FIFA in 1993 and 1994, and he has sometimes been criticized in his native country for not being sympathetic to domestic protests.

17. Jenkins, *The Beautiful Team*.

18. An ITV television crew commenting on the 1970 World Cup had the following exchange: Malcolm Allison, "How do you spell Pelé?" Pat Crerand, "Easy, G-O-D." Jenkins, *The Beautiful Team*, 167.

19. FIFA.com.

20. C. L. R James, *Beyond a Boundary* (Durham, NC: Duke University Press, 1993), is a brilliant study of cricket. It is often cited as one of the best books on sports history ever written.

21. Pelé, *The Pelé Albums: Selections from Public and Private Collections Celebrating the Soccer Career of Pelé* (Sydney: Weldon, 1990).

22. See, for example, "Goal of the Century," cnn.com.

23. Sam Howe Verhovek, "World Cup '94: After Second Test, Maradona Is out of World Cup," *New York Times*, nytimes.com, July 1, 1994.

24. Jimmy Burns, *The Hand of God: The Life of Diego Maradona* (London: Bloomsbury, 1998).

25. As quoted in Burns, *Hand of God*, 243.

26. Matt Dickinson, *Bobby Moore: The Man in Full* (London: Yellow Jersey Press, 2014).

27. Hans Blickendörfer, *Der Kaiser: Die Franz Beckenbauer Story* (Munich: Südwest, 1991).

28. David Clay Large, *Nazi Games: The Olympics of 1936* (New York: W. W. Norton, 2007), 227–94.

29. Kenneth L. Shropshire, *In Black and White: Race and Sports in America* (New York: New York University Press, 1996).

30. Johan Cruyff, *My Turn: A Life of Total Football* (New York: Nation Books, 2016).

31. See, for example, David Winner, *Brilliant Orange: The Neurotic Genius of Dutch Football* (London: Bloomsbury, 2000); and Sanjeev Shetty, *Total Football: A Graphic History of the World's Most Iconic Soccer Tactics* (London: Aurum Press, 2018).

32. As quoted in Winner, *Brilliant Orange,* 46.

33. Cruyff, *My Turn*.

34. Cruyff himself claimed that his father told him about great players of the 1950s, such as Alfredo di Stefano, also of Real Madrid, who "understood everything about how to use space on the pitch." Cruyff, *My Turn*, 4.

35. Rogan Taylor and Klara Jamrich, *Puskás on Puskás: The Life and Times of a Footballing Legend* (London: Robson Books, 1997).

36. Roman Horak and Wolfgang Maderthaner, "A Culture of Urban Cosmopolitanism: Uridil and Sindelar as Viennese Coffee-House Heroes," in *European Heroes: Myth, Identity, and Sport*, Richard Holt et al., ed. (London: Frank Cass, 1996).

37. Horak and Maderthaner, "A Culture of Urban Cosmopolitanism," 147.

38. Goldblatt, *The Ball Is Round*, 401.

39. Patrick Jennings, "Yashin," BBC, bbc.co.uk, June 7, 2018.

40. FIFA.com.

41. Patrick Jennings, "Lev Yashin: Bullet-Maker to Ballon d'Or—The Man Who Reinvented Goalkeeping," BBC, bbc.com, June 8, 2018.

42. Wambach's record may be broken soon by Christine Sinclair of Canada, who is still playing for her national team and has scored over 180 goals in international matches.

43. Abby Wambach, *Forward: A Memoir* (New York: Dey Street, 2016).

44. Wambach, *Forward*, 158.

45. SBNation.com, October 27, 2015.

46. FIFA.com.

47. Roger Gonzalez, "Women's World Cup 2019: Brazil's Marta Delivers Inspirational Speech for Next Generation of Women's Soccer," CBS Sports, cbssports.com, June 24, 2019.

48. Hooliganism and violence were not widely apparent, for example, at the 2018 World Cup in Russia, as the police cracked down on possible instigators, both before and during the competition. Officials had feared violent outbreaks, such as those that occurred at the European Championship in France in 2016. On the other hand, violence comes in many forms. Reports out of England in 2018 claimed that when the national team played, win or lose, domestic violence spiked dramatically. See, for example, Vicky Spratt, "The Truth about Domestic Violence and the World Cup," BBC, bbc.co.uk, July 5, 2018, which cites rates of domestic violence in England rising by as much as 38 percent when England lost a World Cup match.

Conclusion

With the examination of football as sporting spectacle, we have come full circle. We started with a consideration of the deep cultural roots for the game of football by noting the numerous global settings for kicking and ball games. We also noted that the culture of English public schools gave rise to modern football in the second half of the nineteenth century. A game that was supposed to train and civilize Britain's elite quickly spread abroad to the European continent and overseas through the networks of formal and informal empire. Furthermore, in a matter of a few decades, football became a mass sport played before large audiences in organized leagues and in international competitions. The nexus supporting football—audiences, competitions, tournaments, advertising and publications, newspaper reporting—continued to grow throughout the early decades of the twentieth century, and soon football became the world's game.

Against this background, a global tournament, the World Cup, was organized and has become one of the world's premier sporting and marketing events. Football's ability to appeal to a broad spectrum of people has contributed to its spread and global status. The sights and sounds of the spectacle, the participation of the crowd and the ambience of the stadium, the ebb and flow of the game itself, and the attachment to iconic players, images, and moments in the history of the sport have all added to its popularity and position in various global contexts. The spectacle of the sport cannot be divorced from its history.

In addition, our look at the World Cup of football has led us into an examination of modern politics, economics, and race and gender relations, all of which are crucial elements of our contemporary world. From the beginning, football's fortunes have been intertwined with a host of political considerations. For example, the creation of the global tournament as such was a partial recognition that the sport had become an international phenomenon by the 1920s and '30s. The wrangling and behind-the-scenes discussions that went on and go on about the locations for such events reveal much about global relations at any given time. The organization and staging of a global tournament provide a myriad of opportunities for a nation or region to make political statements. Uruguay felt it was announcing itself to the world when it hosted the first competition in 1930. There was a certain confidence about the country's past—its one hundred years of existence—and its future. The fact that the affair was relatively small compared to later events and that Uruguay would not be able to assert itself politically for most of the rest of the twentieth century should not distract us from the motivations that informed its decision to pursue sponsoring the tournament in the first place. Throughout the second chapter of *The World Cup as World History*, we saw how local, regional, and international politics shaped the development of modern football. Our analysis of football as a sport, therefore, has deepened our understanding of contemporary global politics.

Moreover, economic developments and football have been linked in the history of the World Cup since its inception. From the outset, individuals and national organizations had to be concerned about the cost of staging a global sporting event. Initially, sponsoring the tournament was not a lucrative undertaking and the governments of Uruguay in 1930 and Italy in 1934 had to find funds to help make the earliest Cups financially possible. Nevertheless, the popularity of the sport, its ability to draw paying crowds and to hold people's attention and curiosity, were clearly evident in the 1930s. Indeed, the success of football at the Olympic Games in 1924 and 1928 had been one of the economic factors that prompted football's organizations and FIFA to create a global competition to stand on its own.

After the financial disruption of the Second World War, the tournament was reestablished and began to show its true economic potential. Audiences for the competition grew, and television helped the World Cup take on new global dimensions. Between 1958 and 1970, coverage of the tournament grew markedly. The advent of techniques such as color broadcasting, slow motion, and replay technology only added to the game's appeal. Matches could be enjoyed with simultaneous broadcasts and dissected endlessly by commentators and fans. The visual appeal of the game, including its capturing of sporting and cultural icons at play, kept on expanding in the period after 1970. More and more broadcasters and television outlets have been added to cover every tournament, including Brazil 2014 and Russia 2018.

As television broadcasting approached the point of saturated coverage of the World Cup, advertising of the event grew and grew. Companies found a lucrative partner in FIFA, with which they could push their global brands. Coca-Cola's contract with the world organizing body of football is a case in point, but many multinational corporations used the global tournament to expand their share of the world market and to create greater name recognition. Indeed, the dramatic growth of the tournament cannot be separated from its economic sponsors, especially corporate sponsors. Unfortunately, the huge sums of money associated with football's most significant world event have often had a corrupting influence on those charged with organizing and maintaining the tournament. FIFA's success at creating an economic juggernaut has come at the price of subverting many of its basic principles and turning its members into greedy functionaries hoping to drink from the financial trough.

Analyzing the World Cup has also proven to be a useful vehicle for understanding global race and gender relations. The economic growth of the tournament was due in part to its expanding to include more teams from Africa and Asia in particular. The breakthroughs here were slow in coming. The first real success by an African nation, for example, was Cameroon's excellent showing in 1990 in Italy. Be that as it may, the tournament today is unthinkable without the participation of numerous teams from around the globe. It is no longer the preserve of European and South American nations. This expansion in the tournament has come largely as a result of the process of decolonization and the creation of new nation-states in Africa and Asia in the post–Second World War era. It has also come about because of the political and economic pressure applied by these new countries within their continental football organizations and within FIFA itself. The growth in the number of teams in the World Cup, set to rise to forty-eight in 2026, has literally changed the face of the tournament. Teams from Cameroon, Nigeria, Ghana, Ivory Coast, Senegal, South Korea, Japan, and several other countries have had good results and even spectacular individual performances during the matches. Players from around the globe have displayed their talents during the tournament and become attractive to professional leagues worldwide. This development, too, has further internationalized football in recent decades. The increasing number of players from African and Asian countries has changed the racial and ethnic composition of the World Cup and made it, in terms of nationality, a highly inclusive competition. At the same time, the mere presence of a wide diversity of players from numerous nations does not necessarily mean that discussions of race and ethnicity have advanced that far. Racial and even racist assumptions about players still persist. Sports may help to advance racial and ethnic diversity in a global setting, but there is also much resistance to such social and cultural change.

Equally complex in terms of racial awareness and understanding has been the changing composition of various squads. French teams, for example, had a relatively rich ethnic diversity of players early in the tournament, but that does not mean that French society has overcome or even fully dealt with the issue of race and racism. Indeed, the history of the 1998 World Cup–winning side shows that these issues were still very much alive in a country such as France. That team and its role in a global sporting event helped drive a discussion of difficult social and cultural issues. That the discussion is ongoing in France and that its outcome is unknown is hardly surprising and is characteristic of race relations throughout much of the world. Sports can help raise issues about race and racism, but they will clearly not settle them on their own.

Gender relations and the World Cup are equally complex topics. Women's participation in football has grown astronomically in recent decades. In the first half of the twentieth century, women were often discouraged from playing football on an organized basis and found little institutional support for their involvement in the game. Things began to change after the Second World War and dramatically so in the 1960s and '70s, with the rise of global feminism. More young women were given athletic opportunities in general, more international football contests were held, and gradually the formation of a FIFA-sponsored women's tournament took place in 1991. In the last few decades, that competition has become a showcase for women's football and helped solidify their place in the world's game. The introduction and maintenance of women's professional leagues around the globe remains problematic, however. In the United States, for example, where the national team has managed to win four World Cups and several Olympic titles, no fewer than three professional club leagues have been established, with two of them folding in the last twenty-five years. European leagues, in Germany and Sweden, have shown more stability in recent years, even if the crowds they draw to matches remain relatively modest. In some instances, men's clubs have sponsored women's parallel sides, which have helped the latter. The development of women's club football around the globe will be an interesting phenomenon to watch, going forward. Growth and stability are the goals in women's domestic football, and a number of countries are using a variety of models of ownership, sponsorship, and audience appeal to try to achieve them.

The future of the women's game is seemingly bright. The level of play has risen dramatically in the last two decades. More national organizations are building and fielding highly competitive sides that can play attractive and attacking football. Genuine national rivalries—United States vs. Canada, Germany vs. France—have already developed. Asian powers, such as Japan, are part of the footballing landscape, and more African and South American teams are showing promise in the women's game. The women's tournament should continue to grow and establish itself as a global event. The television money and corporate sponsorships for the women's tournament may never reach those of the men's Cup, but they have grown significantly in the last two decades. In a few countries, such as the United States, the women's tournament is often as popular as the men's version.

Sports historians, however, have analyzed much more than just the growing number of women athletes and competitive events for women. Gender analysis has allowed scholars from a wide variety of fields to discuss topics such as feminine and masculine images, sexuality, ideas about normative behavior, and shifts in all of these categories over time and between cultures. Our examination of modern football, especially in chapters 4 and 5 on gender and sport as spectacle, respectively, has also allowed us to see the way gendered images and concepts have filtered into and been shaped by football and its culture. Certain players, for example, have used their images or had their images used to project notions of masculinity or femininity. The advertising campaigns around Cristiano Ronaldo of Portugal or Alex Morgan of the United States, which emphasize their physical attractiveness, would be two cases in point. Abby Wambach, an openly lesbian player, challenges some people's notions of normative or acceptable sexuality, while opening up positive possibilities about sexual identity for others. Looking at the game of football through the lens of gender analysis provides yet other perspectives on global issues, tendencies, and processes in the contemporary world.

By focusing on one major event, football's foremost sporting tournament, one can understand much about political change, economic moves, race and gender relations, and the place of spectacle and sporting icons in modern culture. These themes, which have provided the backbone for this book, are some of the primary perspectives of sports historians analyzing a major event in a world sport. They are also some of the categories that have most concerned world historians in their work in recent decades. One can bring these two fields—sports and world history—together to show how they have many common points of reference. An analysis of one, sports, can help us to gain insight into the other, world history. Sports in general and football in particular have shown many different sides of globalization over the course of the last two centuries. Football's growth has been linked to such developments as changes in work and labor conditions and the advent of more leisure-time opportunities, especially in Western and developing societies. Dramatic developments in technology—transportation and communication, for example—have also radically transformed the way football is played, watched, branded, and consumed. Indeed, football in the modern era has become one of the world's foremost commodities. Tickets, shirts, television rights, images, players, clubs, and leagues are now all for sale. Football is a global product whose appeal stretches from Argentina to Canada, from Iceland to Turkey, from Egypt to South Africa, and from Israel to Japan.

As a commodity, it can be analyzed to reveal much about global patterns of consumption, marketing, and brand awareness.

As an athletic event, football creates images that have elemental appeal to its fans and help create the great attachment to and fervor for it. The sheer spectacle of the game cannot be separated from an analysis of the global reach of football. The flow of the game, the buildup of play, and the physical encounter on the field are all familiar to fans and analysts around the world, even if they sometimes interpret them differently, often through nationalistic eyes. Football is also a modern sport. It has well-known rules that are internationally recognized and organizations that help coordinate and run a large number of tournaments, including the World Cup. Specialists on the pitch have definite functions, even if the definitions of those functions change over time, and many records of past matches give the sport a firm history among its fans. Football has been rationalized in the contemporary world, which has helped make it a global juggernaut. It has developed along many of the same lines as modern work, industry, and leisure in the last two centuries. Yet, as a sport it still retains much of its elemental appeal. One can be caught up in the emotions of the crowd on game day. Nationalist sentiment can grow and sometimes spill over during a competition. The outcome of the game, even with all of its rules, is never known until the contest is actually played. Football moves between the two poles of rational, almost mathematical predictability—its rules and norms—and the sudden, unpredictable nature of its play, the sheer unknowability of its outcome. This is undoubtedly a large part of its popularity in the modern world.

Analyzing the World Cup of football shows how a sport and its practices are related to recent world history. The political, economic, and cultural aspects of staging, playing, and selling football's premier event are closely related to and intertwined with some of the most important global developments of the nineteenth, twentieth, and early twenty-first centuries. The World Cup of football, a truly global event, is therefore clearly and directly related to the way societies and cultures have developed in the modern era.

Bibliography

Agnew, Paddy. *Forza Italia: A Journey in Search of Italy and Its Football.* London: Ebury Press, 2006.

Akpabot, Samuel Ekpe. *Football in Nigeria.* London: Macmillan, 1985.

Alderman, Liz. "Suicide Bombers Tried to Enter Stadium." *New York Times,* nytimes.com. November 14, 2015.

Alegi, Peter. *African Soccerscapes: How a Continent Changed the World's Game.* Athens: Ohio University Press, 2010.

———. "Football and Apartheid Society: The South African Soccer League, 1960–66." In *Football in Africa: Conflict, Conciliation, and Community,* edited by Gary Armstrong and Richard Giulianotti. London: Palgrave, 2004.

Alegi, Peter, and Chris Bolsmann. *Africa's World Cup: Critical Reflections on Play, Patriotism, Spectatorship, and Space.* Ann Arbor: University of Michigan Press, 2013.

Amnesty International. *Argentina: The Military Juntas and Human Rights.* London: Amnesty International, 1987.

Andersson, Torbjörn. "Swedish Football Hooliganism, 1900–1939." *Soccer and Society* 2, no. 1 (2001): 1–18.

Arbena, Joseph L., ed. *Sport and Society in Latin America: Diffusion, Dependency, and the Rise of Mass Culture.* Westport, CT: Greenwood, 1988.

Archer, Michael. *History of the World Cup.* London: Hamlyn, 1978.

Archetti, Eduardo. "Argentinian Football: A Ritual of Violence?" *The International Journal of the History of Sport* 9, no. 2 (1992): 209–35.

Arlt, Roberto. "Soccer and Popular Joy." In *The Argentina Reader,* edited by Gabriela Nouzellis and Graciela Montaldo. Durham, NC: Duke University Press, 2002.

Armstrong, Gary. *Football Hooligans: Knowing the Score.* Oxford: Berg, 1998.

Armstrong, Gary, and Richard Giulianotti, eds. *Fear and Loathing in World Football.* Oxford: Berg, 2001.

———. *Football Cultures and Identities.* London: Macmillan, 1999.

———. *Football in Africa: Conflict, Conciliation, and Community*. London: Palgrave, 2004.

Ashton, Timothy J. *Soccer in Spain: Politics, Literature, and Film*. Lanham, MD: Scarecrow Press, 2013.

Baade, Robert, and Victor Matheson. "The Quest for the Cup: Assessing the Economic Impact of the World Cup." *Regional Studies* 38 (2004): 341–52.

Back, Les, Tim Crabbe, and John Solomos. *The Changing Face of Football: Racism, Identity and Multiculture in the English Game*. Oxford: Berg, 2001.

Bale, John, and J. A. Maguire, eds. *The Global Sports Arena*. London: Frank Cass, 1994.

Banerjee, Rohan, and Adam Shergold. "Suicide Attacks near Stade de France." daily mail.com. November 13, 2015.

Bar-On, Tamir. *Beyond Soccer: International Relations and Politics as Seen through the Beautiful Game*. Lanham, MD: Rowman & Littlefield, 2017.

———. *The World through Soccer: The Cultural Impact of a Global Sport*. Lanham, MD: Rowman & Littlefield, 2014.

BBC News. "Lionel Messi Tax Fraud Prison Sentence Reduced to Fine." bbc.com. July 7, 2017.

Beller, Steven. *A Concise History of Austria*. Cambridge: Cambridge University Press, 2006.

Bensinger, Ken. *Red Card: FIFA and the Fall of the Most Powerful Men in Sports*. London: Profile Books, 2018.

Blickendörfer, Hans. *Der Kaiser: Die Franz Beckenbauer Story*. Munich: Südwest, 1991.

Bondy, Filip. *The World Cup: The Players, Coaches, History, and Excitement*. New York: Mallard Press, 1991.

Bottenburg, Maartan van. *Global Games*. Urbana: University of Illinois Press, 2001.

Bowman, William D. "Hakoah Vienna and the International Nature of Interwar Austrian Sports." *Central European History* 44 (December 2011): 642–68.

Boyle, Nigel. "Teaching History and Political Economy through Soccer." *Soccer and Society* 18, nos. 2–3 (2017): 407–17.

Brandon, Adam. "World Cup Reorganisation: Freshening Up or Diluting Down?" worldfootballindex.com. April 1, 2017.

Brown, Adam, ed. *Fanatics! Power, Identity, and Fandom in Football*. London: Routledge, 1998.

Buford, Bill. *Among the Thugs*. New York: Vintage, 1993.

Burns, Jimmy. *The Hand of God: The Life of Diego Maradona*. London: Bloomsbury, 1998.

Cahn, Susan K. *Coming on Strong: Gender and Sexuality in Twentieth-Century Women's Sports*. Cambridge, MA: Harvard University Press, 1994.

Campomar, Andreas. *Golazo! The Beautiful Game from the Aztecs to the World Cup: The Complete History of How Soccer Shaped Latin America*. New York: Riverhead Books, 2014.

Cantor, Andrés, and Daniel Arcucci. *Goooal! A Celebration of Soccer*. New York: Simon and Schuster, 1997.

Castron, Ruy. *Garrincha: The Triumph and Tragedy of Football's Forgotten Footballing Hero*. London: Yellow Jersey Press, 2004.

Cheeseman, Doug, and Peter Robinson. *This Is Soccer: Images of World Cup USA 94*. London: Gollancz, 1994.

Chisari, Fabio. "When Football Went Global: Televising the 1966 World Cup." *Historical Social Research* 31, no. 1 (2006): 42–54.

Christian, David. *Big History: Examines Our Past, Explains Our Present, Imagines Our Future*. New York: DK Publishing, 2016.

———. *Maps of Time: An Introduction to Big History*. Berkeley: University of California Press, 2004.

Christian, David, Cynthia Stokes Brown, and Craig Benjamin. *Big History: Between Nothing and Everything*. New York: McGraw-Hill, 2014.

Chyzowych, Walter. *The World Cup*. South Bend, IN: Icarus Press, 1982.

Ciria, Alberto. "From Soccer to War in Argentina: Preliminary Notes on Sports-as-Politics under a Military Regime, 1976–1982." In *Latin America and the Caribbean*, edited by A. R. M. Ritter. Ottawa: Canadian Association for Latin American and Caribbean Studies, 1984.

Clack, Neil. *Animals! Argentina vs. England*. Studley, UK: Know the Score Books, 2010.

Clarkson, Wensley. *Ronaldo! Twenty-One Years of Genius and 90 Minutes That Shook the World*. London: Blake Publishing, 1998.

Clignet, Rémi, and Maureen Stark. "Modernization and the Game of Soccer in Cameroon." *International Review of Sport Sociology* 9, no. 3 (1974): 81–98.

CNA. "Football: FIFA Discussing 48-Team Qatar World Cup, Confirms Infantino." channelnewsasia.com. January 18, 2019.

Conn, David. "World Cup Expansion to 48 Teams Could Happen at Qatar 2022, Says FIFA." *The Guardian*. October 31, 2018. https://www.theguardian.com/football/2018/oct/31/fifa-world-cup-expansion-2022-qatar-infantino.

Corner, Paul. *The Fascist Party and Popular Opinion in Mussolini's Italy*. Oxford: Oxford University Press, 2012.

Corner Kick: The Official Newsletter of the 1999 FIFA Women's World Cup. Los Angeles: FIFA Women's World Cup Organizing Committee, 1999.

Cronin, Mike, and David Mayall. *Sporting Nationalisms: Identity, Ethnicity, Immigration, and Assimilation*. London: Frank Cass, 1998.

Cruyff, Johan. *My Turn: A Life of Total Football*. New York: Nation Books, 2016.

Darby, Paul. *Africa, Football, and FIFA: Politics, Colonialism, and Resistance*. Portland, OR: Frank Cass, 2002.

da Silva, Ana Paula. "Pelé, Racial Discourse and the 1958 World Cup." *Soccer and Society* 15, no. 1 (2014): 36–47.

Dauncey, Hugh, and Geoff Hare. *France and the 1998 World Cup: The National Impact of a World Sporting Event*. London: Frank Cass, 1999.

Dickinson, Matt. *Bobby Moore: The Man in Full*. London: Yellow Jersey Press, 2014.

Dimeo, Paul, and James Mills, eds. *Soccer in South Asia: Empire, Nation, and Diaspora*. London: Frank Cass, 2001.

Dobson, Stephen, and John Goddard. *The Economics of Football*. Cambridge: Cambridge University Press, 2001.

Dorsey, James. *The Turbulent World of Middle East Soccer*. Oxford: Oxford University Press, 2016.

Doyle, Jennifer. "Recovering from Soccer's Divorce." Fox Sports. July 7, 2011.

Duarte, Orlando. *The Encyclopedia of World Cup Soccer*. New York: McGraw-Hill, 1994.

Dubois, Laurent. *The Language of the Game: How to Understand Soccer*. New York: Basic Books, 2018.

———. *Soccer Empire: The World Cup and the Future of France*. Berkeley: University of California Press, 2010.

Dunmore, Tom. *Historical Dictionary of Soccer*. Lanham, MD: Rowman & Littlefield, 2015.

Dunn, Carrie. *Female Football Fans: Community, Identity, and Sexism*. London: Palgrave MacMillan, 2014.

Dure, Beau. *Long-Range Goals: The Success Story of Major League Soccer*. Washington, DC: Potomac Books, 2010.

Earnheardt, Adam C., Paul M. Haridakis, and Barbara S. Hugenberg, eds. *Sports Fans, Identity, and Socialization: Exploring the Fandemonium*. Lanham, MD: Lexington Books, 2012.

Edelman, Robert. *Serious Fun: A History of Spectator Sports in the USSR*. Cambridge: Cambridge University Press, 1993.

Elkins, Kathleen. "Soccer Star Cristiano Ronaldo Fined over $20 Million for Tax Fraud." CNBC. cnbc.com. January 22, 2019.

Elsey, Brenda. "Breaking the Machine: The Politics of South American Football." In *Global Latin America*, edited by Matthew C. Gutmann and Jeffrey Lesser. Berkeley: University of California Press, 2016.

———. *Citizens and Sportsmen: Fútbol and Politics in Twentieth-Century Chile*. Austin: University of Texas Press, 2011.

Elsey, Brenda, and Joshua Nadel. *Futbolera: A History of Women and Sports in Latin America*. Austin: University of Texas Press, 2019.

Elsey, Brenda, and Stanislao G. Pugliese, eds. *Football and the Boundaries of History: Critical Studies in Soccer*. New York: Palgrave Macmillan, 2017.

Emery, P. R. "Bidding to Host a Major Sports Event: Strategic Investment or Complete Lottery." In *Sport in the City*, edited by Chris Gratton and Ian P. Henry, 90–108. New York: Routledge, 2001.

Fields of Green. "World Cup Players Compete for Country, and Bonus Money." thefieldsofgreen.com. June 10, 2014.

FIFA. "1950 FIFA World Cup Brazil." FIFA.com. https://www.fifa.com/worldcup/archive/brazil1950/index.html.

———. "2018 FIFA World Cup Russia." FIFA.com. https://www.fifa.com/worldcup.

———. "Classy Cadamuro Bids Football Farewell." FIFA.com. August 14, 2016.

———. "History of the World Cup Final Draw." InfoPlus. FIFA.com. https://www.fifa.com/mm/document/fifafacts/mcwc/ip-201_10e_fwcdraw-history_8842.pdf.

Finn, Gerry, and Richard Giulianotti, eds. *Football Culture: Local Contests, Global Visions*. London: Frank Cass, 2000.

Fishwick, Nicholas. *English Football and Society: 1910–1950*. Manchester: Manchester University Press, 1989.

Foer, Franklin. *How Soccer Explains the World: An Unlikely Theory of Globalization*. New York: Harper Perennial, 2010.

Fortune, Quinton. "South Africa Spent 2.4 Billion Pounds to Host the 2010 World Cup: What Happened Next?" *The Guardian*. September 23, 2014. https://www.theguardian.com/football/2014/sep/23/south-africa-2010-world-cup-what-happened.

Foulds, Sam, and Paul Harris. *America's Soccer Heritage: A History of the Game*. Manhattan Beach, CA: Soccer for Americans, 1979.

Frankl, Walter. "Erinnerungen an Hakoah Wien, 1909–1939." *Bulletin des Leo Baeck Instituts* 64 (1983): 55–84.

Fynn, Alex, and Lynton Guest. *Out of Time: Why Football Isn't Working*. London: Simon and Schuster, 1994.

———. *The Secret Life of Football*. London: Queen Anne, 1989.

Galeano, Eduardo. *Soccer in Sun and Shadow*. Translated by Mark Fried. London: Verso, 1998.

Gardner, Paul. *The Simplest Game: The Intelligent Fan's Guide to the World of Soccer*. New York: Collier Books, 1994.

Gibson, Owen. "FIFA Faces 'Tough Decision' over Qatar World Cup If Human Rights Abuses Continue." *The Guardian*. April 14, 2016. https://www.theguardian.com/football/2016/apr/14/fifa-qatar-world-cup-report-human-rights.

Ginsborg, Paul. *Silvio Berlusconi: Television, Power, and Patrimony*. London: Verso, 2004.

Giulianotti, Richard. *Football: A Sociology of the Global Game*. Cambridge: Polity Press, 1999.

Giulianotti, Richard, Norman Bonney, and Mike Hepworth, eds. *Football, Violence, and Social Identity*. London: Routledge, 1994.

Glanville, Brian. *The Story of the World Cup*. London: Faber and Faber, 2014.

Goldblatt, David. *The Ball Is Round: A Global History of Soccer*. New York: Riverhead Books, 2008.

Goodman, Michael E. *The World Cup*. Mankato, MN: Creative Education, 1990.

Gorn, Elliott J. *The Manly Art: Bare-Knuckle Prize Fighting in America*. Ithaca, NY: Cornell University Press, 1986.

Gorn, Elliott J., and Warren Goldstein. *A Brief History of American Sports*. Urbana: University of Illinois Press, 2004.

Grainey, Timothy F. *Beyond Bend It Like Beckham: The Global Phenomenon of Women's Soccer*. Lincoln: University of Nebraska Press, 2012.

Gratton, Chris, Nigel Dobson, and Simon Shibli, "The Role of Major Sports Events in the Economic Regeneration of Cities: Lessons from Six World or European Championships." In *Sport in the City: The Role of Sport in Economic and Social Regeneration*, edited by Chris Gratton and Ian P. Henry, 35–45. New York: Routledge, 2001.

Guardian. "USA's Hope Solo Given Six-Month Ban for Calling Sweden 'A Bunch of Cowards.'" theguardian.com. August 24, 2016.

Guha, Ramachandra. *A Corner of a Foreign Field: The Indian History of a British Sport*. London: Picador, 2002.

Gumbrecht, Hans Ulrich. *In Praise of Athletic Beauty*. Cambridge, MA: Belknap Press of Harvard University Press, 2006.

Guttmann, Allen. *Games and Empires: Modern Sports and Cultural Imperialism*. New York: Columbia University Press, 1994.

Halifax, Richard. "Platini Vows to Return to Football after Swiss Justice Move." independent.ie. January 16, 2019.

Hallinan, Chris, and John Hughson. *The Containment of Soccer in Australia: Fencing Off the World Game*. London: Routledge, 2010.

Harding, John. *For the Good of the Game: The Official History of the Footballers' Association*. London: Robson, 1991.

Harvey, Adrian. "The Myth of the Public Schools as the Inventors of Modern Soccer: The Ultimate Revisionism." *Soccer and Society* 19, no. 1 (2018): 50–58.

Held, David. *Global Transformations: Politics, Economics and Culture*. Cambridge, UK: Polity, 1999.

Herwitz, Daniel Alan. *The Star as Icon: Celebrity in the Age of Mass Consumption*. New York: Columbia University Press, 2008.

Hill, Dave. *Out of His Skin: The John Barnes Phenomenon*. London: Faber and Faber, 1989.

Holt, Richard, J. A. Mangan, and Pierre Lanfranchi. *European Heroes: Myth, Identity, Sport*. London: Frank Cass, 1996.

Horak, Roman, and Wolfgang Maderthaner. "A Culture of Urban Cosmopolitanism: Uridil and Sindelar as Viennese Coffee-House Heroes." In *European Heroes: Myth, Identity, Sport*, edited by Richard Holt et al. London: Frank Cass, 1996.

Horne, John, and Wolfram Manzenreiter, eds. *Football Goes East: Business, Culture, and the People's Game in China, Japan, and South Korea*. London: Routledge, 2004.

———. *Japan, Korea, and the 2002 World Cup*. London: Routledge, 2002.

Huebner, Stefan. *Pan-Asian Sports and the Emergence of Modern Asia, 1913–1974*. Singapore: National University of Singapore Press, 2016.

Hutchinson, John. *The Football Industry: The Early Years of the Professional Game*. Edinburgh, UK: Richard Drew, 1982.

Inglis, Simon. *The Football Grounds of Europe*. London: Willow Books, 1990.

Irish News. "Joga Bonito: Remembering When Nike Brought 'The Beautiful Game' to Our Screens." irishnews.com. February 9, 2017.

Jackson, Robert B. *Soccer: The International Sport*. New York: H. Z. Walck, 1978.

Jacobs, Barbara. *The Dick, Kerr's Ladies*. London: Robinson, 2004.

James, C. L. R. *Beyond a Boundary*. Durham, NC: Duke University Press, 1993.

Jenkins, Garry. *The Beautiful Team: In Search of Pelé and the 1970 Brazilians*. London: Simon and Schuster, 1999.

Jennings, Andrew. *The Dirty Game: Uncovering the Scandal at FIFA*. London: Century, 2015.

———. *Foul! The Secret World of FIFA: Bribes, Vote Rigging, and Ticket Scandals*. London: HarperSport, 2006.

Jennings, Patrick. "Lev Yashin: Bullet-Maker to Ballon d'Or—The Man Who Reinvented Goalkeeping." BBC. bbc.com. June 8, 2018.

———. "Yashin." bbc.co.uk. June 7, 2018.

Johnes, Martin. "'Heads in the Sand': Football, Politics, and Crowd Disasters in Twentieth-Century Britain." *Soccer and Society* 5, no. 2 (2004): 134–51.

Jones, Stephen. "The Economic Aspects of Association Football in England, 1918–1939." *British Journal of Sports History* 1, no. 3 (December 1984): 286–99.

Jose, Colin, and William F. Rannie. *The Story of Soccer in Canada*. Lincoln, ON: W. F. Rannie, 1982.

Joseph, Seb. "The Media Trends Defining the World Cup, in 5 Charts." digiday.com. June 19, 2018.

Kahn, Roger. *The Boys of Summer*. New York: Harper and Row, 1972.

Keys, Barbara. "Senses and Emotions in the History of Sport." *Journal of Sport History* 40, no. 1 (2013): 21–38.

Kim, Gene, and Clancy Morgan. "Brazil's Empty $300 Million World Cup Stadium." *Insider*. June 27, 2018. https://www.insider.com/300-million-world-cup-stadium -is-nearly-abandoned-2018-6.

Krasnoff, Lindsay Sarah. *The Making of Les Bleus: Sport in France, 1958–2010*. Lanham, MD: Lexington Books, 2013.

Kuper, Simon. *Football against the Enemy*. London: Orion, 1994.

Kuper, Simon, and Stefan Szymanski. *Soccernomics*. New York: Nation Books, 2009.

Lanfranchi, Pierre, and Alfred Wahl. "The Immigrant as Hero: Koa, Mekloufi, and French Football." In *European Heroes: Myth, Identity, Sport*, edited by Richard Holt, J. A. Mangan, and Pierre Lanfranchi, 117. London: Frank Cass, 1996.

Large, David Clay. *Nazi Games: The Olympics of 1936*. New York: W. W. Norton, 2007.

Laughland, Oliver. "FIFA Official Took Bribes to Back Qatar's 2022 World Cup Bid, Court Hears." *The Guardian*. November 14, 2017. https://www.theguardian.com /football/2017/nov/14/fifa-bribery-corruption-trial-qatar-2022-world-cup.

Lewis, Michael. *World Cup Soccer*. Wakefield, RI: Moyer Bell, 1994.

Lineker, Gary, and Stan Hey. *Gary Lineker's Golden Boots: The World Cup's Greatest Strikers, 1930 to 1998*. London: Hodder and Stoughton, 1998.

Lisi, Clemente A. *A History of the World Cup, 1930–2018*. Lanham, MD: Rowman & Littlefield, 2019.

Littlewood, Martin, Chris Mullen, and David Richardson. "Football Labour Migration: An Examination of the Player Recruitment Strategies of the 'Big Five' European Football Leagues 2004–5 to 2008–9." *Soccer and Society* 12, no. 6 (2011): 788–805.

Longman, Jeré. *The Girls of Summer: The U.S. Women's Soccer Team and How It Changed the World*. New York: Perennial, 2001.

———. "A Resilient Team Soothes a Nation." *New York Times*. nytimes.com. July 17, 2011.

———. "Women's World Cup: Norway's Rivalry with the United States Is Intense." *New York Times*. nytimes.com. June 13, 1999.

Los Mundiales de Fútbol: Desde Uruguay 1930 a Francia 1998. Barcelona: Océano, 1997.

Lovett, Samuel. "FIFA Abandons Plans to Expand 2022 World Cup to 48 Teams." *Independent*. May 22, 2019. https://www.independent.co.uk/sport/football/interna tional/2022-world-cup-fifa-48-teams-latest-qatar-a8926266.html.

Luschen, Gunther, ed. *Cross-Cultural Analysis of Sports and Games*. Champaign, IL: Stipes Publishing, 1970.

Maguire, Joseph. *Global Sport: Identities, Societies, Civilizations*. Malden, MA: Blackwell, 1999.

Mangan, J. A. *Athleticism in the Victorian and Edwardian Public School: The Emergence and Consolidation of an Educational Ideology*. London: Falmer Press, 1986.

———. *Europe, Sport, World: Shaping Global Societies*. London: Frank Cass, 2001.

———. *Freeing the Female Body: Inspirational Icons*. London: Frank Cass, 2001.

———. *Making European Masculinities: Sport, Europe, Gender*. London: Frank Cass, 2000.

———. *Tribal Identities. Nationalism, Europe, and Sport*. London: Frank Cass, 1996.

Markowitz, Andrei, and Steven Hellerman. *Offside: Soccer and American Exceptionalism*. Princeton, NJ: Princeton University Press, 2001.

Martin, Simon. *Football and Fascism: The National Game under Mussolini*. Oxford: Berg, 2004.

Mason, Tony. *Association Football and English Society: 1863–1915*. London: Harvester, 1980.

McCormack, Clara, and Kristen Walseth. "Combining Elite Women's Soccer and Education: Norway and the NCAA." *Soccer and Society* 14, no. 6 (2013): 887–97.

McCurry, Justin. "Women's World Cup Victory Brings Joy to Japan." *The Guardian*. theguardian.com. July 18, 2011.

McDougall, Alan. *The People's Game: Football, State, and Society in East Germany*. Cambridge: Cambridge University Press, 2014.

McIlvanney, Hugh, ed. *World Cup '66*. London: Eyre & Spottiswoode, 1966.

Merrill, Christopher. *The Grass of Another Country: A Journey through the World of Soccer*. New York: H. Holt, 1993.

Miller, David. *Cup Magic*. London: Sidgwick and Jackson, 1981.

Miller, Marla. *All-American Girls: The U.S. Women's National Soccer Team*. New York: Pocket Books, 1999.

Moffett, Sebastien. *Japanese Rules: Why the Japanese Needed Football and How They Got It*. London: Yellow Jersey Press, 2002.

Morrison, Ian. *The World Cup: A Complete Record, 1930–1990*. Derby, UK: Breedon Books, 1990.

Murphy, Patrick, John Williams, and Eric Dunning. *Football on Trial: Spectator Violence and Development in the Football World*. London: Routledge, 1990.

Murray, Bill. *The World's Game: A History of Soccer*. Urbana: University of Illinois Press, 1998.

Nadel, Joshua H. *Fútbol! Why Soccer Matters in Latin America*. Gainesville: University of Florida Press, 2014.

Nanji, Noor. "New Qatar World Cup Corruption Scandal over 'Secret $100 Million Deal between FIFA and beIN.'" *The National.* January 21, 2018. https://www.thenational.ae/sport/football/new-qatar-world-cup-corruption-scandal-over-secret-100m-deal-between-fifa-and-bein-1.697343.

Oltermann, Philip. "German Right-Wing Party Apologises for Jérôme Boateng Comments." *The Guardian.* theguardian.com. May 29, 2016.

Palmer, Jon. *Superstars of the World Cup.* Clifton, UK: Parragon, 1998.

Panja, Tariq, and Kevin Draper. "Cristiano Ronaldo's DNA Sought by Las Vegas Police in Rape Investigation." *New York Times.* January 10, 2019. https://www.nytimes.com/2019/01/10/sports/cristiano-ronaldo-lawsuit.html.

Pathak, Shareen. "Rewind: The Day Soccer Came to U.S. Advertising." adage.com. July 10, 2014.

Pelé. *The Pelé Albums: Selections from Public and Private Collections Celebrating the Soccer Career of Pelé.* Sydney: Weldon, 1990.

Pelé, and Robert L. Fish. *My Life and the Beautiful Game: The Autobiography of Pelé.* Garden City, NY: Doubleday, 1977.

Perelman, Marc. *Barbaric Sport: A Global Plague.* London: Verso, 2012.

Pfister, Gertrud. "Sportswomen in the German Popular Press: A Study Carried Out in the Context of the 2011 Women's Football World Cup." *Soccer and Society* 16, nos. 5–6 (2015): 639–56.

Podalsky, Laura. *Specular City: Transforming Culture, Consumption, and Space in Buenos Aires, 1955–1973.* Philadelphia: Temple University Press, 2004.

Porter, Bernard. *The Lion's Share: A Short History of British Imperialism, 1850–2004.* Harlow, UK: Pearson Longman, 2004.

Putnam, Douglas T. *Controversies of the Sports World.* Westport, CT: Greenwood Press, 1999.

Radnedge, Christian. "Özil Retires from International Football Feeling 'Unwanted.'" Reuters. reuters.com. July 22, 2018.

Radnedge, Keir. *The Illustrated Encyclopedia of Soccer.* New York: Carlton Books, 2001.

Redhead, Steve. *Post-Fandom and the Millennial Blues: The Transformation of Soccer Culture.* London: Routledge, 1997.

Reed, Adam. "Brazil Soccer Star Ronaldo Becomes the Majority Owner of a Top Spanish Club." CNBC. cnbc.com. September 4, 2018.

Richter, Felix. "Billions of Dollars for Billions of Viewers." Statista. statista.com. June 21, 2018.

Risoli, Mario. *When Pelé Broke Our Hearts: Wales and the 1958 World Cup.* Cardiff, UK: Ashley Drake, 1998.

Robinson, John. *Soccer: The World Cup, 1930–1998.* Cleethorpes, UK: Soccer Book Publishing, 1998.

Roche, Maurice. *Megaevents and Modernity: Olympics and Expos in the Growth of Global Culture.* London: Taylor and Francis, 2002.

Rollin, Jack. *The World Cup, 1930–1990: Sixty Glorious Years of Soccer's Premier Event.* New York: Facts on File, 1990.

Rookwood, Joel, and Charles Buckley. "The Significance of the Olympic Soccer Tournaments from 1908–1928." *Journal of Olympic History* 15, no. 3 (November 2007): 6–15.

Rosenblatt, Ryan. "7 Questions Now That the USWNT Players and U.S. Soccer Have Agreed to a New CBA." Fox Sports. foxsports.com. April 5, 2017.

Sage, George H. *Globalizing Sport: How Organizations, Corporations, Media, and Politics Are Changing Sports*. Boulder, CO: Paradigm, 2010.

Schomberg, William. "No Regrets for Zico over New, Smaller Maracanã." Reuters. reuters.com. June 16, 2014.

Shetty, Sanjeev. *Total Football: A Graphic History of the World's Most Iconic Soccer Tactics*. London: Aurum Press, 2018.

Shropshire, Kenneth L. *In Black and White: Race and Sports in America*. New York: New York University Press, 1996.

Simmons, Rob, and Christian Deutscher. "Benefits to Local and National Economies from Hosting the World Cup Finals." In *The Oxford Handbook of Sports Economics*, vol. 1: *The Economics of Sports*, edited by Leo H. Kahane and Stephen Shmanske, 453–56. Oxford: Oxford University Press, 2012.

Snyder, John. *Goal! Great Moments in World Cup History*. San Francisco: Chronicle Books, 1994.

Spaaij, Ramon, and Carles Vinas. "Passion, Politics, and Violence: A Socio-Historical Analysis of Spanish Ultras." *Soccer and Society* 6, no. 1 (2005): 79–96.

Spratt, Vicky. "The Truth about Domestic Violence and the World Cup." BBC. bbc .co.uk. July 5, 2018.

Steen, Rob, Jed Novick, and Huw Richards, eds. *The Cambridge Companion to Football*. Cambridge: Cambridge University Press, 2013.

Sugden, John, and Alan Tomlinson. *FIFA and the Contest for World Football: Who Rules the Peoples' Game?* Cambridge, UK: Polity Press, 1998.

———. *Hosts and Champions: Soccer Cultures, National Identities, and the USA World Cup*. Aldershot, UK: Arena, 1994.

Szymanski, Stefan. *Money and Soccer: A Soccernomics Guide*. New York: Nation Books, 2015.

Taylor, Matthew. "Global Players? Football, Migration, and Globalization, c. 1930–2000." *Historical Social Research* 31, no. 1 (2006): 7–30.

Taylor, Rogan, and Klara Jamrich. *Puskás on Puskás: The Life and Times of a Footballing Legend*. London: Robson Books, 1997.

Thompson, Christopher S. *The Tour de France: A Cultural History*. Berkeley: University of California Press, 2008.

Thompson, E. P. "Time, Work, Discipline, and Industrial Capitalism." *Past and Present* 38 (December 1967): 56–97.

Tischler, Steven. *Footballers and Businessmen: The Origins of Professional Soccer in England*. New York: Holmes and Meier, 1981.

Tomlinson, Alan, and Christopher Young. *National Identity and Global Sports Events: Culture, Politics, and Spectacle in the Olympics and the Football World Cup*. Albany: The State University of New York Press, 2005.

Transfer Markt. "Samuel Eto'o." transfermarkt.com.

Trecker, Jim, and Charles Miers. *Soccer! The Game and the World Cup*. New York: Universe Publishing, 1998.

Vamplew, Wray. *Pay Up and Play the Game: Professional Sport in Britain, 1875–1914*. Cambridge: Cambridge University Press, 2004.

Verhovek, Sam Howe. "World Cup '94: After Second Test, Maradona Is out of World Cup." *New York Times*. nytimes.com. July 1, 1994.

Walvin, James. *The People's Game: The History of Football Revisited*. Edinburgh, UK: Mainstream, 1994.

Wambach, Abby. *Forward: A Memoir*. New York: Dey Street, 2016.

Wann, Daniel L., Merrill J. Melnick, Gordon W. Russell, and Dale G. Pease. *Sport Fans: The Psychology and Social Impact of Spectators*. New York: Routledge, 2001.

Wiggins, David K., ed. *Sport in America: From Wicked Amusement to National Obsession*. Champaign, IL: Human Kinetics, 1995.

Williams, Jean. *A Beautiful Game: International Perspectives on Women's Football*. Oxford: Berg, 2007.

———. "Rise Like a Phoenix: The History of Women's Football and the Women's World Cup, 1869–2015." Sport and Translation (blog). Joint blog series on the Women's World Cup with AHRC funded Women, Work, and Value in Europe 1945–2015. University of Bristol, June 2, 2015. http://sportandtranslation.blogspot.com/2015/06/rise-like-phoenix-history-of-womens.html.

Williams, Jean, and Rob Hess. "Women, Football, and History: International Perspectives." *The International Journal of the History of Sport* 32, no. 18: 2115–22.

Williams, John, and Richard Giulianotti, eds. *Games without Frontiers: Football, Identity and Modernity*. Aldershot, UK: Arena, 1994.

Winner, David. *Brilliant Orange: The Neurotic Genius of Dutch Football*. London: Bloomsbury, 2000.

Yallop, David A. *How They Stole the Game*. London: Poetic, 1999.

Yeo, Eileen, and Stephen Yeo, eds. *Popular Culture and Class Conflict, 1590–1914*. Brighton, UK: Harvester Press, 1981.

Young, David. "How the Amateurs Won the Olympics." In *The Archaeology of the Olympics: The Olympics and Other Festivals in Antiquity*, edited by Wendy J. Raschke, 55–73. Madison: University of Wisconsin Press, 1988.

YouTube. "Adidas José + 10 Impossible Team Commercial." youtube.com. April 14, 2017. https://images.app.goo.gl/t4Sf8hRULFgEwyBx6.

Zirin, Dave. *Game Over: How Politics Has Turned the Sports World Upside Down*. New York: The New Press, 2013.

Index

Note: Page references for figures are italicized.

EXPLORING WORLD HISTORY

Series Editors
John McNeill, Georgetown University
Kenneth Pomeranz, University of Chicago
Jerry Bentley, founding editor